Independence for Children

NEW TOPICS IN APPLIED PHILOSOPHY

Series editor:
Kasper Lippert-Rasmussen

This series presents works of original research on practical issues that are not yet well covered by philosophy. The aim is not only to present work that meets high philosophical standards while being informed by a good understanding of relevant empirical matters, but also to open up new areas for philosophical exploration. The series will demonstrate the value and interest of practical issues for philosophy and vice versa.

Independence for
Children

MATTHEW CLAYTON

OXFORD
UNIVERSITY PRESS

Great Clarendon Street, Oxford, OX2 6DP,
United Kingdom

Oxford University Press is a department of the University of Oxford.
It furthers the University's objective of excellence in research, scholarship,
and education by publishing worldwide. Oxford is a registered trade mark of
Oxford University Press in the UK and in certain other countries

© Matthew Clayton 2025

The moral rights of the author have been asserted

All rights reserved. No part of this publication may be reproduced, stored in a retrieval system, transmitted, used for text and data mining, or used for training artificial intelligence, in any form or by any means, without the prior permission in writing of Oxford University Press, or as expressly permitted by law, by licence or under terms agreed with the appropriate reprographics rights organization. Enquiries concerning reproduction outside the scope of the above should be sent to the Rights Department, Oxford University Press, at the address above.

You must not circulate this work in any other form
and you must impose this same condition on any acquirer

Published in the United States of America by Oxford University Press
198 Madison Avenue, New York, NY 10016, United States of America

British Library Cataloguing in Publication Data

Data available

Library of Congress Control Number: 2024948723

ISBN 9780198860549

DOI: 10.1093/9780191892592.001.0001

Printed and bound by
CPI Group (UK) Ltd, Croydon, CR0 4YY

The manufacturer's authorised representative in the EU for product safety is Oxford University Press España S.A. of El Parque Empresarial San Fernando de Henares, Avenida de Castilla, 2 – 28830 Madrid
(www.oup.es/en or product.safety@oup.com). OUP España S.A. also
acts as importer into Spain of products made by the manufacturer.

For Hannah, Joe, and Katherine

Contents

Preface ix
Acknowledgements xiii

1. Parental Morality 1
   1.1 Questions 3
   1.2 Parentalism 10
   1.3 Perfectionism 14
   1.4 The Liberal Consensus 21

2. What Is Independence for Children? 27
   2.1 Ethical Independence 28
   2.2 Moral Direction 32
   2.3 Parental Anti-Perfectionism 40
   2.4 Independence Not Liberation 46

3. The Argument from Self-Rule 54
   3.1 Liberal Anti-Perfectionism 55
   3.2 Parents and Children: A Parallel Case 63
   3.3 Alleged Asymmetries 68
   3.4 Some Misconceptions 78

4. The Attitudinal Requirement 85
   4.1 Enrolment and Intention 85
   4.2 Independence and the Trolley Problem 88
   4.3 The Comprehensive Enrolment of Children 91
   4.4 Intentions and Permissible Parenting 96
   4.5 Non-Parental Influences on Children 102

5. Ethics and Children's Interests 108
   5.1 Appeals to Ethical Scepticism and Subjectivism .. 110
   5.2 Living Well, Dignity and Authenticity 117
   5.3 Self-Rule and Dignity Arguments Compared 123
   5.4 Does Anti-Perfectionist Parenting Harm Children? .. 125
   5.5 The Limits of Independence 134

6. Family Values and Parents' Interests 139
   6.1 Familial Intimacy 139
   6.2 The Interests and Claims of Parents 154
   6.3 Independence and Procreation 164

7. From Parental Morality to Political Morality	167
7.1 A Parental Right to Enrol?	170
7.2 Against Religious Schools	182
7.3 The Phased Abolition of Religious Schools	188
7.4 Religious Associations	193
8. Conclusion: Anti-Perfectionist Parenting beyond Religion	196
8.1 Consumption and Materialism	197
8.2 Work Ethics	200
8.3 Gender	201
8.4 Diet	205
Bibliography	209
Index	219

Preface

I have come to believe that very many children, perhaps most, are unjustly treated by their parents and other adults. I hold this view in part because many parents devote fewer resources to their children's upbringing than they should, and some parents treat their different children unjustly unequally. But in addition to those distributive injustices, I believe parents wrong their children when they make them practise the rites of particular religious doctrines or encourage them to hold controversial beliefs about theology or what makes for a successful life. Parenting should be an anti-perfectionist endeavour in which the child is introduced to the various and sometimes competing views concerning our place in the universe and human flourishing, and raised to be respectful of the diversity of lifestyles within society. Parents have no right to steer their children towards particular religious doctrines or conceptions of human flourishing; children are entitled to an upbringing that respects their ethical independence.

I first defended this conception of parenting in *Justice and Legitimacy in Upbringing* (henceforth *JLU*).[1] In that book, I discussed several other issues in the political philosophy of childrearing: how to decide who has the right to parent; whether a just society must redistribute resources from advantaged parents and non-parents to parents who are poor, who lack parenting skills, or who raise disadvantaged children; whether a legitimate liberal political regime is free to require schools to encourage children to adopt liberal political beliefs, and, if so, what values, beliefs, and skills it should emphasize in ideal and non-ideal contexts; and what is the right way to think about the 'age of majority' or when an individual ought to enjoy the legal rights enjoyed by adult citizens, such as the right to vote.

Chapter 3 of *JLU*, 'Parents and Public Reason', in which I offered a preliminary articulation and defence of anti-perfectionist liberal parenting, received more critical attention than the rest of the book combined. However, when I read the many critical responses to that chapter, it became clear to me that the brevity and unclarity of my discussion made the view appear more vulnerable to objections than I believe it is. Since I continued to believe that the view is a

---

[1] *Justice and Legitimacy in Upbringing* (Oxford University Press, 2006).

distinctive and plausible one, I resolved to try to rectify the ambiguities of my earlier statement, elaborate it at greater length, revise it where required, provide further defence of it, and respond to various objections that have been or might be raised against it.[2] This book is the result of those endeavours.

In the intervening period, philosophical work on the claims of children and parents has burgeoned, and this has enabled me to hone some of the arguments in support of anti-perfectionist parenting and develop others. Here, I want merely to highlight a few developments in my thinking that find expression in this book.

First, I have become more attentive to the different questions that arise when thinking about what we owe to children. Parents owe the children over whom they have custody certain kinds of treatment. What the state owes to children and parents regarding education and upbringing is a different matter. In Chapter 1, I distinguish some of the different questions that require answers before summarizing some prominent responses to them that I reject—what I call 'parentalism', 'perfectionism', and 'the liberal consensus'. In Chapters 2 to 6, for the most part my focus is the relationship between parent and child when questions about the state and the law regarding upbringing are bracketed. I believe this approach gives us a clear view of the moral claims of children and helps us assess whether parents have moral claims against the political community, in particular the right to give their children a religious upbringing or schooling. In Chapter 7, I argue that because they wrong their child when they enrol her into a particular religious doctrine, parents lack an interest in having the legal option of choosing a directive religious education for their child; and I argue for further legal arrangements that ought to govern parents and others with respect to children's education, such as the phased abolition of religious schools.

Second, as the title of this book suggests, I now think it is helpful to think about moral education on the one hand, and religious and ethical education on the other, as informed by the same ideal of independence or self-rule. As I spell it out in Chapter 2, independence for children starts with an account of what it means to set one's own religious and ethical ends and then elaborates a conception of upbringing in which respect for every individual's claim to set her own ends is the guiding moral ideal. Independence for children is a multifaceted conception, I claim, which requires adults to shape children's *moral* convictions so that they are able and motivated to respect the ethical

---

[2] At various places in this book, I indicate in notes where the view defended here, or the arguments for it, differ from those in *JLU*.

independence of others; as their children become more competent end-setters, it requires parents and teachers to increasingly give them the space to pursue their own convictions concerning theology, gender, sexuality, occupation, and so on; and, crucially, it supports an anti-perfectionist conception of parenting.

Third, when elaborating anti-perfectionist parenting, I distinguish more sharply between two tasks. First, we might try to identify the moral principles that govern parental conduct. Second, we can ask whether the motives that guide parents' actions are relevant to an assessment of whether they wrong their children. In *JLU*, I proceeded as if there was not an important distinction between these two questions. In this book, I am more careful to distinguish between them and devote a chapter to each. Chapter 3 defends the core principles of anti-perfectionist parenting by reference to the ideal of individual self-rule. Certain reasons that inform how adults ought to live their own lives are, out of respect for everyone's claim to self-rule, excluded from consideration when we are identifying what parents owe their children. A conception of parenting must, I believe, be developed on the basis of what Rawls calls 'public reasons'. That conclusion is justified, I argue, because the reasons that inform a child's upbringing must not be ones that she might retrospectively reject when she becomes an adult. The 'retrospective rejection' defence of extending public reason to the domain of parenting has received considerable critical attention and, in this chapter, I try to rebut some of the main objections that have been raised against this argument.

Chapter 4 explores the relevance of parents' motives within an account of parental wrongdoing. Does it matter that parents *comply* with or, in other words, are motivated by public reasons if the way they raise their child *conforms* with the behavioural requirements of public reason? I believe that the ends and values that motivate parents to act as they do are morally relevant. I argue that parents wrong their child when they enrol her into a conception of the good: for example, when they ask her to worship *because* they aim to raise her to practise or acquire religious commitments.[3] There has been a lively recent debate in moral philosophy about the relevance of intentions and motives for moral permissibility, which I discuss in the course of defending my claim that parents owe their children a particular attitude.

---

[3] When discussing examples, for purposes of clarity, I tend to use plural pronouns for parents and singular, gendered, pronouns for their child. This is not ideal as, in the conclusion of the book, I present an argument for extending independence for children to matters of gender. If sound, that argument supports the use of third-person singular pronouns that are not gendered. Some languages already have such pronouns, but, unfortunately, not yet the English language.

Finally, I have sought to offer a fuller elaboration and defence of anti-perfectionist liberal parenting in the face of objections that claim that my conception of upbringing is bad for children, violates the rights of parents, or jeopardizes valuable familial relationships. Chapter 5 focuses on whether there is congruence between respecting children's independence and concern for their ethical interests. Trading on Dworkin's account of living well, and his distinction between living well and having a good life, I suggest that anti-perfectionist childrearing is required for children to live well, to live with dignity. I also respond to objections that anti-perfectionist parenting would harm children by failing to give them as good a life as they might enjoy. Chapter 6 turns to the value of the family and the claims of parents. I accept that if the institution of the intimate family were threatened by independence for children, that would be grounds to reject my view. However, I argue that there is no such threat, though I also note that anti-perfectionist childrearing requires parents to have a different understanding of their role compared to that which many parents have today. I then turn to challenge arguments that purport to establish that concern for the welfare or integrity of adults who parent justifies a parental moral permission to direct their child towards their favoured conception of the good. My critique of parent-centred arguments continues into Chapter 7 where I respond to the argument that parents have interests that support the view that the political community is duty-bound not to interfere with their enrolment of their child into controversial conceptions of the good, even if that enrolment wrongs the child.

In very general terms, anti-perfectionist parenting is inspired by the thought that a certain interpretation of respect for individuals' judgements extends to children. Political liberals worry about citizens who regard each other as free and equal becoming estranged from the institutions that govern their lives. Estrangement occurs when the official morality of our governing institutions rests on particular conceptions of religion or human flourishing that some citizens do not understand or cannot endorse in the light of their own views about these matters. Independence for children extends that idea to the young. Children are entitled eventually to adopt and pursue their own conceptions of religion and human well-being. But, in the meantime, they are also entitled to an upbringing that is informed by ideals and reasons they can later accept regardless of the religious or ethical values they go on to hold and pursue as adults. In short, parents and others owe us an upbringing from which we are not alienated later in life.

Acknowledgements

This book was written as part of a research project conducted with Andrew Mason, Adam Swift, and Ruth Wareham, 'Faith Schooling: Principles and Policies', which was funded by the Spencer Foundation (Grant #201500102). I thank the Foundation for its generous support and my fellow investigators for countless productive conversations and for their penetrating comments on draft chapters and papers. I have known Adam and Andy for more than three decades and have learned more than I can say about how to write about the moral and political philosophy of upbringing and education from reading their own work as well as thinking and writing with them on this project. I am also grateful to Precious Williamson for helpful research assistance, and to Debbie Bloxham, Gary Fisher, and Jill Pavey for help in securing and administering the Spencer Foundation grant. I thank my Department and Warwick's Centre for Ethics, Law, and Public Affairs for the marvellous research environments they sustain.

Previous versions of chapters were presented at several seminars and conferences, and I thank the participants on these occasions for their suggestions and objections. These include events at the following universities: Birmingham, Bristol, Central European University, Dortmund, Durham, East Anglia, Glasgow, King's College London, Kyoto, McGill, LMU Munich, Oxford, Pompeu Fabra, Roehampton, Sheffield, Stanford, and University College London. I am especially indebted to Serena Olsaretti for organizing an enormously productive workshop on an early draft of the first five chapters at Pompeu Fabra University; I thank the participants and, in particular, the discussants—Andrée-Anne Cormier, Tim Fowler, Sarah Stroud, and Han van Wietmarschen.

I have also benefitted considerably from conversations with, or written comments offered by, friends, colleagues, and students. With apologies to those I have overlooked, I thank those who have helped me in these ways: Shahnaz Akhter, Richard Arneson, Sameer Bajaj, Didem Bayindir, Enric Bea, Monika Betzler, Nicolás Brando, Harry Brighouse, Kim Brownlee, Giorgia Brucato, Eamonn Callan, Catalina Carpan, Wing Chan, Ben Colburn, Andrew Collins, Phil Cook, Chiara Cordelli, Renske Doorenspleet, Chikako Endo, Brigid Evans, Cécile Fabre, Octavio Ferraz, Alan Finlayson, Andrew Franklin-Hall,

Michael Frazer, Oscar Garcia Jaen, Barbara Goodwin, Michael Hand, Alon Harel, Sabine Hohl, George Iordanou, Shu Ishida, Viktor Ivanković, Hussein Kassim, Ben Kotzee, Cécile Laborde, Steve Lecce, Ida Lübben, Helen McCabe, Trevor McCrisken, Michael Merry, Zoltan Miklosi, Francesca Minerva, Nicola Mulkeen, Amy Mullin, Fay Niker, Shin Osawa, Iason Papaioannou-Turner, Frodo Podschwadek, Shirin Rai, Dean Redfearn, Andrew Reeve, Rob Reich, Massimo Renzo, Emily Rycroft, Abdullah Sahin, Kiyoharu Sakakibara, Liam Shields, the late Tim Sinclair, Adam Slavny, Riccardo Spotorno, Judith Suissa, Lorella Terzi, Areti Theofilopoulou, Patrick Tomlin, Kartik Upadhyaya, Richard Vernon, Jordan Walters, Katy Wells, Martin Wilkinson, and Alexa Zellentin. I am particularly grateful to friends who have been kind enough to talk through issues or arguments that have bothered me, or them, on very many occasions: Paul Bou-Habib, Simon Caney, Paula Casal, Andrée-Anne Cormier, John Cunliffe, Tim Fowler, Anca Gheaus, Sarah Hannan, Hugh Lazenby, Colin Macleod, Chris Mills, Andres Moles, Serena Olsaretti, Tom Parr, Fabienne Peter, Mark Philp, Shirin Rai, Zofia Stemplowska, John Tillson, Andrew Walton, and Daniel Weinstock.

Special thanks are owed to a few further people. I am grateful to the series editor, Kasper Lippert-Rasmussen, and Oxford University Press's Peter Momtchiloff for their patience and generosity, and to Tara Werger for overseeing the production of the book. I'm also grateful to two anonymous reviewers of the book for their helpful suggestions, and to Dan Guillery, Sabine Hohn, and Tom Parr for providing countless insightful comments on a draft of the book, which helped me to identify places where the argument needed to be strengthened.

Since 2006, I have been lucky to have had Victor Tadros as my colleague. Anyone familiar with Victor's work will see how my thoughts about independence and upbringing have been influenced by his ideas. I also thank him for talking through many of the arguments I advance, for his infectious enthusiasm, and for being my guide to the wonderful world of non-consequentialist moral philosophy.

Over the last two decades I have been discussing and writing papers on liberal education with David Stevens. Many of the ideas developed in this book are the product of our regular lunchtime conversations about politics and education; his sage advice, comments, and encouragement have been invaluable.

It continues to be my great good fortune to count among my closest friends one of the world's smartest and most generous philosophers: Andrew Williams. I know of no one who sees the moral landscape more clearly than Andrew. In particular, many moons ago, during a car journey from York to Leamington, he pointed out a distinction that led me to adopt the idea of independence for children. More generally, since we met in 1987, he has been a brilliant tutor in moral and political philosophy. Without his inspiration, insights, and encouragement I would have abandoned the goal of writing something interesting in the philosophy of upbringing years ago.

Most of all, I want to thank my family—Katherine, Joe, and Hannah. The book has been so long in the writing that I've had the benefit and enormous pleasure of discussing the position I defend with all three of them. I thank them for their insights, encouragement, sense of perspective, and much more besides. For the sake of Hannah and Joe, I hope I am at least nearly right.

I am grateful to the following publishers—and Andres Moles and David Stevens—for permission to draw on or adapt material first published in the following papers:

'Debate: The Case Against the Comprehensive Enrolment of Children', *Journal of Political Philosophy* 20 (2012): 353–364. © 2011 Blackwell Publishing Ltd.

'When God Commands Disobedience: Political Liberalism and Unreasonable Religions' (written with David Stevens), *Res Publica* 20 (2014): 65–84. © Springer Netherlands.

'Anti-Perfectionist Childrearing', in Alexander Bagattini and Colin Macleod, eds., *The Nature of Children's Well-Being* (Dordrecht: Springer, 2015), 123–140. © Springer Science + Business Media Dordrecht 2015.

'Neurointerventions, Morality, and Children' (written with Andres Moles), in David Birks and Thomas Douglas, eds., *Treatment for Crime: Philosophical Essays on Neurointerventions in Criminal Justice* (Oxford: Oxford University Press, 2018), 235–251. © Oxford University Press.

'Against Religious Schools', in Matthew Clayton, Andrew Mason, and Adam Swift, with Ruth Wareham, *How to Think About Religious Schools: Principles and Policies* (Oxford: Oxford University Press, 2024), 74–106. © Oxford University Press.

1
Parental Morality

In recent years, moral, political, and educational philosophers have made significant progress in articulating and defending different ideals of upbringing and parenting. What has emerged from that literature is what I call *the liberal consensus*, which, briefly stated, contends that children have rights and, in particular, the right to 'an open future'. The consensus describes a profoundly important truth, which as we shall see constitutes a significant improvement on common, more permissive, views of parenting. That truth is that we are morally required to provide children with the wherewithal—the skills, understanding, virtues, and opportunities—to decide for themselves as adults what kinds of relationships, goals, or religious commitments to pursue. However, the liberal consensus also asserts that, subject to certain other moral constraints, parents enjoy a reasonably wide-ranging moral right to raise their child as they like provided they satisfy her interest in having the opportunity to abandon the way of life into which she is enroled as a child. For example, religious parents may raise their child in their faith so long as they allow her to be educated such that, on achieving maturity, she has the intellectual and other resources to make free, rational, and informed choices between the different religious and ethical options that are available within society.[1]

---

[1] The term 'open future' was introduced by Joel Feinberg in 'The Child's Right to an Open Future', reprinted in his *Freedom and Fulfilment: Philosophical Essays* (Princeton, NJ: Princeton University Press, 1992). Notwithstanding the sometimes profound differences between them, prominent writers who I interpret as members of the liberal consensus include: David Archard, 'Children, Multiculturalism, and Education', in *The Moral and Political Status of Children*, edited by David Archard and Colin Macleod (Oxford: Oxford University Press, 2002); Richard Arneson and Ian Shapiro, 'Democratic Autonomy and Religious Liberty: A Critique of *Wisconsin v. Yoder*', in *NOMOS XXXVIII: Political Order*, edited by Russell Hardin and Ian Shapiro (New York: New York University Press, 1996); Harry Brighouse, *School Choice and Social Justice* (Oxford: Oxford University Press, 2000); Eamonn Callan, *Creating Citizens: Political Education and Liberal Democracy* (Oxford: Clarendon Press, 1997); Meira Levinson, *The Demands of Liberal Education* (Oxford: Oxford University Press, 1999); Colin Macleod, 'Conceptions of Parental Autonomy', *Politics & Society* 25 (1997): 117–140; Ian MacMullen, *Faith in Schools? Autonomy, Citizenship, and Religious Education in the Liberal State* (Princeton, NJ: Princeton University Press, 2007); Rob Reich, *Bridging Multiculturalism and Liberalism in American Education* (Chicago: University of Chicago Press, 2002); and Daniel Weinstock, 'How the Interests of Children Limit the Religious Freedom of Parents', in *Religion in Liberal Political Philosophy*, edited by Cécile Laborde and Aurélia Bardon (Oxford: Oxford University Press, 2017). Many others hold a similar view. Other writers articulate views that proceed from an account of upbringing geared towards creating

My aim in this book is to challenge the liberal consensus and to elaborate and defend a different, though still recognizably liberal, conception of how children should be raised. I'll argue for what I call the ideal of *independence for children*. The fundamental thought that animates this ideal is that individuals are entitled to set and pursue their own ethical goals. Each of us has a view about what a good life involves. Many in our community hold religious convictions and regard their lives as successful to the extent that they honour their god's commands. Others who are atheist or agnostic have occupational ambitions or particular beliefs and tastes that determine how they use their leisure time, for example. To live independently means that it is the individual herself who determines the character of these aspects of her life; and, crucially, that others do not choose for her. The distinctive claim of the ideal of independence for children is that parents are not permitted to make their child participate in particular religious practices or encourage her to develop religious commitments, say, even if that upbringing is consistent with the child's having the opportunity later to abandon that religion as a mature, rational adult. Rather, they ought to respect their child's independence by raising her according to principles that neither affirm nor deny particular religious or ethical views. Simply put, they have no moral right to raise her to endorse or practise a particular religion or conception of ethics.

Because independence for children is an unfamiliar conception of upbringing and education, much of this book will be devoted to describing and clarifying the ideal to present it in an attractive light. But I also provide various arguments for the ideal. In particular, I advance arguments that rest on particular ideas that have been advanced in moral and political philosophy. In Chapter 3, I set out an argument for independence for children that trades on the similarities between the relationship between governments and citizens on the one hand and parents and children on the other. And, in Chapter 5, I suggest that there might also be ethical reasons to embrace the ideal.

---

liberal or democratic citizens, which is similar in practice to the open future view in that the beliefs and dispositions required for citizenship also provide individuals with the wherewithal and opportunity to choose between different conceptions of religion or ethics. See, for example, Amy Gutmann, *Democratic Education* (Princeton, NJ: Princeton University Press, 1987); and Stephen Macedo, *Diversity and Distrust: Civic Education in a Multicultural Democracy* (Cambridge, MA: Harvard University Press, 2000).

1.1 Questions

Before we begin to examine the merits of competing conceptions of parenting, I need to clarify the different questions of parental morality I intend to address. First, we may distinguish between moral questions concerning the legal regime that governs the upbringing and education of children, on the one hand, and the moral principles that apply to parents directly, which, among other things, ought to guide them when they exercise their legal options. Among the former is the question of what kinds of parental conduct the political community, the citizenry, is morally permitted to require or forbid. In many countries, parents are legally required to do various things for their child that go beyond the general legal responsibilities citizens have to each other. For example, parents are often under a legal requirement to provide their child with adequate food and shelter and to ensure that she is educated to a particular standard. In many jurisdictions, there is ongoing debate over whether parents ought to be legally forbidden from withdrawing their child from lessons or schools that are provided or regulated by the government—to withdraw them from religious or sex education classes, or to homeschool, for example.[2]

When we discuss legal matters, it is helpful to draw a distinction between the political community's *authoritative commands* and its *use of force, coercion, and manipulation*. Some moral questions about the law are questions about whether lawmakers—voters and the politicians they elect—are morally permitted to issue particular commands that citizens are under a duty to obey. Consider an example that does not involve parenting: drug laws. Many societies prohibit the consumption of cannabis. The government instructs its citizens not to consume the drug and, assuming it has justified authority, citizens have a moral obligation to obey its instruction. One question is whether it is morally permissible for the government to pass a law prohibiting the consumption of cannabis; another is whether it is morally permissible for citizens to campaign or vote for such a ban.

Laws are often backed up by force and coercion—threats of punishment if the law is broken, for example—but they need not be. It might be that, sometimes, the government is morally permitted to issue particular obligation-conferring

---

[2] On the moral issues concerning homeschooling, see Reich, *Bridging Multiculturalism and Liberalism in American Education*; Graham Badman, *Report to the Secretary of State on the Review of Elective Home Education in England* (London: The Stationary Office, 2009); James G. Dwyer and Shawn F. Peters, *Homeschooling: The History and Philosophy of a Controversial Practice* (Chicago: University of Chicago Press, 2019).

commands but not to force us to conform to what the law requires. The government might, for example, indicate publicly that, even though its citizens are under a political obligation to obey drug laws prohibiting the consumption of cannabis, it will not punish cannabis users or physically prevent them from consuming the drug. In a similar fashion, one question about family law concerns what the political community is morally permitted to instruct parents to do or not do. Another set of questions is whether the government is morally permitted to manipulate, coerce, or force parents to conform to its instructions, and to what extent. A moral assessment of parental law needs to address both issues. Of course, in most cases, if the government is not morally permitted to pass an obligation-generating law that requires a particular activity, it is also impermissible for it to manipulate, coerce, or force its citizens to perform the activity in question.[3] Thus, normally, the first moral issue concerning parental law concerns whether the government may issue authoritative instructions regarding how parents must act. If it is morally permitted to demand certain parental conduct—that parents must ensure that their child attends school, for example—then we must examine whether and how the government is morally permitted to enforce its instruction and, specifically, what instruments it may use to produce conformity with the law. It might be that, unlike other areas of law, family law ought to be particularly sensitive to the distinction between issuing authoritative instructions and enforcing conformity with the law, because of the difficulty of changing parental behaviour without jeopardizing valuable relationships between parents and children, or otherwise harming children.

Parental morality also covers the principles that apply to parents directly, which, among other things, determine how parents ought to exercise the legal options they enjoy. In most jurisdictions, the law gives parents broad discretion regarding how they raise their child—discretion with respect to where she grows up, what activities she pursues, with whom she has relationships, and the beliefs and desires they encourage her to form. Yet, plainly, there are moral questions about how parents should use that discretion. Are parents morally

---

[3] Hobbes's account of political authority challenges this claim. He argues that the Sovereign is always morally permitted to enforce its will, even in cases in which the subject is not morally required to obey its commands: for example, the Sovereign is morally permitted to kill a subject even if she is not morally obligated to obey a command to kill herself or to allow the Sovereign or someone else to kill her. See Thomas Hobbes, *Leviathan*, ed. Richard Tuck (Cambridge: Cambridge University Press, 1991), Ch. 21. Although Hobbes's view is too extreme, there might be some cases in which, although the government is not morally permitted to issue a particular obligation-generating instruction, it may use force to achieve conformity with its policy. However, in most cases, the moral permission to use coercion to achieve a particular outcome is absent if the community lacks the moral permission to command its citizens to follow the policy.

required to use their legal options in a manner that promotes their child's well-being as much as they can? Are there moral principles that constrain what parents can permissibly do to, or for, their child? Are they morally *permitted* to act in the best interests of the child? Do parents enjoy *moral options* such that they are morally permitted to raise their child in a particular way or not as they choose? If so, with respect to what range of activities do they have moral options? For example, many people believe that parents have moral options with respect to whether to take their child to a religious event or a football match, but they lack other options—they are morally required to ensure that their child is well nourished. These, then, are some of the fundamental questions of parental morality regarding how parents ought to use their legal options.

For the most part, in this book I tackle questions concerning the moral principles that apply directly to parents—what parents owe to their children when questions about the law are bracketed. I do this, in the first place, because these questions have received less attention than they merit. Perhaps because of the prominence of certain legal cases, particularly in the USA, much academic discussion about upbringing and education has concerned what a just state would require or permit parents to do regarding their child's schooling.[4] How parents ought to treat their children *within the law* tends to receive less attention, at least in moral and political philosophy.[5] But, secondly, I evaluate what parents owe to their children when legal issues are bracketed—taken off the table, so to speak— because issues concerning the laws that ought to apply to parents should be informed by an account of what parents are morally permitted or required to do to or for their children. This is because, as in other domains, our laws should often enable us to comply with the moral duties we have to each other. Once we have a settled account of what parents owe to their children, we will be in a better position to identify what laws governing parenting we ought to have.

---

[4] The most famous legal case is *Wisconsin v Yoder* 406 US 205 (1972), in which the US Supreme Court allowed Amish parents to withdraw their children from education at the age of 14, two years before the Wisconsin minimum school-leaving age, which has generated considerable philosophical discussion. Other notable US cases are *Mozert v Hawkins*, 827 F.2d 1058 (6th Cir. 1987), which concerned religious objections to the required reading expected of pupils in state schools, and *Kitzmiller v Dover Area School District*, 400 F. Supp. 2d 707 (M.D. Pa. 2005), which upheld the view that the teaching of intelligent design as an alternative to evolution within the science curriculum of state schools is unconstitutional within the USA.

[5] For related observations about recent liberal political philosophy's inattention to non-legal questions concerning upbringing, see Steven Lecce, 'How Political is the Personal? Justice in Upbringing', *Theory and Research in Education*, 6 (2008): 21–45, at 26–27. To be sure, there are countless popular publications and websites that purport to tell parents how they should raise their child in the light of what we know about developmental psychology. However, that literature is rather inattentive to the moral principles that apply to parenting. For a fascinating discussion of its limitations, see Stefan Ramaekers and Judith Suissa, *The Claims of Parenting: Reasons, Responsibility, and Society* (Dordrecht: Springer, 2012).

Two further distinctions are helpful to clarify the subject matter of this book. The first is between *directive* and *non-directive* parenting or education. As I'll understand it, directive parenting is parenting that involves raising a child such that she acquires particular beliefs, desires, and intentions, or performs actions, that satisfy certain substantive standards about the matters in question. Parents who encourage their children to worship, to accept or reject religious propositions, or to comply with moral duties, engage in directive parenting. By contrast, an upbringing is non-directive to the extent that the reasons governing parents or other responsible adults do not include the aim of shaping the child's beliefs, desires, intentions, or actions to satisfy particular standards.[6]

In our world, most parents direct their children towards particular religious or ethical ends. They take steps to get their children to adopt and pursue particular religious goals, cultural preferences, or occupational ambitions. I sometimes call this kind of directive parental activity the religious or ethical *enrolment* of children. Such enrolment is often performed in a formal ceremony, such as paedobaptism in which parents ask their church to receive their child as a member, undertake to govern her life according to the rites of the religion, and encourage her to believe in and practise the tenets of the religion in question. But ethical enrolment can take less formal routes, as when parents agree between themselves to raise their child to conform to, and to develop, an atheist or humanist worldview, for example. Ethical or religious enrolment is an intentional activity in which parents steer their child towards particular ethical or religious conceptions, and they make or encourage her to practise the rituals associated with them. Either explicitly or implicitly, most people in the world take religious and ethical enrolment to be morally permissible.

Different kinds of directive parenting might be distinguished according to the *content* of the beliefs, desires, or actions towards which children are directed—they might be *religious, moral, prudential, ethical, aesthetic,* and so on. We might also distinguish between kinds of direction according to *object* of the direction. It might be that the aim of parents is to shape their child's *behaviour, actions, desires,* or *beliefs.* Some parents try to ensure that their child

---

[6] My distinction between directive and non-directive parenting is informed by Michael Hand's taxonomy of different kinds of teaching in his *A Theory of Moral Education* (London: Routledge, 2017). Hand draws the directive/non-directive distinction when discussing 'moral inquiry' in schools—the *beliefs* children should be encouraged to hold—which he treats separately from 'moral formation', which concerns shaping children's desires, intentions, and behaviour. I use the terminology somewhat differently by stipulating that directive parenting and education include both moral formation and teaching that aims to get children to hold certain beliefs. Nothing of substance turns on this terminological difference.

behaves in a certain way. In that endeavour, it might be helpful for them to shape her beliefs and desires such that she is motivated to behave in the prescribed way. But that might not always be necessary: perhaps the child can be encouraged to behave in that particular way without her parents' interfering with her beliefs or desires. They might, instead, control features of the environment in ways that automatically trigger the favoured behavioural response.[7] And, thirdly, we might distinguish between different *mechanisms* of direction. Parents might *physically make* their child behave in a certain way; they might *coerce* her by threatening an unwelcome outcome should the activity in question not be performed; *induce* her to abide by certain standards by subsidizing the costs of particular activities or raising the costs of engaging in others; use *nudge* techniques to trigger an automatic behavioural response in their child; *encourage* her through selective deployment of their appraising attitudes—praising conformity to the standards and expressing blame or resentment in response to non-conformity. To change their child's beliefs and desires, they might force her to have certain experiences that are likely to lead to the formation of the favoured beliefs or desires, which may include preventing her from being exposed to competing experiences; they might seek to affect her attitudes or conduct directly through drugs that change her brain chemistry; they might try to *persuade* her of the merits of having particular desires or the truth of particular propositions.

The central question of this book concerns the moral limits of directive parenting and education and, particularly, the *content* of permissible parental direction. To which standards may parents permissibly get their child to subscribe and conform? I argue that while certain standards of morality and political morality justify directive parenting, directing children towards other standards—particular religious or ethical standards, for example—is morally impermissible. Ethical or religious enrolment is morally wrong.

Since it is crucial to my argument, I need to elaborate this second distinction—between morality and political morality, on the one hand, and ethics and religion, on the other. As above, I'll stipulate how I understand these domains for the purposes of presenting my argument. Moral standards tell us what we owe to each other or how we should treat others. Ethical standards tell us how we ought to live our lives and what counts as a good life.[8] Of course, the words 'morality' and 'ethics' are sometimes used to refer to the

---

[7] See §2.1 where I briefly discuss recent findings in behavioural science and the 'nudge' agenda it has spawned.
[8] Here I follow Ronald Dworkin. See his *Justice for Hedgehogs* (Cambridge, MA: Harvard University Press, 2011), 191.

same subject matter or, at least, to issues that overlap considerably: when we study 'medical ethics' or 'business ethics', for example, an important part of our enquiry is what I call morality—how doctors ought to treat their patients or what employers are morally required to do for, or not do to, their employees or customers. I do not draw the distinction as I do as an account of how people ordinarily use these words. Rather, I do so because the distinction between morality and ethics has relevance for the distinction between directive and non-directive parenting. Direction in morality is often morally permissible and, indeed, required, but direction in the details of ethics, or how one should live one's life, is morally wrong. Or so I'll argue.

It might be thought that drawing the distinction in the way I do is unhelpful, because morality is central to ethics in the sense that an individual ought to live her life by complying with moral standards. But I do not deny this. All I need is that ethics is not exhausted by moral considerations, and to see that this is the case imagine someone like Robinson Crusoe living alone on an island. Crusoe need not worry about morality, let us suppose, because there is no one to whom he owes anything.[9] Still, he faces many ethical questions. He can live well or poorly, his life can go better or worse, and the standards to which he subscribes may well affect his level of well-being. To be sure, when interaction with others is introduced into his life, our ethical evaluation of the way he lives will be sensitive to his treatment of others, because moral wrongdoing may well make his life go worse, for both instrumental and non-instrumental reasons.[10] Nevertheless, whether he lives well or has a good life are matters that are assessed in a way that is at least partly distinct from whether he fulfils his duties to others (and himself).

How do religions fit into this landscape? Religions represent worldviews that consist of several non-normative beliefs about the nature and origin of the world or universe as well as normative and evaluative claims concerning morality and ethics. At least, that is the way in which religious conceptions are of interest for the purposes of my argument. Religious individuals affirm particular beliefs about the world and its creation—that there is a god who

---

[9] In the imagined case, I set aside the question of whether morality is exhausted by what we owe to each other. Some claim that there are impersonal or non-person-affecting moral reasons. It might be morally wrong, for example, for Crusoe to destroy a beautiful gorge on his island as his last act even if no one else will benefit from the gorge's continued existence. In addition, I assume that Crusoe has no self-regarding moral duties and no duties to the non-human animals with whom he shares the island, both of which are false. For discussion of these matters, see Derek Parfit, *Reasons and Persons* (Oxford: Oxford University Press, 1984), part IV; T. M. Scanlon, *What We Owe to Each Other* (Cambridge, MA: Harvard University Press, 1998), Ch. 5.

[10] For defence of this view, see Thomas Nagel, *The View from Nowhere* (New York: Oxford University Press, 1986), Ch. 10; Ronald Dworkin, *Justice for Hedgehogs*, Ch. 9.

is powerful, omniscient, and benevolent, for example; they hold particular moral convictions, such as the view that individuals should treat others as they would wish to be treated—some affirm these views because they believe that God inspires or commands them to do so; they also hold particular ethical views—that one should worship God regularly, that one ought not to waste one's talents, and that it is sinful to engage in gay sex, for example. In virtue of their ambition to offer more or less complete accounts of all the virtues, values, and moral norms of human life and beyond, Rawls calls religious views 'comprehensive doctrines'.[11]

Of course, there are countless non-religious comprehensive doctrines that share these features with religious views—several humanist conceptions that provide non-normative, scientific accounts of our place in the world as well as distinctive moral and ethical standards for guiding and evaluating our lives. In the argument I offer, religions should be seen as analogous to ethics or what are sometimes called 'conceptions of the good'. I argue that parents and educators should take a non-directive stance towards such conceptions, at least in so far as doing so does not conflict with citizens' honouring their duties to each other and the wider world. In what follows, then, I use 'religion', 'conception of ethics', 'conception of the good', and 'comprehensive doctrine' interchangeably. For example, I discuss 'religious' or 'comprehensive' enrolment. In these cases, I am interested in whether it is morally permissible for parents to direct children towards particular actions or beliefs that are ethical in character; in other words, towards views about how we ought to live our lives that go beyond how we ought to treat each other. Comprehensive claims go beyond moral ones by telling us how we ought to choose between different morally permissible options; they also provide further justifications of the moral norms that apply to us, justifications that refer to claims about God or the nature of human flourishing.

For the most part, I discuss issues concerning parental morality by taking *religious* and *anti-religious* comprehensive views as my points of reference. That is not because I believe there are special reasons to object to *religious* enrolment. I treat religion as my central case because, first, it has been and continues to be an important kind of comprehensive enrolment of children, and, second, the well-established world religions have produced arguments for the enrolment or non-enrolment of children with which I engage. Nevertheless, if independence is the right conception of how children should be raised, its objections to the comprehensive enrolment of children have more general

---

[11] Rawls, *Political Liberalism* (New York: Columbia University Press, 1996), 13 and passim.

implications and bring into question the way in which children are gendered by their parents and others; they also offer a distinctive critique of children's enrolment into materialist values, which, though routinely practised in many societies, receives less scrutiny. In the conclusion, I briefly address these wider questions.

These, then, are the questions that interest me. What do parents owe to their children? In particular, is it permissible for them to direct their child towards particular moral, ethical, or religious standards? Once we have answers to these questions, we can assess how parents' legal options ought to be configured.

1.2 Parentalism

In the remainder of this chapter I outline three conceptions of parental morality. In Chapter 2 I elaborate the conception I seek to defend: *independence for children*. But to show how my view is distinctive, I need first to introduce three alternative views, which I call *parentalism, perfectionism*, and *the liberal consensus*.

Parentalists hold that parents enjoy a wide range of moral options with respect to how children are raised. Specifically, they are morally permitted to give their child a religious or non-religious upbringing as they choose. They are permitted to enrol their child into particular religious practices and to encourage her to develop a belief in and motivation to follow the teachings and rituals of that religion, even if the religion in question is mistaken.[12] Unlike the liberal consensus I describe later, some members of which also hold reasonably permissive views with respect to parental conduct, parentalism allows parents to raise their child in ways that fail to provide their child with an 'open future': it contends that parents may shield their child from exposure to alternative lifestyles to their own and to raise her in ways that close her mind to them.

Some might object that no one believes in parentalism so defined, particularly once we draw a distinction between moral permissibility and permissible interference by third parties such as the state. These critics might argue that many accept that the government may not pass laws requiring parents to refrain from enrolling their child into particular comprehensive doctrines, or

---

[12] Different views are available here. On a very permissive parentalist view, parents are morally permitted to transmit to their offspring religious doctrines that they know to be false. On a less permissive view, they may transmit a doctrine that is false only if they sincerely believe it to be true.

forcibly prevent them from engaging in such enrolment, or punish parents who direct their child towards particular religions. But it does not follow that parents are *morally* permitted to direct their child towards a religious life, for example. The objection rests on the claim that almost everyone believes that whether or not parents enjoy a moral permission to enrol their child into Christianity, say, depends on whether a Christian upbringing would benefit their child, which might turn on the truth of Christianity.

Indeed, parentalism as a claim about *political* morality—the view that parents ought to enjoy the *legal* freedom to direct their child's upbringing as they believe appropriate, at least provided the upbringing does not expose her to abuse or neglect and is consistent with maintaining liberal democratic institutions over time—is a view that is widely held in popular and philosophical discourse.[13] I'll consider this view in §7.1 when I turn from moral matters to questions about politics and the law. However, it seems to me that the parentalist conception of *political* morality does not exhaust what many believe. Though my evidence for this is anecdotal, many people I encounter believe that parents do not wrong their child in any way when they enrol her into a particular conception of religion or ethics and shield her from exposure to what they take to be harmful alternative conceptions; and they hold that view even when they believe the conception to be mistaken and that the child's life would go better if she were liberated from erroneous beliefs: many Christians do not believe that atheists wrong their child when they encourage her to reject religion. On this view, the *moral* permission to enrol one's child into a particular religion does not turn on whether the child is benefitted or harmed by being so enrolled. As a claim about the principles that parents should abide by when exercising their legal options, I believe parentalism is a widely accepted view.[14]

There is a family of parentalist views with different conceptions asserting different views concerning the content, objects, and instruments of the permissible parental direction of children. For example, with respect to

---

[13] Two prominent defences of this position, which do not deal directly with the question of the moral principles that govern parenting, are William Galston's *Liberal Pluralism: The Implications of Value Pluralism for Political Theory and Practice* (Cambridge: Cambridge University Press, 2002), Ch. 8, and Melissa Moschella's *To Whom Do Children Belong? Parental Rights, Civic Education and Children's Autonomy* (Cambridge: Cambridge University Press, 2016).

[14] As with many issues involving normative matters, consulting survey evidence concerning people's attitudes is of little help, because surveys rarely isolate the particular attitude we want to identify. I know of no attitude survey, for example, that distinguishes between people's beliefs about what the law should be with respect to allowing or forbidding directive education or upbringing and their beliefs about whether parents are *morally* permitted to engage in religious direction within the limits of the law.

considerations of content, a very permissive parentalist view might hold that parents may try to get their child to subscribe to any view of morality, religion, or ethics that they choose. This view must be rejected, however, because it holds that it is morally permissible to encourage one's child to be racist. A less permissive parentalism contends that although parents are morally required to raise their child to subscribe to *certain* moral standards, with respect to other matters concerning morality, ethics, and religion they are permitted to direct or not direct their child as they see fit; they may seek to raise their child as close-minded by shielding her from exposure towards alternative conceptions of religion and ethics, for example.

Various defences of parentalism have been offered. I'll return to some of these later in the book when I try to rebut certain objections to the conception of parental morality I defend (§6.2). For now, it is enough for us to have a sense of the reasons that might motivate the view. Historically, some have defended parentalism by an appeal to the view that moral principles may reflect the power relations between different people. On one version of this view, parents are morally permitted to direct their children as they choose because their children (tacitly) consent to their authority due to the differences in power that obtain between them. Children agree to be directed in return for their security.[15] But views of that kind are no longer seriously entertained: we no longer think that might can be converted into moral right so easily.

A different argument for parentalism, at least with respect to young children, is that there is a difference between parent and child with respect to moral status. A young child's capacities are not nearly as well developed as her parents', and that difference makes a difference to the moral importance of their respective interests or claims. Although it might be true that the child has interests in developing and exercising a sense of morality and a view of what it means to live well, because her interests count less in virtue of her diminished capacities, they may be disregarded or discounted by parents and others. However, again, although this view has received some advocates, I'll

---

[15] See Hobbes, *Leviathan*, 138–141. Interestingly, Hobbes is not patriarchal in his conception of parental rights. He writes that in the state of nature in which there are no civil laws, mothers have at least initial dominion over their child: 'seeing the Infant is first in the power of the Mother, so as she may either nourish, or expose it; if she nourish it, it oweth its life to the Mother; and is therefore obliged to obey her, rather than any other; and by consequence the Dominion over it is hers. But if she expose it, and another find, and nourish it, the Dominion is in him that nourisheth it. For it ought to obey him by whom it is preserved; because preservation of life being the end, for which one man becomes subject to another, every man is supposed to promise obedience, to him, in whose power it is to save, or destroy him.' For discussion, see Tommy L. Lott, 'Patriarchy and Slavery in Hobbes's Political Philosophy', in *Philosophers on Race: Critical Essays*, edited by Julie K. Ward and Tommy L. Lott (Malden, MA: Blackwell, 2002).

follow the common assumption that, compared to adults, children have equal moral status at least from birth.[16]

Perhaps the most intuitively plausible parent-centred case for parentalism involves an appeal to the costs parents would have to bear if they were denied the moral permission to enrol their child into the ethical or religious practices they believe to be valuable.[17] A familiar principle endorsed by many is that individuals are morally permitted to pursue the ethical or religious conceptions they endorse. Since many ethical views include judgements about the value of procreation and raising children to subscribe to particular practices, it would be bad for parents if it were morally impermissible for them to act on their ethical convictions with respect to how they ought to parent. Moral principles that prohibited parents' directing their children towards their favoured ethical standards would, in effect, be preventing those parents from pursuing their conception of the good or fulfilling duties they believe themselves to be under.[18] A related defence is that, given that they care so much about their own child, parents can reasonably reject principles that demand they stand by and allow the child to adopt a view they regard as mistaken when they could instead protect her from perceived harm.

These are merely some prominent arguments for parentalism; others are available.[19] Here, it is worth noting a couple of different criticisms of parentalism. One objection is that, although it might be morally permissible for individuals to make a mess of their own lives by adopting and pursuing activities that diminish, or fail to enhance, the quality of their lives, their making their child's life go worse by directing her towards ethical activities that diminish her well-being seems harder to justify. This is an objection that *perfectionists* press.

---

[16] In 'Abortion and Infanticide', *Philosophy and Public Affairs*, 2 (1972): 37–65, Michael Tooley famously argues that a neonate lacks the right not to be killed because she lacks a conception of herself as 'a continuing subject of experiences and other mental states'. Thus, he argues that infanticide in the short period following birth is morally permissible.

[17] Notice that this defence suggests that parents may not transmit views they know to be false to their child, because it is hard to believe that it would be a cost to them to be denied that opportunity.

[18] For a statement of this argument, see David Bridges 'Non-paternalistic Arguments in Support of Parents' Rights', *Journal of Philosophy of Education*, 18 (1984), 55–61. Like others, Bridges' aim is to defend a parentalist conception of legal options. Nevertheless, if sound, his arguments might extend to defend the moral options that I have taken to be constitutive of the parentalist view. Similarly, although their focus is on moral questions about the law, some of the arguments of Galston, Moschella, and others for parental rights appeal to the costs, such as a loss of integrity, that parents would incur if ethical or religious enrolment were prohibited.

[19] John Locke and David Archard criticize what the latter calls the 'proprietarian' conception of parenting, which I interpret as a view that defends parentalist conclusions on the basis of an assumption or argument that children are the property of their parents. See Locke, *Two Treatises of Government*, II, Chs. 6 and 16 and passim; David Archard, *Children: Rights and Childhood*, 2nd edn. (London: Routledge, 2004), Chs. 1 and 10.

A different objection is that each individual is entitled to adopt and pursue the religious or other ethical goals she finds attractive irrespective of whether they are in fact worth pursuing; because everyone is entitled to set her own ends, others are not morally permitted to choose goals for other people, children included. On this view, it is wrong for parents to enrol their child into a particular set of religious practices, because ethical enrolment is inconsistent with her having her life governed by the ethical conception she finds attractive. This is the objection that I develop in my conception of *independence for children*.[20]

1.3 Perfectionism

Perfectionism can be expressed as conception of parental morality or as a conception of political morality, a view of what justifies the authoritative rules of the political community. I discuss these views—*parental* and *political* perfectionism—in turn.

To many, it seems obvious that parents ought to promote the well-being of their children, to act in ways that enable their children to have good lives. This is the perfectionist view of parenting.[21] Parental perfectionism defends the view that parents are morally permitted, sometimes morally required, to enrol their child into certain comprehensive doctrines—those that enhance the goodness of her life. Unlike parentalism, it does not permit bringing up children to hold religious or ethical convictions or participate in comprehensive practices that diminish their well-being compared to available alternatives. For example, Tim Fowler holds that 'perfectionism requires designing children's

---

[20] Another possible defence of parentalist parental morality appeals to the interests of children rather than those of adults or parents. The argument would be that children have interests or claims that justify parents being morally permitted to choose whether to raise their child as, say, a Muslim or atheist. But it is hard to believe that such a view can survive both of the objections given. If a child has a claim to independence or an interest in living a good life, then it is hard to believe that parents are morally permitted to choose to raise her in ways that disrespect her independence or fail to enhance her well-being.

[21] See, for example, Paul H. Hirst, 'From Revelation and Faith to Reason and Agnosticism', in *Religious Upbringing and the Costs of Freedom*, edited by Peter Caws and Stefani Jones (University Park, PA: Pennsylvania State University Press, 2010), and Tim Fowler's, *Liberalism, Childhood and Justice* (Bristol: Bristol University Press, 2020), which is perhaps the most thorough perfectionist account of what parents and others owe to children. In addition, although he does not engage with the debate between perfectionism and anti-perfectionism, John Tillson defends a distinctive conception of parental perfectionism in his *Children, Religion and the Ethics of Influence* (London: Bloomsbury, 2019). For perfectionist accounts of schooling, see John White, *Education and the Good Life: Beyond the National Curriculum* (London: Kogan Page, 1990), and Francis Shrag's critique of secular public schooling on the basis of an appeal to diverse, sometimes conflicting, kinds of human flourishing in his 'Diversity, Schooling, and the Liberal State', *Studies in Philosophy and Education* 17 (1998): 29–46.

upbringing to raise the probability that they will choose to live good lives'.[22] On his view, there is an objective list of items that enhance the goodness of our lives, including, among other things, relating to others as equals, personal autonomy, 'an accurate understanding of important features of the world and one's place in it', 'interaction with the natural world', 'the ability to create new objects', and sexual intimacy between consenting adults regardless of sex or gender.[23] Fowler argues that parents are morally required to 'engage in value shaping to promote their children's well-being' understood by reference to this (non-exhaustive) list.[24]

Parental perfectionism has considerable currency in public discourse where it is sometimes stated as the claim that parents ought to act in the best interests of their child. Nevertheless, there are several different interpretations of that seemingly simple claim, and it helps to understand the appeal and limitations of parental perfectionism if we distinguish between them. One interpretation of 'the child's best interests' view is that parents are morally *required* to act in ways that maximize fulfilment of their child's interests. Alternatively, we might understand it as the view that parents do nothing morally wrong by acting in their child's best interests, that they are morally *permitted* maximally to promote her well-being. Nevertheless, it is worth noting that despite its currency, when people reflect on it, the view that parents are morally required or morally permitted to act in the best interests of their child is, rightly, universally rejected. Everyone accepts that there are moral limits to the extent to which parents and others are morally permitted to promote their child's well-being. Some of those limits are generated by the claims of third parties. As in other domains of morality, it is generally impermissible to use or intentionally harm other people in certain ways to advance one's child's well-being. For example, although my child's well-being might be improved if I kidnapped an effective mathematics tutor or cricket coach and forced her to perfect my child's arithmetic or spin bowling, I am not morally permitted to do so. A second limit relates to parents whose concern for their child leads them to perform acts that set back the interests of others as a side effect. Suppose that taking my child for a walk in a wood to enhance her understanding of the natural world would foreseeably release hundreds of wasps that would inflict harm on other people in the wood. If the harm done to others were reasonably serious, I would not be permitted to improve my child's well-being in that way. The interests and

---

[22] Fowler, *Liberalism, Childhood and Justice*, 67.
[23] Fowler, *Liberalism, Childhood and Justice*, 80.
[24] Fowler, *Liberalism, Childhood and Justice*, 123.

claims of third parties, then, limit the extent to which parents are permitted to advance the well-being of their child.[25]

Nevertheless, parental perfectionism might be reinterpreted as claiming that parents do not wrong *their child* if they maximize her well-being. This view is compatible with various further views of how parents ought to act, which are more or less demanding. The most demanding parental perfectionist view asserts that, bracketing moral questions concerning third parties, parents are morally required to act in the way that maximizes their child's well-being. The demanding perfectionist view seems too demanding, however, because it requires parents to make huge sacrifices with respect to their own well-being if that would generate even minor improvements in their child's well-being. On any plausible view of morality, parents have interests as adults that are separate from those of their child, and their reason to pursue these interests is not always defeated by their duty to promote their child's well-being.

A more plausible, less demanding, conception of parental perfectionism asserts that, bracketing their duties to third parties, parents are morally *permitted* to act in ways that maximize their child's well-being. However, we might object that this view needs some revision for two reasons. First, the child has a moral claim to be treated in certain ways even if the consequence of such treatment is that her well-being across her life is set back: parents would not be permitted to beat their child even if this were necessary to instil in her a work ethic that maximized her well-being in the long run. Second, parents are not morally permitted completely to sacrifice their own interests as non-parents for the sake of their child. This objection has force if we believe that we have self-regarding duties. If I am under a moral duty to live a dignified life, then it is sometimes impermissible for me to accept an offer of employment in which I am dominated or abused in a way that is inconsistent with my dignity, even for the sake of enhancing my child's well-being.[26]

Accordingly, a plausible account of parental perfectionism will claim that, bracketing the duties described above, parents are morally permitted to act in ways that maximize their child's well-being. However, this is an incomplete description, because perfectionists contend that parents are often under *a duty* to promote their child's well-being. For that reason, they need to supply an

---

[25] For a thorough discussion of these issues in the context of questions concerning whether elite inequality-generating private schools should be legally permissible and, if such schools exist, whether parents are morally permitted to buy such expensive schooling for their children, see Adam Swift, *How Not to be a Hypocrite: School Choice for the Morally Perplexed Parent* (London: Routledge, 2003).

[26] Note that the duty to live a dignified life might require parents not to place their dignity in jeopardy for the sake of minor enhancements to their child's well-being but permit them to do so to save her life, for example.

account of when parents are morally required, and not merely permitted, to promote their child's well-being. In addition, if a version of parental perfectionism were adopted we would need to know more about individual well-being, and we would need to understand well-being at different parts of the life cycle. Some suggest that there are certain goods that can be enjoyed only, or particularly, in childhood.[27] Childrearing also involves imparting the capacities, beliefs, and desires that will enhance the child's well-being in her life as an adult. If there are different life-cycle-relative goods that cannot all be reconciled, then questions arise as to whether trade-offs can be made between them and, if so, which trade-offs should be made. These are questions that those attracted to parental perfectionists must address. But since I reject both parental and political perfectionism, I leave these matters for others to clarify.

Although I'll not discuss parental perfectionism any further, one important feature of it is worth noting. Some embrace parental perfectionism because they assume that it permits parents to enrol their child into the practices and goals they (the parents) believe to be worthy of pursuit. That assumption is mistaken, because perfectionism is a *fact*- or *evidence*-relative, not a *belief*-relative, view.[28] For example, if we suppose that a life without Christian worship is an impoverished one, is it morally permissible for parents to raise their child to be irreligious? If such an upbringing would diminish the child's well-being, then the reason that motivates parental perfectionism—that parents ought to act to improve rather than diminish their child's well-being—suggests that it may well be morally impermissible to raise one's child in that way. Perfectionism is a set of claims about what we ought to do given the facts or the evidence available to us. In the case above, it does not permit parents to raise their child as an atheist merely because they *believe* that doing so is good for her; to be permissible their belief must be correct or indicated by the available evidence. Thus, parental perfectionism might condemn many practices that are commonly thought to be acceptable, such as parents' pursuing their own religious or ethical goals with their child regardless of the worth of those goals.

Perfectionism is sometimes elaborated as a conception of *political* morality.[29] In this guise it is an account of what justifies the community's laws. The central perfectionist claim is that, because an important role of political

---

[27] I briefly discuss childhood goods in §5.4.
[28] For the distinction between these three ways of understanding moral permissibility, see Derek Parfit, *On What Matters*, vol. 1 (Oxford: Oxford University Press, 2011), §21.
[29] See, for example, Raz, *The Morality of Freedom* (Oxford: Oxford University Press, 1986); Thomas Hurka, *Perfectionism* (Oxford: Oxford University Press, 1996); Steven Wall, *Liberalism, Perfectionism, and Restraint* (Cambridge: Cambridge University Press, 1998).

and legal institutions is to enable citizens to live good lives, the laws we have in place should be ones that enhance the quality of our lives. As in the parental case, political perfectionism needs to be qualified in various ways. For example, our reason to have laws that promote citizens' well-being is sometimes overridden by the general duty we are under to ensure that everyone's basic needs are satisfied, including the basic needs of non-citizens and non-human animals. Furthermore, we must consider distributive questions about whose well-being to promote if there are conflicts of interest within the community between different individuals or groups. Suppose that our political institutions can choose between a policy that increases to a modest extent the well-being of those who are poor and another that delivers greater benefits to those who are already well-off. Because the moral requirement to promote the well-being of citizens does not tell us how to choose between these policies, perfectionists must address distributive questions concerning what would be a fair distribution.[30] The political perfectionist, then, tries to identify laws that would enhance in a fair way the well-being of its citizens, consistently with the community's honouring its duties to non-citizens.

The implications of political perfectionism for family law will turn on countless empirical facts that tell us what arrangements would enhance the goodness of children's and others' lives. They will also be sensitive to how we answer distributive questions about whose well-being should be given priority or greater weight in the context of children's upbringing—is it the child's, the parents', or the well-being of third parties? These are complicated issues. And there is a further question about political morality, the question of enforcement, that needs attention. For the sake of argument, suppose that the right elaboration of political perfectionism settles on the authoritative rule that parents should not raise their child to be atheists because that belief system diminishes the child's well-being. Parents ought to defer to that rule, let us suppose, when deciding how to parent, because doing so produces the right distribution of well-being promotion in society. Still, it might not be appropriate for the state to force parents to conform to that rule if they disobey it, by taking their child from them for instance; it might make the outcome worse if it punished parents

---

[30] For the best survey of conceptions of distributive fairness that is agreeable to perfectionists, see Derek Parfit, 'Equality or Priority?' in *The Ideal of Equality*, edited by Matthew Clayton and Andrew Williams (Basingstoke: Macmillan, 2000). Some believe that Parfit's taxonomy can be used even if we abandon the perfectionist view that the goods to be distributed are ones that relate to individuals' well-being. For a different view that is sceptical of the idea that we can specify what G. A. Cohen calls a 'currency of justice', see Ronald Dworkin, *Sovereign Virtue: The Theory and Practice of Equality* (Cambridge, MA: Harvard University Press, 2000), Chs. 2, 7, and 9, and *Justice for Hedgehogs*, 354–356. (For Cohen's ideas about the currency of justice, see his 'On the Currency of Egalitarian Justice', *Ethics* 99 (1989): 906–944.)

who raised their child as an atheist. As mentioned above, one question is 'what should the law be?'; another is 'would the enforcement of those rules by force, threats, or punishment be morally permissible?'

I'll not delve further into the issues about how best to characterize the political perfectionist conception of parenting, because I believe political perfectionism to be mistaken. Its central mistake is its assumption that a normally decisive aim of political and legal institutions is to make people's lives go better. That assumption is mistaken because citizens have two basic moral entitlements that support the rejection of political perfectionism. The first is that individuals are morally entitled to set their own religious and ethical ends even if the ends they set themselves are less good than the ends they would have if they deferred to the state's directives. I am morally permitted to act on my misguided beliefs about what would improve my life—to pursue a career as a commercial litigator rather than as a teacher, for example, even though teaching would enhance my well-being more. I am morally permitted to act in ways that fail to improve my well-being, and the government is not entitled to enact laws that require me to serve or pursue ethical ends that I reject, notwithstanding the fact that my well-being would be enhanced if it did so.

Second, citizens who honour their duties to treat others with concern and respect are entitled to live under a political system that is acceptable to them. This entitlement trades on the fact that political communities are coercive and have significant effects on how we understand ourselves and our opportunities. Given those facts, the law should be elaborated and justified in a manner that is acceptable to citizens who treat each other with concern and respect.[31] I'll elaborate this acceptability requirement, inspired by Rawls's work, in more detail in Chapter 3.

These two basic entitlements support the rejection of political perfectionism. It does not follow from the fact a particular law or its enforcement would enhance an individual's well-being that the government is morally permitted to enact or execute that law. Rather, our legal rules must respect each individual's moral claim to set her own religious and ethical ends, and they must be elaborated and justified in a way that is acceptable to citizens who regard and treat each other as 'free and equal persons' and in the light of the different religious and ethical ends they endorse. In Chapter 3, I argue that these anti-perfectionist entitlements support the rejection of parental perfectionism as well as perfectionism in politics.

---

[31] For Rawls's remarks on the need for profoundly important institutions to be defended according to reasons acceptable to 'free and equal persons', see *Political Liberalism*, 68.

Although I believe that both parental and political perfectionism are mistaken they can, as I briefly noted above, serve as plausible alternatives to the parentalist view. Indeed, certain perfectionists raise an important challenge to that view. They claim that parents ought to make their child's life go better, and they argue that whether enrolment into a particular religion benefits the child depends on whether the religion in question is worthy of adoption. According to these perfectionists, parents ought to enhance the quality of their child's life by identifying and promoting ethical or religious goals, activities, and relationships that are worthwhile; we must affirm a *content-dependent* conception of permissible parental conduct according to which the moral permissibility of enrolment depends on the nature of the doctrine into which the child is enrolled.

One way to resist this perfectionist challenge to the parentalist view involves embracing a somewhat different account of perfectionism, one that insists that the child benefits from being enrolled into their parents' religious doctrine regardless of the truth or falsity of the religion, and regardless of whether the specific activities of the religion—the forms of worship, study, and other observances—are worth pursuing. There are various strategies that might be deployed to try to reconcile perfectionism and parentalism. For example, a perfectionist might appeal to the idea that it is valuable for parents and children to share an ethical life or religious practices.[32] I'll discuss versions of a similar argument later in the book. For now, I simply observe that these attempts to reconcile perfectionism with the parentalist view appear unlikely to succeed. Parental perfectionism is a view about how parents ought to decide between the various options open to them with respect to what they do for or with their child. Even if their child would benefit from being enrolled in a religion she can share with her parents, for example, it is also the case that, other things equal, it is better for the child to be enrolled into a religion whose beliefs, traditions, and practices are worth pursuing. If that is the case, then perfectionists must be committed to the view that parents ought to pursue *worthwhile* ethical or religious activities with their child, not merely the activities that parents believe have value. So, even if perfectionists appeal to the value of shared ethical practices between parents and their children, it would seem that that value fails to rescue the parentalist view that gives parents free rein with respect to the religious or ethical views towards which their child is directed.

---

[32] For a perfectionist who argues that parents are sometimes morally permitted to encourage their children to share their mistaken religious views, see Fowler, *Liberalism, Childhood and Justice*, 132. Note, however, that Fowler rejects the view that parents have wide-ranging moral options with respect to the religious and ethical direction of their children.

1.4 The Liberal Consensus

What I call 'the liberal consensus' holds that the political community should protect an 'open future' for every child but allow parents to raise their child as they choose provided that the proposed upbringing preserves for her an open future and does not set back her other important interests, such as her health or the development of her sense of justice, for example.

The consensus represents a claim about the *legal* options parents should enjoy; it is not primarily a conception of the moral principles that apply to parents directly. As we shall see, some views within the consensus also set out principles that should guide parents, yet some are simply silent on those matters. In this section, I discuss some of the variants of the liberal consensus. My review is by no means complete, and I'll not discuss particular defenders of it.[33] As with parentalism and perfectionism, my aim is to offer a sense of the different positions within this conception and to highlight some of the arguments for them with a view to contrasting this account with the ideal of independence for children, which I defend.

First, it is worth noting that although the consensus supports a *conditional* legal entitlement for parents to enrol their child into a particular religious or ethical outlook, there are several different ways of interpreting that entitlement. Certain versions of the view claim that the political community should not prevent parents from establishing, or sending their child to, a school that has a religious character, for example. Other versions go further by arguing that such schools should receive funding from the taxpayer or that religious schools that are expensive to maintain should be subsidized. But more restrictive interpretations of the consensus are also possible. The conditional legal right comprehensively to enrol one's child might apply only within the home or religious organizations. On this view, parents would lack a legal right to opt for a religious school for their child.[34] In addition, some members of the liberal consensus draw distinctions between different stages of education. For example, MacMullen argues that although parents should have the legal option to send their child to a religious school in the first few years of their child's schooling, thereafter schools should be more heavily regulated in order to expose students to alternative world views on which they might reflect autonomously.[35]

---

[33] See the first footnote in this chapter for an incomplete list of prominent members of the liberal consensus.
[34] Daniel Weinstock defends this view. See his 'A Freedom of Religion-Based Argument against Religious Schools', in *Religion and the Exercise of Public Authority*, edited by B. Berger and R. Moon (Oxford: Hart, 2016).
[35] See Ian MacMullen, *Faith in Schools?*, Part III.

Second, it is worth noting that the consensus view might be shared by perfectionists and anti-perfectionists. A perfectionist might hold that individuals' lives go well if, or only if, they live autonomously, and protecting an open future for children is necessary to have the opportunity to lead an autonomous life.[36] For those who defend this view, it is consistent with the development of autonomy for parents to enjoy the legal option to make their child practise particular ethical or religious activities and to seek to ensure that their child develops certain convictions about religion. Perfectionist members of the liberal consensus offer different reasons for the state to allow parents to direct their child towards their chosen religious or ethical convictions. Some argue that preventing parents from choosing would have detrimental consequences for the child, because it would prevent children and parents sharing a life, or because parents are the best judges of the interests of their child. Others argue that disallowing ethical enrolment would make parents' lives go worse.

Some anti-perfectionists also sign up to the liberal consensus. Such a view acknowledges the importance of citizens' affirming the rules that govern their lives. For this reason, anti-perfectionists insist that the political community's laws ought not to be justified by or aim to promote any controversial conception of what a good life involves, even if the view is sound: it should not be the business of the state to try to identify the truth about individual well-being and to arrange societal institutions to enhance citizens' enjoyment of it. Church and state should be separated: there ought not to be a particular religion or conception of human well-being that is treated as the *official* doctrine that animates our political and legal institutions.

Anti-perfectionist members of the liberal consensus also insist on the legal requirement that children be raised and educated in a way that enables them to develop and exercise a sense of morality and justice and the capacity to develop and pursue convictions and plans concerning how they ought to lead their own religious and ethical lives. Thus, the political community ought to require parents to educate their child, or allow her to be educated, in such way that she becomes motivated to attend to the certain moral claims of others. The child should also develop various intellectual capacities such that she is able to form her own ideas about how her life ought to go: which religion to pursue, if any, and which occupational and leisure activities are worth pursuing. Because they are morally entitled to an open future, children should be equipped with skills and understanding such that, as adults, they are able to fashion for themselves

---

[36] For autonomy-based perfectionist accounts education, see Levinson, *The Demands of Liberal Education*; Brighouse, *School Choice and Social Justice*; Fowler, *Liberalism, Childhood and Justice*.

a lifestyle that they find attractive on the basis of their own reasoned reflection on the alternatives available.

According to those anti-perfectionists who align themselves to the liberal consensus position, the legal options of parents should be limited by the requirement that children have a sense of morality and justice and an open future. These limited options have been the subject of considerable debate in the context of certain high-profile legal cases about whether parents may restrict their child's exposure to certain kinds of education—particularly the science and literature curriculum, for example—that articulate views that they reject as evil or mistaken.[37] Nevertheless, the political community faces another question. Granted, it ought legally to require parents to educate their child such that she internalizes certain moral norms and enjoys the wherewithal for an open future; but should an anti-perfectionist government allow or deny parents the opportunity to enrol their children into particular religious practices that are consistent with those legal requirements? On this question, anti-perfectionist members of the liberal consensus give arguments for parents' having the legal right to enrol their child into a particular religious conception. One parent-centred argument is that parents are morally permitted to pursue their conception of ethics provided it does not set back their child's important interests. A different, child-centred, defence is that the child benefits from being brought up to endorse the ethical or religious convictions held by her parents. According to this argument, parents are *morally* permitted (perhaps morally required) to enrol their children into their values and the legal framework ought to enable them to act accordingly by making enrolment legally permissible—by not criminalizing it, by not discouraging it, by not raising the costs of enrolment activities, or by legally allowing the creation of religious schools (perhaps with funding from the government).[38]

But it is also open for anti-perfectionists legally to allow religious enrolment for a different reason. They might simply say that the business of the state is to ensure that our interests as free and equal persons are fulfilled. The government does that by using legal instruments to maintain an educational system that gives every child a school environment that promotes her sense of justice and protects for her an open future. It is simply not the state's business to do anything more. On this view, parents remain legally free to enrol their child by default: because it is an issue on which the law is silent, parents are legally

---

[37] See the legal cases to which I referred earlier: *Wisconsin v Yoder*, *Mozert*, and *Kitzmiller*.
[38] For a nice articulation of an anti-perfectionist conception of the liberal consensus, see Ian MacMullen, *Faith in Schools?*

free to enrol or not as they choose in virtue of their general custodial rights over their child that protects from interference by others their entitlement to govern their child's upbringing. Unlike the previous anti-perfectionist conception, here the parents' legal permission to enrol is not justified in virtue of their having a moral permission or requirement to enrol. Rather, the community takes no stand on that issue. Thus, on this version of the liberal consensus the question of whether parents are morally free or ought to exercise their legal right to enrol is simply not addressed.[39]

In Chapters 3 and 4, I elaborate and defend a conception of anti-perfectionist liberal political theory that is less permissive with respect to parents' comprehensive enrolment of their children. I argue that the reasons that motivate anti-perfectionist liberalism—that the principles regulating coercive and influential institutions should be ones that cannot be rejected by citizens who regard each other as free and equal—extend beyond the political domain to govern parenting, and I explain why parents' religious enrolment of their children is impermissible. But, here, I simply want to record the fact that many anti-perfectionist liberals align themselves with the consensus among liberal philosophers of upbringing.

In sum, there are several versions of what I call the liberal consensus and various ways of endorsing it. Some defences assume or argue for the view that parents are morally permitted to direct their children towards particular ethical or religious ideals. Others do not address that question but restrict their focus to how the political community should act. And the view that parents ought to enjoy a conditional legal permission to enrol their child into a particular religious conception might be defended by an appeal to perfectionist or anti-perfectionist ideals.

I finish my brief review of the liberal consensus with three comments. The first relates to those who affirm the last version of the consensus I reviewed, which sets out a view of how children's upbringing should be regulated by the government, but offers no guidance on how parents ought to exercise their options within the law. Whatever else we think about that view, it is clear that we need to move beyond it because it is incomplete. Parents would benefit from guidance as to how they ought to exercise the legal options they enjoy. Should parents direct their child towards particular ethical or religious standards—would they wrong their child by enrolling her into particular

---

[39] On this view, one might be an anti-perfectionist with respect to political morality, which concerns the principles that govern the law and its enforcement, but perfectionist about parental morality—the principles that guide parents in raising their child.

ethical or religious practices, for example? If not, should they direct her towards the standards they affirm or to standards that pass some additional test of correctness, for example? We need answers to these further questions. Of course, members of the liberal consensus are free to offer more complete moral conceptions of parenting by defending various claims about what parents are morally permitted or required to do within the limits of the legal options they enjoy. Nevertheless, because the focus of this version of the consensus view is only the law, these questions about parental morality tend to receive less attention than they merit.

Second, as noted, certain variants of the consensus are premised on claims about what parents are morally permitted to do to or for their child. The conditional legal permission to enrol one's child has been defended by claiming that parents are either morally permitted or morally required to enrol their child, which, in turn, is defended by appealing to the value of parents' and children's sharing ethical convictions or pursuits, parents' entitlement to pursue their own conception of religion or ethics, or the interests of the child in having an upbringing in which she is encouraged to adopt the ethical values of her parents. These variants of the consensus provide accounts of what parents owe to their children that compete with the ideal of independence for children that I aim to defend; they are sources of objections to the ideal that must be rebutted.

Finally, the view I defend over the next few chapters denies that parents are *morally* permitted to enrol their children into particular religious or ethical practices or to encourage them to form particular religious beliefs. Now, in principle, that view is compatible with the liberal consensus as I have stated it, which asserts that parents should be *legally* permitted to enrol. That compatibility holds because their enjoyment of the legal option to enrol is consistent with their not exercising that option. Nevertheless, the ideal I'll defend is hostile to the liberal consensus, because it asserts that the legal options available to parents should be informed by considerations of morality that apply directly to parents: because parents wrong their child when they direct her towards particular controversial conceptions of religion or ethics, it is less objectionable than the liberal consensus claims for the state to prohibit or to refuse to fund schools that afford parents the opportunity to enrol their child into such views. It might be that the state should not get into the business of policing homes to ensure that children are not enrolled into particular comprehensive doctrines—advocates of independence for children must be mindful of the distinction between legal and moral options discussed at the beginning of this chapter. But if it is morally impermissible for parents to engage in religious enrolment, there would seem to be a case for the prohibition of faith schools (see §§7.1–7.3).

No doubt, my discussion of different conceptions of parental morality might be considerably more subtle. The taxonomy of positions I have presented is merely a shorthand way of identifying some salient points of disagreement about parental morality. It is more important, I think, to have a clear view of the questions that need answering and the order in which they should be addressed. In particular, I have argued that our first task is to identify the moral principles that apply directly to parents; once we have a clear understanding of those principles, we can then address what legal framework governing the upbringing of children we ought to have.

This book falls a long way short of identifying all of the most important principles of parental morality. For example, one politically significant issue I do not systematically examine concerns how resources or goods should be distributed between different children—both within a family and between families—and between children and adults.[40] The central issue I address concerns the content of children's upbringing and education; in particular, is it morally permissible for parents to direct their children towards particular conceptions of morality, religion, and ethics? I have suggested that parentalism, perfectionism, and the liberal consensus provide somewhat different answers to that set of questions. In the next chapter, I outline the ideal of independence for children, which I believe offers a more attractive conception of what parents owe to their children.

---

[40] I sketch an anti-perfectionist conception of how to distribute resources between children and adults in 'How Much Do We Owe to Children?', in *Permissible Progeny? The Morality of Procreation and Parenting*, edited by Sarah Hannan, Samantha Brennan, and Richard Vernon (New York: Oxford University Press, 2015).

2
What Is Independence for Children?

In this chapter, I set out the main features of independence for children before, in later chapters, adding further detail and defending the ideal. The view I advocate is close to the liberal consensus in terms of the ideas that animate it, that individuals should develop a sense of justice and the capacity to deliberate about, adopt, revise, and pursue their own conception of what a successful live involves. But it departs from that consensus in one crucial way. It is not silent on the question of whether parents enjoy the moral option to enrol their child in, or direct her towards, a particular religious or ethical view. It denies that they have that option and, instead, asserts that their aim should be to raise their child to be just and independent but not to force or encourage her to practise or endorse a particular comprehensive view.

Independence for children requires parents and other adults to raise children according to a particular configuration of directive as well as non-directive norms. It requires moral direction—an education that steers children towards certain standards concerning what we owe to fellow citizens and others. However, it morally forbids direction in comprehensive matters, towards particular conceptions of ethics and religion.

Independence for children extends the idea of the separation of church and state to the family. It proposes an interpretation of the separation of church (and other comprehensive doctrines) and parenting. Plainly, parents are not only parents; they are also adults who have their own lives to live. As independent adults they are morally permitted to form and pursue their own religious goals. My claim is not that when they become parents individuals must give up the project of trying to identify what makes a life successful or enquiring into the existence and nature of gods. Those endeavours are protected by the moral entitlement of each person to set and pursue her own ends in life. Rather, the restriction is that these pursuits are activities that they are permitted to have as independent agents, but not in their conduct as parents. Thus, parents are not morally permitted to enrol their child into particular ethical or religious conceptions: they may not make or encourage her to practise Christianity, Islam, or any other religious doctrine; their aim should not be to direct her towards a belief in atheism, humanism, theism, or the value of particular ethical norms that might guide her choice of career, leisure activities, or partner.

2.1 Ethical Independence

I begin by outlining my interpretation of an independent life *for an adult*. Such a life is one in which the individual sets and pursues her own ethical goals or ends. As mentioned above, 'ethical' is understood by reference to ideals of what makes a life a good one or what it means to live well. People have very different views about what kinds of lifestyle are worth pursuing: some are devout while others reject religion as unhelpful superstition; some believe that money is the marker of success, others that wealth corrupts one's sense of what is valuable; while some regard same-sex or -gender relationships as superior or preferable, others believe them to be sinful, and so on. The ideal of independence does not take a stand on which of these ethical views is true, if any. Rather, it asserts that each individual is entitled to answer these questions for herself.

To elaborate ethical independence we might, first, describe what it means to set and pursue one's own ethical goals. In the first place, an independent life requires that the individual in question pursues her ethical goals and projects because she endorses them.[1] Endorsement goes beyond her believing that her goals, project, or relationships have value, because she might believe that several different goals are worthy of pursuit but, nevertheless, pick one out as best for her or the one to which she has committed herself. In these cases, she endorses the goals and projects she decides to pursue. The endorsement condition means that forcing an individual who implacably favours sporting achievement over musical prowess to train to become an accomplished pianist violates her independence. Relatedly, independence requires everyone to have the resources that enable her to overcome internal obstacles—her unwanted

---

[1] The view that, ideally, individuals should endorse the lifestyle they lead is widely accepted: Dworkin, *Sovereign Virtue*, Ch. 6, and *Justice for Hedgehogs*, 209–213; Raz, *The Morality of Freedom*, 288–294; Will Kymlicka, *Liberalism, Community and Culture* (Oxford: Oxford University Press, 1989), 12–13. These thinkers disagree about the way in which endorsement is ideal. For some, it is a condition of having a good life; on this view, projects that are pursued without the individual's endorsement do not enhance the quality of her life. Others claim that endorsement is an ethical duty that might depart from having a good life: pursuing the projects and goals that strike the individual as the most valuable or right for her is constitutive of living a life of dignity in which she tries to identify and pursue a good life, even if her life would go better if she did not follow her beliefs about the good. For this view, see Dworkin, *Justice for Hedgehogs*, Ch. 9. I discuss Dworkin's view in §5.2.

addictions, for example—that interfere with her pursuit of the goals she endorses.

In addition to pursuing activities she endorses, independence demands that an adult's ethical convictions are her own. To set her own ethical ends she must have certain mental capacities and exercise them, such that we can say of her that she holds and pursues her own ethical commitments rather than having ones that simply happen to fall on her. To see the contrast, suppose that there is a variety of pollen that is a natural hypnotic, which when inhaled causes chemical changes to the brain such that the consumer becomes committed to particular ethical ends, a commitment that is immune to revision following the individual's rational reflection on the alternatives available to her. In this case, although she is not subject to anyone else's influence or interference, the individual fails to set her own ends. An independent life is one in which a person's ethical commitments are the product of her exercising her capacity for rational deliberation: she exercises the capacity to form reliable beliefs about various aspects of the non-normative world, such as the mental states of other people and the likely consequences of performing particular actions; she is capable of understanding and assessing in the light of her other convictions the ethical views that others affirm; she has the capacity to order her different ambitions in importance and to identify how various intermediate goals are more or less effective in realizing her final ends; and she is capable of revising her ethical convictions if the consequence of her rational reflection is that she believes some other ethical lifestyle is more worthy of pursuit.

Independence has a third, interpersonal dimension I call *non-usurpation*, which insists that an individual's ethical ends are not set by others. Independence is absent if others take charge of an individual's ethical life without her agreement, or if they seek to shape her ethical choices without allowing her the opportunity to exercise and act upon her well-developed capacities for reflection. Much of this book is an exploration of the demands of non-usurpation in the context of parenting. Here, it is worth briefly sketching its implications for interpersonal relationships between adults and between the political community and individual adult citizens. Interpersonally, we might distinguish between independence-compatible and independence-jeopardizing ways of affecting people's convictions and behaviour. Once an individual possesses the capacity ethically to reflect, other citizens' trying rationally to *persuade* her of the errors of her ethical ways in favour of a different kind of life is consistent with her retaining her independence. By contrast, *forcing* her to engage in particular practices, or changing her convictions by bypassing her ethical deliberation without her knowledge, are examples of usurpation. Usurpation is an intentional activity that has two key features. First, others aim to shape the ethical behaviour or commitments of the individual in question. Second, they do not treat her having the opportunity to engage in reflection, or her endorsement of a particular comprehensive lifestyle, as constraining how they pursue that aim. Persuading another individual with well-developed capacities for rational thought to pursue a different ethical life aims to change her ethical commitments and actions, but it does so by engaging her reflective powers and does not deny the importance of her endorsing her lifestyle. But there are various ways in which others might ride roughshod over her reflection or endorsement. A clear example is when advertisers seek to impart to a person a desire for their products without giving her fair warning of the nature of their manipulative activities and the opportunity to avoid them. Similarly, direct manipulation through neurointerventions is often usurpatory, at least when it changes our convictions or actions by bypassing our deliberative capacities without our agreement. Organizations that change the environment to nudge us towards particular activities can usurp for the same reason.[2]

With respect to the relationship between the political community and an individual citizen, criminalizing an ethical practice is a clear case of usurpation: the state must not prohibit ethical activities just because it believes, rightly perhaps, that the activities in question are sinful, ethically despicable, or bad for people. More generally, the state usurps an individual's independence when it makes her serve ethical ideals she rejects: for example, when it imposes taxes on her to fund policies that are justified by appealing to a conception of ethics or religion that she believes to be false. And we can go further by observing that whereas reasoned persuasion by others does not jeopardize independence when it is practised by other individuals, it becomes usurpatory when it is practised by the state in the name of the political community. Because the citizen's relationship to the state is non-voluntary, to be consistent with an individual's independence understood in terms of self-government, the state must govern on the basis of reasons and principles that are not rejected by citizens who regard and treat each other as free and equal. I return to these aspects of independence—the political morality of anti-perfectionism—in §2.3 and Chapter 3.[3]

---

[2] Note, however, as Fay Niker does, that certain kinds of nudge are consistent with ethical independence as I understand it. See her PhD thesis, *Living Well by Design: An Account of Permissible Public Nudging* (University of Warwick, 2017).

[3] The thought that citizens' ethical independence can be usurped by policies that tax them is emphasized by Dworkin. See Dworkin, *Justice for Hedgehogs*, 355.

As others insist, usurpation should not be equated with influencing or affecting another's beliefs or behaviour. It is inevitable that one's life will be affected by the activities of others. The goals and projects that are available to us are shaped by history and geography, and, particularly, by how others lead their lives. We do not have access to certain goals or lifestyles unless the corresponding social practices are in place. More generally, we must frame our lives in the light of the options available to us, which are often a side-effect of the activities of others. This is because the goals other people pursue generate meaningful options for us: participation in a flourishing piping band is harder to accomplish in England than in Scotland, for example. To be sure, there are moral issues about the extent to which others may permissibly affect us or influence our opportunities, which we'll consider in later chapters. However, the mere fact that a person's life is affected by others is not sufficient to establish that her independence has been usurped, because usurpation requires her changed convictions or behaviour to be part of someone else's plan.[4]

Ethical independence, as I understand it, involves living a life characterized by ethical endorsement, rational deliberation, and the absence of usurpation by others. But we might pause to distinguish different claims that might be made about the relationship between these different elements. According to one view—*the interaction account*—the validity of a particular requirement depends on the satisfaction of another. For example, it might be said that endorsement of one's lifestyle is independence-conferring only if one's convictions are the product of rational deliberation. Or it might be claimed that usurpation jeopardizes independence only if the individual in question endorses a particular ethical conception on the basis of rational reflection. On a different view, *the additive account*, at least some of the different elements have independent importance: most relevantly for us, an individual's independence might be jeopardized by usurpation, by others' forcing her to participate in ethical activities, even when the individual in question is incapable of reflecting rationally on the different ethical conceptions that are available. The argument from self-rule set out in Chapter 3 defends this conclusion: that others violate a person's independence when they make her serve a particular ethical ideal even when she is currently incapable of directing herself according to her own informed ethical judgements. On this kind of additive view, one's independence can be violated before one possesses the capacities required for rational

---

[4] Here I follow Dworkin's conception of ethical independence as outlined in *Justice for Hedgehogs*, 212. For discussion of our dependence on social forms for goals and projects, see Raz, *The Morality of Freedom*, Ch. 12, Section 5.

deliberation, which has clear implications for the permissible treatment of young children.

Before we continue, it is worth explaining why I describe my view as the ideal of ethical independence rather than an account of personal autonomy. Part of the reason for avoiding the language of autonomy is that the term has been interpreted in very many different ways by people who disagree about how to understand concepts in general and autonomy in particular.[5] To sidestep those conceptual disputes, it is helpful for me simply to set out what I take to be an attractive ideal that ought to guide our moral judgements and give it a label to which we can refer as shorthand. Secondly, although many conceptions of autonomy share some of the requirements of the ideal of independence as I stipulate it, some of them have additional features that do not feature in ethical independence. For example, some equate an autonomous life with a life of ongoing self-examination and choice as opposed to a life of commitment or deference to authority.[6] But independence is a more limited idea. It is compatible with independence to commit oneself to a particular practice or religious institution and, thereafter, defer to the instructions of one's spiritual leader. True, the decision to do so must be unmanipulated and the product of reasoned reflection about the available alternatives.[7] Nevertheless, there is no incoherence in the idea that an individual can live an independent life whilst submitting herself to another's authority with respect to ethical or religious matters.

2.2 Moral Direction

Having described the character of an ethically independent life, I turn to address the issue of what citizens owe to each other if everyone has a moral claim to live an independent life. I discuss part of that moral conception, which is associated with anti-perfectionism, in the next section. Here I explore certain general matters concerning the moral requirements demanded by independence.

---

[5] For an excellent survey of the many different conceptions of autonomy in moral and political philosophy, see Ben Colburn, *Autonomy and Liberalism* (London: Routledge, 2010), Ch. 1.

[6] This is often the conception of personal autonomy that is highlighted by critics of autonomy. See, for example, Galston's account of autonomy in his *Liberal Pluralism*, 21, where he writes that '[l]iberal autonomy is frequently linked with the commitment to sustained rational examination of self, others, and social practices—whence Mill's invocation of Socrates as liberal hero'.

[7] We might add that the deferential individual must have a meaningful exit right, such that she may terminate her involvement in the authoritative relationship at any time, for example.

First, although I'll not argue for this view, I take it as given that every individual who has the latent capacity to set and pursue her own comprehensive ends has, at least from birth, a weighty claim to develop and later exercise that capacity.[8] That entitlement correlates with others' being under moral requirements to provide her with educational and other resources to help her realize the capacity to set and pursue ethical ends.[9] Once individuals have acquired the capacity to deliberate about, adopt, revise, and pursue ethical goals, others are morally required not to prevent them from exercising that capacity. In addition, I'll assume that each citizen is entitled to a fair share of resources and opportunities, which she may use further to enhance her deliberative faculties and to pursue her ethical conception. Thus, citizens are under a duty to promote and comply with political, social, and economic arrangements that secure for everyone a fair share of resources and other goods that enable her to set and pursue her own ends.

A further question is whether our moral obligations and duties to promote and respect others' independence are *enforceable*. In the case of ethical decisions, independence requires that rational and informed individuals be legally free to make mistakes; each individual must enjoy the legal permission to adopt and pursue religious and ethical conceptions that do not maximally enhance her quality of life. Does that requirement extend to making *moral* mistakes— forming judgements and performing actions that fail to honour her duties to other citizens? No: the ideal of independence does not insist that individuals must set and pursue their own *moral* ends. That is, it does not protect the individual from interference by the community such that she has the opportunity to act in accordance with her own considered judgement of what she owes to others and the opportunity to come to her own considered judgement about the demands of morality and justice. In short, our behaviour and moral judgements may be directed by the community, at least when the community is a more competent judge of morality than the individual herself. Let me elaborate and provide some defence of this view, which has considerable importance for the kind of direction children should receive within a compulsory schooling regime.

First, let us clarify the questions under consideration. When, if ever, is the community morally permitted to change an individual's moral behaviour or

---

[8] Of course, there is a question of whether that entitlement exists before birth, but I propose not to explore that issue here. I simply assert the widely accepted view that persons have equal moral standing at least from birth.

[9] Here, there is the issue of how the costs of such an upbringing should be distributed between people. This issue has generated a large literature. Nevertheless, I do not address those distributive issues here.

attitudes? And, if it is morally permitted, what techniques may it use to enhance her sense of morality or justice? May it use techniques that permanently bypass her reasoning capacities by, for example, instilling in her a sense of guilt that makes her automatically baulk at the prospect of doing wrong; or must it use techniques that leave open the possibility of her coming to appreciate the demands of justice or morality through her own deliberation?

A traditional model of directive education involves parents' or educators' *persuading* the child of the merits of the right view of justice by offering reasons for it that she can appreciate and which leads her to adopt the view as her own. Action follows belief in the sense that once the child endorses a particular account of morality, that conception will normally guide how she behaves towards others. Of course reality is not nearly as neat as this, because we are sometimes weak-willed—our behaviour sometimes fails to match what we believe we ought to do. Nevertheless, something like this model of persuasive education is often the picture we have in mind when we think about moral improvement.

The findings of cognitive science over the past few decades have cast doubt on this view of moral enhancement by persuasion, at least as a complete description of the options available to us. We now know that a considerable part of our everyday lives is *automatic*.[10] That is, our behaviour is often directly triggered by external stimuli. There are various processes that describe our automatic responses. One is mimicry: people often find themselves rubbing their knees or faces in the company of those who do the same. Another is behaving in ways associated with particular stimuli: individuals who read words that connote politeness interrupt conversations less frequently than those who read words that connote rudeness.[11] A third involves stereotyping, our relating to individuals of a given group according to certain perceived characteristics of the group: many individuals who avow anti-racist or anti-sexist views, for example, *implicitly* hold racist or sexist biases. For example, in the Implicit Association Test developed at Harvard University it is harder for many to relate a person of colour with positive words such as 'joy', 'love', and 'peace' than with negative words such as 'nasty', 'evil', or 'failure'.[12] It is not that these people

---

[10] See, for example, John Bargh and Tanya Chartrand, 'The Unbearable Automaticity of Being', *American Psychologist* 54 (1999): 462–479.

[11] See John Bargh, Mark Chen, and Laura Burrows, 'Automaticity of Social Behaviour: Direct Effects of Trait Construct and Stereotype Activation on Action', *Journal of Personality and Social Psychology* 71 (1996): 230–244, at 230.

[12] See Mazarin Banaji and Anthony Greenwald, *Blindspot: Hidden Biases of Good People* (New York: Bantam Books, 2016). See also the Project Implicit work at Harvard: http://implicit.harvard.edu/implicit/index.jsp.

are lying when they affirm anti-racist views. Rather, it is that they are in the grip of automatic stereotyping associations that bypass their reasoning processes.

Our growing understanding of automaticity has led to what is known as the 'nudge' agenda.[13] Because we often react automatically to environmental stimuli, one way to improve an individual's conduct is to change the environment such that she automatically behaves in better ways. A famous illustrative example is cafeterias improving our diet by rearranging the display of different foods such that healthier foods appear in our eye-line, because we are more likely to choose foods in easy view. Nudging can also be used to enhance our moral behaviour by using the environment to trigger automatic behavioural responses that improve our conformity with moral norms. For example, displaying pictures of 'watching eyes' has been shown to decrease the incidence of free riding in cooperative settings, such as littering in cafeterias, and to decrease the incidence of bicycle theft.[14] In the educational context, the arrangement of seats within the classroom has been shown to affect children's behaviour towards their classmates, for example.[15]

A second way of effecting moral enhancement, which is beginning to receive some critical attention, involves neurointervention: shaping our judgements and behaviour by introducing chemicals into our brains. For example, oxytocin, a neurotransmitter and hormone, whose presence enhances child-mother bonding, has been linked to feelings of empathy and social cooperation; some studies suggest that it increases people's generosity and reciprocity in social interactions, though others suggest that it also increases their in-group bias.[16] Other research suggests that propranolol reduces one's propensity to implicit racial bias;[17] and serotonin has been linked to certain kinds of pro-social behaviour.[18] Although this research is in its infancy, it may well

---

[13] See Richard Thaler and Cass Sunstein, *Nudge: Improving Decisions about Health, Wealth and Happiness* (New York: Penguin, 2009).

[14] Max Ernest-Jones, Daniel Nettle, and Melissa Bateson, 'Effects of Eye Images on Everyday Cooperative Behavior: A Field Experiment', *Evolution and Human Behavior* 32 (2011): 172–178; Daniel Nettle, Kenneth Nott, and Melissa Bateson, '"Cycle Thieves, We Are Watching You": Impact of a Simple Signage Intervention against Bicycle Theft', *PLoS ONE* 7 (2012): e51738.

[15] See Rachel Wannarka and Kathy Ruhl, 'Seating Arrangements Promote Positive Academic and Behavioural Outcomes: A Review of Empirical Research', *Support for Learning* 23 (2008): 89–93.

[16] See Paula Casal, 'Love Not War: On the Chemistry of Good and Evil', in *Arguing about Justice: Essays for Philippe Van Parijs*, edited by Axel Gosseries and Philippe Vanderborght (Louvain-la-Neuve: Presses Universitaires de Louvain, 2013); Jorge A. Barraza and Paul J. Zak, 'Empathy toward Strangers Triggers Oxytocin Release and Subsequent Generosity', *Annals of the New York Academy of Sciences* 1167 (2009): 182–189; Carsten K. W. De Dreu et al., 'Oxytocin Promotes Human Ethnocentrism', *Proceedings of the National Academy of Sciences* 108 (2011): 1262–1266.

[17] Sylvia Terbeck et al., 'Propranolol Reduces Implicit Negative Racial Bias', *Psychopharmacology* 222 (2012): 419–424.

[18] Molly J. Crockett, 'The Neurochemistry of Fairness', *Annals of the New York Academy of Sciences* 1167 (2009): 76–86.

be that, in the not too distant future, we will be able to enhance people's conformity to morality by neurointerventions rather than traditional educational techniques.[19]

With these non-normative facts in place, let us return to the question of whether individuals should be free to set and pursue their own *moral* ends. My claim that they lack that entitlement is supported by our intuitive reaction to various cases. The duty not to kill or seriously hurt others is enforceable: it is often morally permissible, and sometimes morally required, for third parties to prevent a person from killing, for example. We hold the same view about certain positive duties we have to others. If there is a drowning child in a shallow pond that Ailsa might save at little cost to herself, her duty to save the child is enforceable: it would be permissible for me to shove her into the pond if she refused to wade in and my shoving her is the only other way of effecting the child's rescue—I am morally permitted to prevent Ailsa from acting on her own judgement about what she owes to the drowning child.

Our actions, then, can sometimes justifiably be constrained to conform to what we owe to others. What about our moral judgements? Suppose that the only way in which I can get Ailsa to go into the pond is to get her to inhale a chemical spray that causes her to form the action-producing belief that she is morally required to save the child. At first sight, spraying Ailsa appears to be morally permissible: it seems that the spray is no less harmful than a shove, and it is morally permissible for us to shove her in this case.

We interfere with Ailsa's beliefs in this case for instrumental reasons. Fundamentally, we are interested in her actions; her beliefs are relevant only to the extent that they are causally important to how she acts. But there might also be cases in which the community is morally permitted to enhance an individual's moral attitudes for non-instrumental reasons. These are cases in which we are morally required to develop certain beliefs or, more specifically, to act with certain intentions or to reason in certain ways. For example, consider the case of a clearly unqualified black applicant for a job who is denied the job, not because the selector realizes that he is unqualified and appreciates that this is a decisive reason to deny him the job, but because the selector is a racist. The black applicant is not wronged in virtue of being denied the job, but the selector nevertheless wrongs him because she rejects his application for the wrong reasons. The selector has a duty not to be motivated by racist animus

---

[19] On this subject, and its possibly transformative implications for education policy, see Allen Buchanan, 'Cognitive Enhancement and Education', *Theory and Research in Education* 9 (2011): 145–162.

when deciding between different applicants; and it is reasonable to claim that the selector's duty to reason in an impartial way is enforceable. Accordingly, if there were a spray that reliably removed her racist beliefs without causing disproportionate side effects, then, prima facie, it seems permissible for others to administer the spray or to require her to accept the spray.

These examples suggest that at least some of the moral duties we have to act in particular ways or to hold certain attitudes are enforceable: the community is morally permitted to make us fulfil the duties in question. Our intuitive view of these cases suggests that these enforceable duties are justified by the claims of other individuals to be treated or regarded in particular ways.

Might there also be coerced-party interests to enforce such duties in educational contexts? Consider first a paternalist argument for the enforcement of morality that appeals to the interests of the person whose freedom is constrained. Rawls claims that as citizens one of our two basic interests is to develop and exercise a sense of justice, which he defines as 'the capacity to understand, to apply, and to act from (and not merely in accordance with) the principles of political justice that specify the fair terms of social cooperation'.[20] Rawls's claim chimes with the thought that it is valuable for a person to express her nature as a moral person. The argument is that it is permissible for third parties to interfere to develop an individual's understanding of justice so that she can comply with its demands.

The difficulty with this argument is that even if having a sense of justice is in an individual's interest, it does not follow that it is morally permissible for that good to be imposed upon her without her consent. To see this, we need only consider cases of paternalism with respect to ethics, such as whether one pursues a religious life, in the light of our earlier discussion. According to the ideal of independence it is morally impermissible to force an individual to adopt the right view of religion on the grounds that holding such beliefs improves her well-being. But if paternalism is morally problematic in the case of the good, then it also seems problematic in the case of justice and morality.

One reply to this argument is that our interest in having a sense of justice, or at least in avoiding a seriously impoverished sense of justice, is very weighty, whereas our interest in pursuing a sound conception of the good is (often) less weighty, and paternalism is morally permissible when the interests at stake are very weighty. If that argument is forceful, then there might be an interest-based argument for giving individuals a sense of justice.

---

[20] Rawls, *Justice as Fairness: A Restatement* (Cambridge, MA: Harvard University Press, 2001), 18–19.

There is a second coerced-party interest in being directed towards the right norms of justice. In the next section and Chapter 3, I elaborate the view that individuals have a claim to rule themselves, which I flesh out partly in terms of their endorsement of the ideals and rules that govern their lives. This Rousseauian and Rawlsian idea of 'political autonomy' gives us an important, though often overlooked, reason to engage in the directive moral education of citizens. As established above, we have enforceable moral duties: others are permitted to exercise coercion over us to ensure that we do what we owe to others. Given the existence of enforceable moral duties, it serves our interest in political autonomy for our moral convictions to be aligned with those duties. If it is appropriate for others to force us to fulfil certain duties, then it is important that there are moral educators who teach directively and thereby bring us to understand and accept both that we have those duties and that others are permitted to force us to honour them. Such teachers enable us to regard the rules we live under as our own rather than alien constraints.

The political autonomy defence regards mere *conformity* with our duties as less than ideal. An agent conforms with a reason or duty just in case she behaves in the way demanded by the duty.[21] However, political autonomy requires more than conformity: the agent in question must at least understand and accept the principles she is forced to follow. Thus, moral teachers have the vital role of imparting to us an appreciation of morality and justice, without which we would lack political autonomy in a rule-governed society. For example, schools and parents must do more than merely sustain an environment that ensures that we behave morally as children and adults. Every child has a claim to an education in morality that enables her to understand and accept sound moral principles that justify the legal constraints under which she ought to live—her claim to political autonomy demands nothing less.

I have cited some cases that show that it is sometimes morally permissible to constrain individuals' activities and shape their attitudes so that they fulfil their duties to others and endorse the way in which the political community ought to constrain their liberty. But it is also the case that individuals have interests in having at least some opportunities to come to understand the moral duties and obligations that apply to them *on the basis of their own reasoning* and to

---

[21] For an account of conformity with reasons or duties, see Raz, *Practical Reason and Norms* (with a new postscript) (Princeton, NJ: Princeton University Press, 1990), 178–182. Raz contrasts conformity with compliance, which is where an agent's fulfilment of a duty is motivated by her recognition that the duty applies to her. The kind of relationship between the agent and her duty-fulfilment that is required by political autonomy differs in some respects to Raz's conception of compliance. For political autonomy, what matters is that we endorse the reasons that justify the constrains under which we live.

express themselves as moral agents. To see this, let us return to our simple pond case. Suppose that Alan has an enforceable duty to rescue the child; he fully recognizes that he has a duty to rescue children in cases like this but is presently unaware of the fact there is a child in need of rescue. Now suppose that Beth, who is unable to save the child herself, is capable of either alerting Alan of the need for a rescue or giving him a hypnotic spray that makes him to walk into the pond (which, suppose, is sufficient to rescue the child). In this case, since Alan is capable of recognizing and acting on his duty to save the child, Beth ought to give him the opportunity to exercise his sense of morality.[22]

A similar reason applies in cases in which the individual is deciding what to believe is a sufficient reason for action, rather than which action to perform. Suppose that Alan has not given any thought to the question of whether he is morally required to save young children from ponds when the costs to him are low. Beth has a choice between using a neurointervention to give him that belief, or leaving Alan to come to that conclusion by his own reasoning in the light of a conversation with her. In this case, I believe she ought to do the latter, at least if it is clear that he will come to the right belief through his own deliberation.

If we have an interest in having opportunities for moral accomplishment of these kinds, we have a moral claim to institutions that enable us to deliberate about and pursue our own moral goals insofar as doing so is consistent with our honouring the moral requirements we are under. We have a valid claim, in other words, to an environment in which we can come to appreciate and act on our moral duties. For this reason, we might prefer what have been, to date, the usual methods for achieving moral enhancement—directive moral teaching that seeks to persuade us of the merits of particular moral positions and teaching by example—over alternative methods that are increasingly discussed in public discourse, like nudges and neurointerventions, which bypass our deliberative faculties.

I have advanced two central claims concerning the idea of independence. First, I have summarized the features of what it means to live an independent life. Such a life is one in which the individual endorses the ethical practices she engages in, forms her own ethical conception through a process of deliberation

---

[22] To be clear, I am not arguing that it is always the case that third parties' forcing individuals to do their duty is second best. For example, it is valuable for the state to enforce a tax policy that succeeds in realizing a just scheme of social cooperation which citizens owe to one another. Even if the same distributive outcome might be realized by individuals' voluntarily contributing an appropriate amount of their pre-tax income to a social pot, an enforcement scheme would be preferable because it publicly expresses the nature of every citizen's status and her entitlement to a fair share of resources.

about the available alternatives, and others do not engage in ethical usurpation. But, second, I have argued that although we have reasons to enable individuals to become moral agents capable of understanding and complying with the demands of morality and justice, there is no unconditional moral permission for individuals to set and pursue their own *moral* ends. If we care about our independence then we must take steps to ensure that citizens fulfil their duty to respect, protect, and promote, and not to usurp, others' independence.

2.3 Parental Anti-Perfectionism

In this section, I examine in more detail the duty of non-usurpation that follows from everyone's having a moral claim to independence. The non-usurpation requirement claims that others must not take charge of our lives by making us practise or serve a particular conception of ethics or religion without our consent or endorsement. In the next chapter, I'll defend a conception of non-usurpation that requires parents and teachers to provide children with what can be called an *anti-perfectionist* upbringing: an upbringing whose justification does not draw on particular controversial ethical ideas, such as particular theological claims. To see what this requires it is useful to consider, as an analogy, anti-perfectionist *political* morality. Anti-perfectionists claim that the reasons that are relevant when we make certain decisions ought to be excluded from consideration when we make political decisions. For example, suppose that there is no god and, because there is no god, a life of Christian worship would not make one's life go as well as pursuing various other comprehensive goals. If true, those facts give us a weighty, and perhaps a decisive, reason not to believe in God and not to engage in Christian worship. But there is a separate question of whether those reasons extend to inform how we ought to vote when electing politicians: if there is no god, do citizens have a weighty reason to vote for politicians who will enact laws that seek to discourage belief in god via, for example, an education policy that mandates schools to direct children away from religion, or through the funding of public campaigns to convert the devout, or by subsidizing non-religious activities to induce individuals to give up their religious pursuits? Political anti-perfectionists deny that citizens have such reasons. Rather, religious and ethical reasons are excluded from consideration, notwithstanding the fact that they are relevant for other decisions we take—in leading our own lives, for example. The exclusion of these reasons from the political domain is morally appropriate, they claim, because politics is centrally concerned with the generation of authoritative rules and their enforcement, and engagement in those activities makes a difference to the kinds of reason to which we may appeal. One prominent argument for political anti-perfectionism, which I find plausible and develop in the next chapter as the basis of my argument for *parental* anti-perfectionism, proceeds from the claim that citizens have a moral claim to live under legal constraints that they can endorse in the light of their own beliefs and their status as free and equal persons. Given that disagreement about religion seems to be a permanent feature of our society, if our legal rules are to be acceptable to every reasonable citizen they must not depend on reasons that some citizens reject. Thus, even if there is no god, many in our society do in fact have religious convictions. To treat the non-existence of God as a reason when making political decisions is to proceed as if citizens are not entitled to live under legal rules that they understand and elicit their endorsement. But that would be a moral mistake.[23]

Parental anti-perfectionism extends these ideas to parents. Controversial religious and ethical ideals are excluded from the domain of parenting. If we suppose, again, the non-existence of God then we have a reason to hold atheist convictions and not to worship as many theists do; but we ought to exclude those reasons from consideration when we try to identify how children ought to be raised. These particular religious and ethical reasons do not operate in the context of parenting: how a child should be raised is determined by the reasons in play, but neither the existence nor non-existence of God counts as one of those reasons.

If parents are not morally permitted to appeal to controversial ethical conceptions when deciding how to raise their child, what kinds of reasons determine how they ought to act? How are we to evaluate whether particular parents are discharging their duties to their child well or poorly if we cannot appeal to conceptions of their child's ethical or religious interests? My remarks in the previous section suggest an answer to these questions. Although independence for children insists on the exclusion of certain ethical ideals from the domain of parenting and education, it also offers a positive vision of parenting in which children are entitled to an upbringing that enables them to develop a sense of justice and the mental and physical wherewithal to lead an independent life. Since I have discussed morality and justice reasonably extensively, I'll briefly illustrate the positive vision with reference to the entitlement to set and pursue one's own ends.

---

[23] For discussion, see Andrew Williams, 'Constructivism in Political Philosophy', *The Stanford Encyclopedia of Philosophy*, edited by Edward N. Zalta and Uri Nodelman (Spring 2024 Edition): https://plato.stanford.edu/archives/spr2024/entries/constructivism-political/, Section 5.

In the first place, as I understand it, independence requires individuals themselves to set their own goals in life. If they are to set their own goals, they must have what Rawls calls 'a capacity for a conception of the good': the capacity to deliberate rationally about the various goals, projects, and relationships that are available to them and the intellectual and physical wherewithal to pursue the ends that they come to endorse.[24] It is clear that we can use the capacity for a conception of the good as the foundation for judging whether parents and teachers are effective in raising a child. Plainly, for the purposes of developing a public guide to evaluate individuals in these roles we would need to disaggregate several different features of the capacity. For example, the capacity for rational thought needs further elucidation. Is the child rational only if her thought conforms to the requirements of expected utility theory, or are the requirements of rationality for the purposes of conferring independence less demanding? Second, the intellectual and physical capacities that constitute the capacity for a conception of the good need to be characterized in more detail. Is it better from the point of view of independence if the child has an advanced understanding of mathematics or literature, for example, or better to the extent that she is physically stronger or faster?

First, it should be noted that the rational, intellectual, and physical powers required for ethical independence are *threshold* requirements. Independence requires that individuals have enough of these powers: just because Bertrand is a better philosopher, logician, linguist, and mathematician than Brian does not mean that his life is more independent, because Brian might possess sufficient rationality and intellectual and physical capacity to satisfy the conditions for independence. The capacity for a conception of the good demands a certain threshold of capability with respect to rationality: individuals should understand that their goals are nested in structures in which certain goals serve others, and they should have the ability generally to avoid adopting goals that are mutually inconsistent and to choose effective means of realizing their fundamental goals. The rationality required for this capacity need not, then, be the kind of rationality that is demanded by certain variants of expected utility theory in which individuals maximize their risk-neutral expected preference-satisfaction. The rationality required for independence is less demanding and consistent with individuals' adopting different attitudes towards preference-satisfaction. They may be satisficers rather than maximizers, or be averse to certain kinds of risk, or regard their practical reasons as given by their ethical duties to others regardless of their preferences, without jeopardizing their

---

[24] Rawls, *Political Liberalism*, 18–20.

independence. What matters is that their goals are chosen in a way that faithfully reflects their own ambitions.

Below the threshold, we might say that individuals might deliberate and act more or less rationally and, accordingly, be closer or further away from full independence. One example of this is the development of children. In our infancy, when we lack well-developed deliberative and rational powers, we lack the mental capacities to form and revise a comprehensive conception and others must control our lives and conduct so that we acquire these capacities. As we develop deliberative and rational powers, that control lessens until the point at which we have sufficient powers to develop and pursue our own goals according to the standards of independence (see §2.3 for further remarks on the moral relevance of the gradual development of independence). In addition, we might evaluate different kinds of parenting and education to assess whether they are well designed to assist the development of these powers such that individuals acquire them in a timely fashion: parenting arrangements that fail to facilitate their acquisition or that take longer to do so might be subject to criticism or reform.

I have argued that independence requires possession of the capacity for a conception of the good. But some have suggested that the capacity is itself a conception of the good and, therefore, if it is morally impermissible to enrol children into a particular ethical conception then surely it is morally impermissible to shape the child's life so that she is able and willing rationally to embrace and pursue the particular goals that strike her as worthwhile. The objection is that anti-perfectionist childrearing cannot without contradiction advocate the development of the child's capacity for a conception of the good.

This objection can be rebutted by observing that it overlooks the fact that anti-perfectionism operates with a distinction between *ethical ideals* and a *moral conception* of how individuals are entitled to relate to their ethical lives and to other individuals. It asserts that there is a set of ethical ideals—conceptions of what makes a life a good one and views concerning the existence and implications of deities, for example—with respect to which parents should take no stand in their capacity as carers or educators of children. But this set does not include the moral ideal of independence or self-rule. It is coherent to hold that there is a moral ideal that should guide the choices of parents and, at the same time, hold that parents should not be guided by concrete ethical ideals, such as those involving religious claims. Indeed, the argument above is that the ideal of independence, which recognizes an individual's moral claim to sets her own ends, explains and justifies the distinction that is drawn. Independence is possible only if we are able rationally to adopt and pursue our own goals. That explains the importance of the development and exercise of the capacity for a conception of the good. An upbringing that goes further and enrols the child into a particular conception of the good is not inconsistent with her acquisition of that capacity, but it is ruled out by a further requirement of independence: that others do not force her to serve particular ethical ends without her agreement. Thus, independence for children has a positive vision of upbringing and education to which we shall return at various stages of the argument, as well as a negative, anti-perfectionist agenda.[25]

I now want to introduce a further controversial feature of the view I defend, which goes beyond the claim that certain ethical reasons that inform other parts of their lives are excluded when we address how parents and other adults ought to raise children. The moral entitlement to independence is not merely a claim about the reasons that are relevant to what parents do for their child. It also claims that parents should display an anti-perfectionist *attitude*. That is, when they deliberate about how to exercise the legal discretion they enjoy and form their aims as parents, they ought to regard themselves as under a duty to exclude religious and ethical considerations: they ought to be saying to themselves 'when deciding how to raise my child I must put aside my convictions about whether god exists and my other controversial beliefs about, say, which occupations are intrinsically worth pursuing'.

The idea of an anti-perfectionist attitude is a claim about how parents ought to deliberate, the kind of reasoning process they ought to engage in when deciding how to use their discretion under the law. The general thought behind the attitudinal requirement is that parents can wrong their child even when what they otherwise do to, or for, their child is required by the relevant (anti-perfectionist) reasons. As illustration, consider the racist hiring case introduced earlier in which the selector rejects the candidate's application not because she realizes that he is unqualified and appreciates that this is a decisive reason to deny him the job, but because she is a racist. If we consider only whether her refusal to hire the applicant is supported by the reasons in play, it is clear that she acts permissibly. Nevertheless, her decision to hire or not hire is not the only thing the selector does; she also deliberates in a particular, impermissible way because she is motivated by animus against people of colour when she evaluates the applications. Indeed, her racist motivation denies black candidates something to which they are entitled, namely, that their applications are read impartially by selectors. The

---

[25] For more discussion of whether the ideal of ethical independence is a comprehensive doctrine, see §3.5. My view here, that political liberalism does not rest on even a partially comprehensive conception, differs from the view I defended in *JLU* at 24–27.

selector is morally required to deliberate in a non-racist way and to act on the basis of non-racist intentions.

Independence for children asserts something similar for parents. Parents ought to do various things for their child. Among other things they should display a particular attitude towards her—they are morally required to acknowledge their child's claim to live an independent live, which includes an undertaking on their part not to evaluate different kinds of parental decision open to them by treating as relevant the value of controversial conceptions of religion or of what makes a life go well. Consider the following case.

Local Schooling: The Carters and the Dixons are two sets of Christian parents. They send their respective children to the local Christian school. The Carters send their child, Carly, to the school because it is the local school. They would send her to the school even if it were a school that did not favour any particular religious or ethical doctrine. The Dixons send their child, Dan, to the school because it is a Christian school where the Gospel will be taught. Were it not a Christian in character, they would send Dan to a different school.

Suppose that sending one's child to the local school is, in this case, supported by the (non-excluded) reasons in play: for instance, it is supported by environmental reasons—one's carbon footprint is significantly lower if one's children walk to school rather than travel by car—and let's imagine that, although we might think that it is not ideal because it prioritizes Christian values, taking into account all the relevant factors, the school is the most appropriate for both children to attend. Nevertheless, in this case, although the Dixons send Dan to the right school, they have the wrong attitude towards him and select the school for the wrong reason. They violate their duty to exclude Christian values from their deliberations when they evaluate the educational choices they face. They do not wrong Dan in their choice of school, but they do wrong him in how they arrived at their decision to send him to that school.

For a real-world case, consider the views of the Muggletonians.[26] The Muggletonians were a religious sect started in the 1650s by John Reeve and Lodowicke Muggleton who claimed to be the 'Last Two Witnesses' documented in the Book of Revelation. Among the several distinctive religious

---

[26] My understanding of Muggletonianism is from William Lamont, 'The Muggletonians 1652–1979: A "Vertical" Approach', *Past & Present* 99 (1983): 22–40, and Andrew Bradstock, *Radical Religion in Cromwell's England: A Concise History from the English Civil War to the End of the Commonwealth* (London: I. B. Tauris, 2011), 144–145. I thank Andrew Williams for pointing out the Muggletonian features of my view, at least behaviourally, and Bernard Capp for further advice.

views the Muggletonians held were particular conceptions of salvation and evangelism. They held the view that, although salvation does not require belief, those exposed to the word of the Muggletonian God but who consciously reject it are irredeemably damned. Because they held this view alongside an appreciation that one cannot be confident that one's child will embrace Christianity, to preserve their children's opportunity for salvation Muggletonian parenting involved not attempting to steer children towards Christian beliefs, and even shielding them from exposure to such views. Unsurprisingly, the Muggletonians did not gain many followers.

The Muggletonian view of morally required parental behaviour resonates with some of the features of independence-based parenting as will become clear in later chapters.[27] However, even if the Muggletonians can be interpreted as conforming with the parental activities required by independence for children, such as the non-disclosure of their religious views to young children, they did not exclude their religious beliefs when parenting: they did not refrain from treating as a reason the fact that some action, in their case non-disclosure, increases the chances of salvation for their offspring; rather, they believed in the wrongness of disclosure because they thought that shielding their children from knowledge of 'the Word' was the best bet with respect to their children's salvation. Although Muggletonian parents might have *behaved* well according to independence for children in virtue of not imparting their religious convictions to their children, they were not fully compliant with the ideal because their conduct did not exhibit the right exclusionary attitude. I shall return to defend this aspect of anti-perfectionist parenting in Chapter 4.

2.4 Independence Not Liberation

I finish my introduction to the ideal of independence for children by briefly comparing and contrasting it with a different conception of how parents and other adults should relate to the young: the *liberation* of children. Child liberationists object to the restrictions that are placed on children by parents, teachers, and society more generally—through the law, for example. In most societies, the law denies children opportunities available to adults: only those above certain age thresholds are legally permitted to vote, marry, engage in

---

[27] See, in particular, my discussion of parent-child intimacy and parents' revelation of their ethical and religious convictions in §6.1, where I claim that, if certain psychological facts are true, Muggletonian behaviour might be supported by independence for children, at least for very young children.

consensual sex, work, choose where they live, give or withhold consent to medical procedures, decide whether and what to study, and so on. In addition, parents and teachers often constrain the young in various ways: schools tell pupils what they may and may not wear, how they are to address their teachers, what they study, and when they may break for lunch or use the toilet; parents influence their child to engage in particular activities or relationships that do not always conform to the child's wishes—for example, some cajole their child to take up a musical instrument or play a particular sport, and they steer them away from playing video games or maintaining friendships with other children that they believe will lead their child astray. According to child liberationists, preventing individuals from setting and pursuing their own goals is a kind of oppression from which everyone—the young included—should be emancipated.[28]

At first sight there seems to be a good deal of common ground between the *liberation of* children and securing their *independence*. Both ideals seem to be motivated by the thought that each individual is entitled to set and pursue her own ethical goals, that others are duty-bound to respect her decisions and not impose upon her rules justified by ethical ideals she rejects. However, first appearances are deceptive. Independence for children is, in fact, hostile to the conclusions that child liberationists draw from the ideal that individuals should set and pursue their own goals, at least given the need for paternalistic restrictions on children's lives in virtue of certain non-normative facts about the developmental needs of young children.[29]

Because it is central to the issues under discussion, consider first the right to control one's own learning. In most societies, the education of individuals below a particular age is a legal requirement. Up to the relevant age, parents are required to send their child to a school or to educate her themselves according to certain standards defined in terms of the child's acquisition of particular attitudes, skills, dispositions, and understanding. Notwithstanding certain exceptions, above the relevant age the political community is not permitted to require individuals to make themselves available to be educated.[30] Child

---

[28] Prominent child liberationists include John Holt, *Escape from Childhood: The Needs and Rights of Children* (New York: Ballantine Books, 1975); Richard Farson, *Birthrights* (London: Collier Macmillan, 1974); Howard Cohen, *Equal Rights for Children* (Totowa, NJ: Rowman & Littlefield, 1980).

[29] The critique of child liberationism that follows draws on David Archard's excellent discussion, though it should be noted that he does not share my positive conception of parental morality. See Archard, *Children: Rights and Childhood*, Part II, especially Chs. 5–6. See, in addition, Laura Purdy, *In Their Best Interests? The Case Against Equal Rights for Children* (Ithaca, NY: Cornell University Press, 1992).

[30] Conscription is an exception: the political community might be entitled legally to require an adult to train to be a combatant. Adults who drive under the influence may be required to undertake a drug awareness course as a condition of escaping a fine or imprisonment.

liberationists object to these arrangements. They do not object to the universal provision of education for children. However, they insist that children should be legally permitted to refuse any kind of formal education offered to them. For some liberationists, this follows from a commitment to freedom of thought. For example, John Holt claims that everyone has a right to mental freedom: to decide what to think about.[31] We may refuse to subject ourselves to preachers or teachers who seek to try to get us to believe certain things or to act in certain ways; we are also morally permitted to decide the activities or fields of inquiry to which we devote our energies. So, for Holt, there is a fundamental human right from birth to refuse to be schooled or educated.

By contrast, the ideal of independence asserts that a certain kind of compulsory education does not wrong children. As discussed above, ethical independence requires the child to have certain mental and physical capacities that are constitutive of her setting and pursuing her own ethical goals and relationships in the right way—that is, in an informed and rational way. Thus, children need the capacity to understand and consider the merits of the different ethical ends that are feasible, and a grasp of means-ends reasoning so that they can figure out which activities would enable them to realize their ends. We can say of them that they lead an independent life only when they possess such capacities. Since that is the case, the ideal of ethical independence asserts an inalienable entitlement to the conditions that are conducive to developing the capacities required for individuals to set and pursue their own ethical goals. Once an individual possesses these capacities to the required level, it might be that she may independently choose not to exercise them on a daily basis, by submitting herself to an ethical authority for example. Still, that choice would be an exercise of independence that shapes how we understand her life under the authority: she can be viewed as self-governing to the extent that she makes an informed and rational choice to pursue a life of deference. Ethical independence requires the individual to make choices of a certain kind; there is, therefore, normative space for compulsory education if that is necessary for the acquisition of the capacities that are constitutive of the kind of choice in question. In addition to these capacities, I have argued that the political community is permitted to engage in moral enhancement by using educational institutions and, in some circumstances, perhaps other instruments, such as nudging, to get us to act in ways and adopt beliefs that respect the freedom and equality of everyone.

---

[31] See Holt, *Escape from Childhood*, 186f.

Of course, these observations are not enough to rebut the claims of certain child liberationists, particularly those who insist that these ethical and moral considerations apply as much to adults as they do to the young. If compulsion is required to get an individual to satisfy these ethical and moral requirements for independence, they might say, then so be it; the age of the individual in question is irrelevant. A prominent argument of some child liberationists is that age-based discrimination is morally unjustified.[32] If there is a case for restricting a person's freedom, that is always in virtue of her lacking certain qualities. To deny an individual freedom because most who are of a similar age to her lack the relevant qualities is a form of unjust discrimination akin to racism and sexism. Thus, there is a different child liberationist view that is not hostile to compulsory education. Rather, it claims that just as some but not all children should be educated compulsorily, some adults who lack required qualities that might be developed by education should be required by law to submit themselves for education. Moreover, it is morally impermissible to impose compulsory education on many who are young, particularly somewhat older children, who satisfy the threshold of understanding and ability for independence.

One could accept the ideal of independence for everyone and yet side with critics of age-based discrimination and the more sophisticated version of child liberation described in the previous paragraph. However, that view seems unconvincing, because age-based discrimination seems to lack the features that make racism or sexism wrongfully discriminatory. The age of an individual seems to be a good proxy for the presence or absence of certain morally relevant abilities and motivations in people—with respect to whether the individual will vote in an informed and politically engaged manner, for example.[33] Furthermore, unlike other kinds of discrimination, age-based discrimination does not disadvantage some and advantage others, at least if we assume that people live through both childhood and adulthood, and it need not involve demeaning or subordinating treatment.[34] There are reasons, then, to retain

---

[32] John Harris is a leading advocate of this view. See his 'The Political Status of Children', in *Contemporary Political Philosophy: Radical Studies*, edited by Keith Graham (Cambridge: Cambridge University Press, 1982); 'Liberating Children' and 'Reply to Purdy' in *The Liberation Debate: Rights at Issue*, edited by Dan Cohn-Sherbok and Michael Leahy (London: Routledge, 1996). For a nice discussion of this argument, see David Archard, 'Children, Adults, Autonomy and Well-Being', in *The Nature of Children's Well-Being*, edited by Alexander Bagattini and Colin Macleod (Dordrecht: Springer, 2015).

[33] See Tak Wing Chan and Matthew Clayton, 'Should the Voting Age be Lowered to Sixteen? Normative and Empirical Considerations', *Political Studies* 54 (2006): 533–558.

[34] This important difference between ageism and other kinds of discrimination, such as sexism or racism, is emphasized by Norman Daniels in *Just Health Care* (Cambridge: Cambridge University Press, 1985), Ch. 5. For further discussion, see *JLU*, 181–191. For conceptions of wrongful discrimination that make reference to demeaning or subordinating treatment, see Deborah Hellman, *When Is Discrimination Wrong?* (Cambridge, MA: Harvard University Press, 2013); Benjamin Eideslon,

age-based criteria in the administration of certain social policies and reasons for believing that age-based policies lack the features that make racism or sexism unjust. Still, we need not delve deeper into these issues here. What matters for our purposes is whether the compulsory education of the young is morally permissible, not whether compulsory education should be extended to some adults. And it seems clear that to the extent that we care about ethical independence, the young—at least very many of the young and perhaps all of the very young—should not have the legal right to control their own learning. Independence demands that children be protected from their own choices such that they develop the wherewithal to live a just life and to set and pursue their own ethical goals.

Independence for children does not, then, agree with child liberationists who hold that young children should be legally permitted to refuse to attend school or particular lessons, for example. However, it should be noted that ethical independence is sensitive to some of the same concerns that motivate child liberationists.

In the first place, child liberationists claim that dominant conceptions of childhood in modern society seriously underestimate the cognitive and emotional maturity of the young; they claim that children are capable of setting and pursuing ambitions and relationships. Even if we agree that the liberationists are mistaken in proposing to extend all or most legal rights enjoyed by adults to children, there remains the issue of how much weight to give to children's ethical views and goals when decisions are made within the family or school. An independence-respecting society does not gainsay the values of train-spotting adults; why may it deny the train-spotting ambitions of young children by insisting that they take reasonably advanced courses in mathematics, English, and so on? It is too simplistic to hold that there is a single point in our lives before which we have the capacity to set and pursue our own goals and after which we possess that capacity. Rather, the acquisition of the relevant capacities is gradual. Since that is the case, it would appear that the degree to which parents and teachers respect the wishes of the child should increase as her capacity to form, revise, and pursue ethical convictions in a rational and informed manner develops.[35]

Discrimination and Disrespect (Oxford: Oxford University Press, 2015); and Sophia Moreau, *Faces of Inequality: A Theory of Wrongful Discrimination* (New York: Oxford University Press, 2020).

[35] Here I follow Samantha Brennan who develops this view in the context of a discussion of the rights of children: 'Children's Choices or Children's Interests: Which Do Their Rights Protect?', in *The Moral and Political Status of Children*, edited by David Archard and Colin Macleod (Oxford: Oxford University Press, 2002).

We need a more nuanced understanding of the idea of 'growing respect' for children's ethical views. David Archard proposes that we take decisions regarding children and adolescents by weighing two separate considerations: the individual's interests and her convictions. Her interests can be understood in various ways, which will be determined by the larger conception of morality we hold. For example, perfectionists understand interests by reference to the complete truth about what makes a life a good one. The ideal of independence claims that individuals have an interest in developing and exercising the capacity to set and pursue their own ends and to respect the similar interest of others. Whichever view is taken, to the extent that the interests of a young person are very weighty and her own views about her interests are not rational or informed, then parents and teachers may override her desire to act in ways that would fail to realize her interests: notwithstanding her objections, they may force her to go to school to develop her ethical capacities or undergo a necessary medical procedure to improve her health. But, with respect to ethical matters, to the extent that the child's views and preferences are well informed and the product of appropriate deliberation, and her pursuit of those ambitions leave her developmental interests relatively unaffected, parents and teachers are morally required to respect the wishes of the child.[36]

This gradualist account of the acquisition of the capacity to set and pursue one's own ends has significant implications for parents and schools. As children grow in maturity, their views and ambitions should be accorded more weight just in virtue of the fact that they are the views of individuals who are more capable of deliberating about ethical matters—matters concerning sexuality, gender, appearance, occupation, religion, and so on. At some point in their development, individuals pass a threshold of maturity such that others are required fully to respect their entitlement to decide ethical matters for themselves. But those close to the threshold of maturity should be afforded considerable respect. According to this view, it is difficult to see how school uniform codes respect the views of teenage students. As children grow in maturity the

---

[36] Archard, 'Children, Adults, Autonomy and Well-Being', 11–13. For a similar view, see Paul Bou-Habib and Serena Olsaretti, 'Autonomy and Children's Well-Being', 27–29, in *The Nature of Children's Well-Being*, edited by Alexander Bagattini and Colin Macleod. See, in addition, Amy Mullin, 'Children, Paternalism and the Development of Autonomy', *Ethical Theory and Moral Practice* 17 (2014): 413–426. For a thorough empirically informed exploration of the agency rights of children, see Thomas Peto's DPhil thesis, *Children's Rights: A Liberal Framework* (Oxford University, 2018). Andrew Franklin-Hall offers a somewhat different account of respect for the decisions of adolescents in which an individual's 'stage of life' is relevant to how she is treated. See his 'On Becoming an Adult: Autonomy and the Moral Relevance of Life's Stages', *The Philosophical Quarterly* 63 (2013): 223–247. Franklin-Hall's thoughtful essay raises a series of questions that any account of the age of majority must address, but I believe that it is compatible with the gradualist account.

scope of parents' and schools' moral permission to deny children the opportunity to pursue their own goals with respect to education, occupation, sexuality, gender, appearance, and religion becomes increasingly narrower.

A second way in which child liberationist concerns chime with those of advocates of independence for children is revealed in the former's critique of prevailing attitudes towards children. Holt describes how the child is seen by adults 'as a mixture of expensive nuisance, slave, and super-pet'.[37] The dependence and vulnerability of children are viewed by many adults as representing an opportunity to control children and to decide what would make their lives go well. In the belief that they are freed from the moral principle of respect for individuals' independent judgement, adults regard themselves as entitled to decide what ethical goals children pursue and what ethical convictions they are directed towards. Many parents regard themselves as morally free to impose upon their child their own views of how she should appear—how long her hair should be and what clothes she wears—what she should learn, and what religious institution she should be a part of, if any, and so on. They regard themselves as free to express their own ethical and religious views through their child. That attitude reminds us of the certain versions of the liberal consensus and the parentalist conception of parental morality outlined in the previous chapter. Perfectionists hold similar beliefs to the extent that they claim that the immaturity of the child gives adults more opportunity to improve her life by getting her to adopt and pursue worthwhile ethical goals than they have with respect to adults who have their own independent ethical perspective. Yet this is to view children in the wrong way. Instead, we should respect the fact that everyone has a life to live and is entitled to have the character of her ethical life decided by herself and no one else. Of course, individuals might be prevented from choosing lifestyles that wrong others. But within the set of morally permissible ethical options, it is up to each individual to answer ethical questions herself rather than have someone else's answer imposed upon her.

The child liberationist elaboration of the thought that parents ought not to impose a conception of ethics or religion on the child takes the form of extending adult freedoms with respect to ethical pursuits to children: children should enjoy the same opportunities as adults to pursue their own ethical ambitions, regardless of the level of development of their deliberative capacities, even if the consequence of that freedom is that the development of their capacity to make informed decisions later in life is jeopardized. I have argued against that account with the observation that young children lack the

---

[37] Holt, *Escape from Childhood*, 1.

capacities that justify a duty on others to allow them free rein to pursue their ethical goals. Children need to be constrained in various ways to enable them to develop the capacities that are constitutive of leading an independent life. Nevertheless, there is an alternative elaboration of the thought that parents and teachers should not impose a conception of ethics or religion on the child: independence for children. Parents owe it to their child to constrain her in ways that are conducive to her leading an independent and just life, but they also owe it to her to acknowledge that the character of her ethical life is for her, not them, to decide. True, they may make their child postpone making momentous choices until she has sufficient capacity to deliberate rationally and in an informed manner about ethical and religious decisions. Still, parents and teachers must take an anti-perfectionist stance. The upbringing they give their child must be justified without appealing to the intrinsic merits of particular ethical or religious conceptions.

In this chapter, I have set out the central features of independence for children. Parents and teachers are morally required to provide young children with an education and upbringing that develops their capacity to lead just and independent lives. They must also take an anti-perfectionist stance by not enrolling them into particular ethical and religious practices that are controversial within society, because to do so would usurp children's entitlement to govern themselves. And I have argued that, although it shares certain similarities with the views of child liberationists, independence for children justifies placing various constraints on the young so that they can become just and independent.

As mentioned at the outset of this chapter, the positive vision of independence for children—the development of individuals' capacity to lead a just life and to set and pursue their own comprehensive ends—is close to the liberal consensus. The radical nature of the ideal is due to the idea of parental anti-perfectionism. In the self-conception of most parents the child's vulnerability and dependence presents an opportunity for them to improve her life by getting her to practise and endorse ethical and religious ideals that are good for her or aligned with their own. They have greater opportunity to do this because, unlike most adults who are protected from the interference of others in virtue of having their own rationally held convictions, the young child lacks the capacity to set and pursue her own ends in the right way. Independence for children rejects those assumptions about parenting by insisting that parents should be guided by an anti-perfectionist principle that forbids them from appealing to the soundness of particular conceptions of religion or what makes for a good life.

3
The Argument from Self-Rule

My argument for independence for children trades on an idea in political philosophy that was first expressed in Rousseau's *On the Social Contract* and developed by John Rawls in his *Political Liberalism*. The basic idea is that, ideally, individuals should affirm the ideals and rules that constrain them. In this chapter, I set out what I take to be an attractive interpretation of what Rawls calls 'political autonomy' and explain how it is nested within a larger account of political morality. I then use that account to support the particular moral principles that apply to parents that are affirmed by the ideal of independence for children, which I argue follow from the fact that the relationship between parent and child is relevantly similar to the relationship between the political community and individual citizens.

Before proceeding, a caveat. Readers will notice that my argument invokes various features of Rawls's conception of political liberalism, such as his ideal of 'political autonomy' and his accounts of 'the burdens of judgement', 'reasonable comprehensive pluralism', and 'public reason'. It is worth noting at the outset that, although I trade on many of his insights, my use of them and view of their implications for upbringing depart considerably from Rawls's own conception.[1]

What I call the *argument from self-rule* for parental anti-perfectionism begins with an elaboration of *liberal anti-perfectionism*. Like Rawls, I start with the claim that citizens have various moral entitlements in virtue of their status and interests as 'free and equal persons'. They are entitled to live under institutions that (a) enable them to develop and exercise the capacity appropriately to reflect on, revise, and pursue their own view of what a good life involves and (b) cultivate in them an understanding of, and motivation to comply with,

---

[1] Rawls famously wrote little about normative matters concerning the family and the upbringing and education of children. He distinguishes between 'familial' and 'political' domains. I briefly discuss that view in §3.3. He also comments on schooling within political liberalism when discussing whether his view collapses into comprehensive liberalism. There, he suggests that political liberalism's requirements with respect to the compulsory school curriculum are reasonably modest and appear to afford parents wide-ranging discretion with respect to how they educate and raise their children. See Rawls, *Political Liberalism*, 199f.

various moral norms, including the recognition that they are duty-bound to respect the entitlements of others to pursue their own conception of the good. I then introduce the idea of political autonomy, which requires us to provide reasons for political and legal institutions that are acceptable to free and equal individuals. Given the inevitable religious pluralism produced by political institutions that protect our interests as free and equal citizens, political autonomy demands that we avoid appealing to comprehensive reasons when thinking about how political and legal institutions should be arranged. Instead, identifying the right political principles should be done by appeal to what Rawls calls a 'political conception of justice' or 'public reason', both of which are constituted by reasons that derive from our interests as free and equal citizens, reasons that do not depend on the truth of particular controversial conceptions of religion. Political philosophers and citizens should refrain from regarding the law and politics as arenas for perfecting people's lives; institutions designed according to that aim would wrong many citizens by imposing on them laws and policies that are justified on the basis of religious or ethical ideals they reject.

After elaborating and defending liberal anti-perfectionism, I turn to the question of *parental* morality. I argue that the relationship between parents (and certain other adults) and children exhibits morally relevant similarities to the relationship between the political community and citizens, and if political autonomy supports the adoption of public reason for politics it also supports its adoption for understanding the rights and duties of parents.

In the final two sections, I consider certain arguments that liberal anti-perfectionists might mount to resist my extension of public reason from political to parental conduct, and I raise and discuss some other objections to parental anti-perfectionism.

3.1 Liberal Anti-Perfectionism

Political philosophy is centrally concerned with identifying the principles that ought to govern the choice of legal and political institutions, institutions that assert the right to rule over citizens, exercise coercion over individuals, and have long-term and significant effects on their lives. A familiar liberal conception of political morality has the following two features. First, included as part of the package of principles that ought to regulate the political community is a principle that protects various civil and political freedoms: (a) the right to participate in democratic institutions that determine the law—to vote, stand for office, petition one's representatives, and so on; (b) freedom of religion or conscience, including freedom of thought and the legal right to adopt and pursue the ethical life of one's choice; and (c) freedom of expression and association—the right publicly to bear witness to one's religious and ethical convictions, to join with others to pursue one's goals, and to try to persuade others to share one's view. And, second, the political community ought to be governed by principles that protect every individual's enjoyment of various social and economic goods—educational opportunity, health care, and wealth and income.[2]

In addition to these two institutional requirements, liberals who describe themselves as *political anti-perfectionists* offer a distinctive account of the reasons that ought to inform political actors. They argue that even if it is the case that we have a reason to practise a Christian lifestyle, there is a weighty reason for us to exclude that reason from consideration when identifying the principles that ought to regulate significant coercive institutions, like a society's political and legal arrangements. Political actors should, instead, operate on the basis of 'public' reasons. As the 'anti-perfectionist' label suggests, the upshot of this account of political morality is that we should not regard political and legal institutions as instruments to be used to perfect the lives of citizens. In Rawls's famous phrase, when theorizing about politics we should not appeal to 'the whole truth' about religion or what makes our lives go well.[3]

Political anti-perfectionists draw a distinction between our public and comprehensive reasons. The latter include our ethical reasons, what leading a good life for oneself consists in, and our religious reasons—the existence or non-existence of a deity and, if a deity exists, its implications for how we ought to live our lives.[4] By contrast, our public reasons are limited to our interests and conduct as citizens, politicians, and law enforcers. When acting in these roles, our conduct ought to conform to public reason, which excludes reasons that have their source in religion or a conception of what it means to live a good life.

---

[2] See, in particular, the writings of John Rawls and Ronald Dworkin who describe their own views as 'liberal'. Nothing of importance hangs on that description, and I shall not defend my characterization of this view as liberal. Others have described positions exhibiting these features as 'left-liberal' or 'social democratic' or simply 'democratic'. I am not interested in debating the meaning of liberalism. Political philosophy has focused far too much on the project of demarcating different kinds of political view and sorting different thinkers into the respective ideologies. The point of political philosophy is to offer arguments for conclusions about how we ought to act as citizens, politicians, law-makers, and parents. Using labels is sometimes useful, as shorthand, in that endeavour. Nevertheless, if my understanding of the point of political philosophy is right, it is rarely instructive to engage in debates about whether one's conception of political morality really is a 'liberal' view or some other kind of view.

[3] Rawls, *Political Liberalism*, 216f, 224f, 242.

[4] As before (§1.1), when I refer to 'ethical' ends it is important to note that I am discussing ethics in a thin sense as referring to what it means to live a good life for oneself, which excludes what 'ethics' is sometimes interpreted as including, namely, a conception of how we ought to treat each other.

For a different example of the idea of the exclusion of reasons, consider jurors who are asked to exclude from consideration their, perhaps sound, judgements concerning the moral probity of the accused formed on the basis of their religious judgements and limit their attention to whether a crime has been committed given the facts presented in court.

There is a very sizeable literature on the nature and scope of public reason. For present purposes, I'll make use of the idea as follows. Citizens, law makers, and political philosophers are under a duty to explain how the principles, laws, and policies they propose are supported by political values that respond to our status and the interests we have as 'free and equal persons', but to refrain from proposing laws and policies whose justification requires appealing to religious ideals or conceptions of what a good life involves.[5] They should address political questions by reference to a restricted set of reasons, those that refer to the moral ideal of cooperation between free and equal citizens.

Having outlined the essential features of liberal anti-perfectionism, I turn now to explain its attractions. Consider, first, the proposed entitlement to various civil and political freedoms and socioeconomic resources, which, following Rawls, I defend by reference to the interests of 'free and equal' individuals. If the foundation of our political morality is the idea of free and equal citizens, then we recognize individuals as entitled to set and pursue their own religious or ethical ends but duty-bound to ensure that others have fair opportunity to set and pursue their own ends and to participate in democratic self-government.[6] That entitlement justifies several important civil and political liberties. For example, freedom of expression is required if we are to set our own ethical and religious ends in an informed manner, as well as to examine different legislative proposals, to improve our understanding of the demands of justice, and to bear witness to and seek to persuade others of the merits of our particular conception of just social cooperation. Freedom of association and rights of democratic participation are supported by similar considerations.[7]

---

[5] Rawls calls this the 'duty of civility': see Rawls, *Political Liberalism*, 217. Rawls appears to limit the duty of civility to fundamental political matters: 'constitutional essentials and matters of basic justice'. However, he is non-committal about the extension of public reason beyond fundamental matters. His aim is to defend the public reason requirement for these matters. If they can be shown to be appropriate for those, then we can proceed to other matters to gauge whether they apply to those as well. See Rawls, *Political Liberalism*, 214–215. In what follows, I extend public reason beyond fundamental matters—indeed, beyond what is usually understood as the political domain—because the reasons that support public reason for fundamental matters appear to demand such an extension. For a defence of the broad view of public reason—though it should be noted that he does not systematically address the question of parenting—see Jonathan Quong, 'The Scope of Public Reason', *Political Studies* 52 (2004): 233–250.

[6] Rawls elaborates these requirements by reference to our interest in developing and deploying two 'moral powers': our 'capacity for a sense of justice' and our 'capacity for a conception of the good'. See Rawls, *Political Liberalism*, 19.

[7] See Rawls, *Political Liberalism*, Lecture VII.

Further liberties and the entitlement to social and economic resources follow from our interest in setting and pursuing our own comprehensive goals. Rawls describes this as our interest in developing and exercising our capacity for a conception of the good—the capacity 'to form, revise, and rationally pursue a conception of the good', our religious and ethical ends.[8] In order to set and pursue our own ends, we need educational and other related institutions that enable us to develop and exercise certain mental and physical capacities, such as the capacity to deliberate about which ethical ends are worthy of pursuit; and we need various legal freedoms and material resources that enable us to pursue the ends we select—freedom of conscience or religion, freedom of expression and association, occupational opportunity, and monetary and other resources that can be used to fund the various activities that are useful for, or integral to, the successful pursuit of one's ethical ends.

Let us turn to anti-perfectionism, which, recall, claims that within politics our conduct ought not to be informed by reasons given by comprehensive doctrines. Consider the example of Christianity. Suppose it were true that living a Christian life is always worse for individuals than living some alternative life. In those circumstances, the question is whether the political community ought to use its legal powers, over educational institutions, say, to promote suitable non-Christian lifestyles, if such promotion were shown to be successful in enhancing the well-being of its citizens. Anti-perfectionists claim that the government has a weighty reason not to do so.

What I call the argument from self-rule for anti-perfectionism proceeds from what Rawls calls *political autonomy*, which asserts that every free and equal person should endorse the legal and political institutions that govern her life.[9] To introduce that ideal, note first that, usually, we are born into a society and our life chances and self-understandings are significantly affected by particular legal, social, and political institutions that force us to do various things, exercise coercion over us, and shape the opportunities available to us. In short, we do not choose the coercive political arrangements that regulate our lives in profound ways.

Perhaps the most important question of political philosophy, originally posed by Rousseau who called it 'the fundamental question', is whether it is possible to reconcile the fact that an individual's relationship to the state is both non-voluntary and coercive with her freedom or independence.[10] Rousseau's

---

[8] Rawls, *Political Liberalism*, 30.
[9] Rawls, *Political Liberalism*, 66–68.
[10] Rousseau, *On the Social Contract*, Book I, Chs. vi–viii.

answer is that political authority and independence can be rendered fully compatible only if legal and political institutions are regulated by principles that every citizen endorses. Such endorsement would be ideal, he claims, because, when the political principles that regulate society are accepted by every free and equal citizen, each may view herself as self-governing rather than subject to principles she cannot understand or which she regards as alien to her.

Rousseau's solution is developed by Rawls who understands independence in the context of a richer account of our duties to arrange social institutions so that they distribute social goods and bads fairly. As we have seen, he claims that just political institutions must protect a range of familiar civil and political freedoms—democratic rights, and the rights of free expression, association, and conscience—as well as distribute social and economic goods so that everyone enjoys the opportunity to be healthy and has the wherewithal to pursue her goals. Rawls notes that if such institutions are maintained then a diversity of convictions about comprehensive ends will inevitably develop—this is due to what Rawls calls 'the burdens of judgement': individuals who think about these ends under conditions of freedom are, he claims, bound to disagree over which ones are worthy of adoption and pursuit.[11] Given that we have a weighty reason to arrange political institutions in a way that is compatible with the maintenance of everyone's political autonomy, it appears that those institutions must not be designed to serve any particular comprehensive end. Because citizens disagree about religion, for example, if political institutions adopted and promoted a particular view of religion, then those citizens who reject that view would no longer be constrained by rules whose justification they endorse. The upshot of this argument is political anti-perfectionism. The political community has a weighty reason to refrain from appealing to the 'whole truth' about individual well-being or our religious obligations; and it should not aim to promote the comprehensive well-being of its citizens, because that would violate the political autonomy of many of them. The *official* political morality of an ethically diverse society—the moral principles that govern its choice of laws and policies and the fundamental moral ideals that support those principles—must not depend on controversial ideas about religion or the details of personal well-being.

That, in summary, is the nature and justification of liberal anti-perfectionism. It is a conception of political morality that combines an insistence on certain moral ideals and institutional requirements but also, importantly, tells us what reasons are included or excluded in politics. Our claims to freedom

---

[11] Rawls, *Political Liberalism*, 54–58.

and equality are weighty reasons to maintain political institutions that protect various freedoms and ensure that everyone has a fair share of socioeconomic goods; our political autonomy as free and equal persons is a weighty reason when acting politically in an ethically diverse society to set aside reasons that apply to us in other domains, such as whether I should follow the instructions of a particular church when deciding what I should do for my own sake. Even if I have a reason to frame my own ethical life around the teachings of a particular religious institution, the ideal of political autonomy requires that, when I act politically, I must do so on terms that are acceptable to other free and equal citizens in virtue of their distinctive religious and ethical convictions, which may conflict with my own.

Before examining how parents fit into this view, it is worth briefly commenting on a couple of different objections to the Rawlsian conception of political morality as I have presented it. Both objections are associated with so-called convergence liberalism, which differs from the 'shared reasons' or 'consensus' conception of liberal anti-perfectionism I have outlined.[12] The first objection insists that we—political philosophers and citizens—need not exclude from consideration comprehensive convictions when judging the justice of political institutions. Some argue that laws can be justifiable to different people given the beliefs they hold even if they do not endorse these arrangements for the same reasons.[13] For instance, every citizen might view as justifiable laws that protect individuals in practising their distinctive comprehensive convictions, but whereas some will argue for such laws by appeal to the value of their own religion, others might endorse them because they believe that autonomous choice is necessary for human flourishing, or because they believe that comprehensive pluralism helps us to become more enlightened, or because there are no right or wrong answers when it comes to religious or ethical matters.

On this view, all that matters is that citizens endorse the law; from a moral point of view, we need not enquire whether they endorse the law for the same

---

[12] Prominent advocates of convergence liberalism include Gerald Gaus, *The Order of Public Reason* (Cambridge: Cambridge University Press, 2011); Kevin Vallier, *Liberal Politics and Public Faith: Beyond Separation* (London: Routledge, 2014). Other than Rawls, prominent defenders of the 'shared reasons' conception include Jonathan Quong, *Liberalism without Perfection* (Oxford: Oxford University Press, 2011); Andrew Lister, *Public Reason and Political Community* (London: Bloomsbury, 2013); Lori Watson and Christie Hartley, *Equal Citizenship and Public Reason: A Feminist Political Liberalism* (New York: Oxford University Press, 2018), Ch. 2. For helpful discussion, see Paul Weithman, 'Convergence and Political Autonomy', *Public Affairs Quarterly* 25 (2011): 327–348.
[13] For helpful commentary, see Andrew Mason, *Living Together as Equals: The Demands of Citizenship* (Oxford: Oxford University Press, 2012), Ch. 6; Paul Billingham, 'Convergence Justifications Within Political Liberalism: A Defence', *Res Publica* 22 (2016): 135–153.

reasons. But that view fails to fully capture the ideal of individual self-rule. Laws are selected and justified on the basis of more fundamental moral, religious, or ethical ideals that favour the laws in question. Similarly, individual self-rule consists in setting and pursuing one's own ends; we choose to act in certain ways to realize particular final ends. Thus, an individual's self-rule can be thwarted by others' making her pursue final ends she rejects, even if the actions they make her perform are ones she acknowledges are conducive to realizing the ends she does in fact endorse. To illustrate, consider a society with an established church in which the state enacts a law prohibiting euthanasia because the state believes that God forbids the taking of innocent human life. Suppose that many non-theistic people agree that euthanasia should be legally prohibited, but they hold that view for different reasons—they might, for example, believe that it is a just rule to adopt given the harm individuals suffer if their flourishing lives were to end prematurely and the difficulty of distinguishing between harmful and helpful euthanasia. Such citizens do not rule themselves if they live under political institutions that prohibit euthanasia for Christian reasons that they do not understand or endorse. Thus, it is morally important that the justification of the law, as well as the content of the law, be acceptable to citizens who regard themselves as free and equal.

Imagine a society in which, noting the citizenry's unanimous support for a particular law with different groups having different comprehensive reasons for their endorsement of it, a justification of the law is simply not supplied on the grounds that any justification would be rejected by some. Would that arrangement accommodate individual self-rule? Possibly. But we should acknowledge that it is often necessary to appeal to more fundamental ideals to justify particular laws. For example, it is right to prohibit murder and assault because people have an interest in not being killed or physically harmed; it would be unclear why we have those rules if people did not have those interests. So, we need an account that elaborates the ideals to which we may and may not appeal when designing political and legal rules. To the extent that we take universal self-rule seriously, that account must exclude reasons that are not acceptable to every free and equal citizen.

A second objection asserts that political liberalism does not provide justifications that are sufficiently sensitive to *actual* people's beliefs. This objection proceeds by accepting that it is appropriate to elaborate a moral and political framework that every citizen endorses. However, it rejects the Rawlsian understanding of who are owed justifications or laws that are acceptable to them in light of their own beliefs. The Rawlsian view is that the constituency consists of 'free and equal citizens' who, as noted above, are committed to regarding each other as having moral claims to a fair share of social goods that enable them to fulfil their interests in developing and deploying a sense of justice and the ability to form and pursue their own ethical convictions.[14] By contrast, justification to *actual* people takes people more or less as they are. Those who defend this view insist that individuals' thought processes must conform to certain *procedural* standards of rationality, but they do not require the *content* of their beliefs to satisfy particular requirements, moral or otherwise. Provided their views are rational in that procedural sense, even people who hold horrific views—the view that socioeconomic inequalities should be encouraged because the existence of both conspicuous privilege and poverty is valuable for the development of the arts and sciences, for example—are owed legal and political arrangements they can accept in light of their distinctive views.

It is hard to believe that the broad conception of the constituency supported by certain convergence liberals is right. If the standard for membership of the group that is owed a justification includes people who exhibit more or less the full spectrum of moral beliefs—from fascism and racism to libertarian and egalitarian conceptions—it is difficult to see how any moral claim to rule can be justified: it is not clear, for example, how this view can establish that religious fanatics who believe that heretics should be killed are under a moral or political obligation to refrain from acting on their beliefs.[15]

By contrast, the liberal anti-perfectionism I have described asserts that our reason to supply justifications acceptable to everyone is conditional. It starts with a statement of our interests and claims as free and equal citizens—that everyone has a claim to a fair share of resources to pursue just and independent lives. It proceeds to offer an account of individual self-rule that limits the imperative to offer justifications that everyone can endorse to citizens who already accept that they have a normally decisive reason to support and comply with legal and political arrangements that attend to those interests and claims. Of course, it is unfortunate if real people who live under such arrangements do not endorse the constraints they live under. Nevertheless, as I argued earlier (§2.2), that fact gives us a reason to educate these citizens to accept that they have enforceable duties to respect other citizens' freedom and equality. It does not give us a reason to be reticent about insisting that they respect

---

[14] For an elaboration of the Rawlsian conception of the constituency, see Quong, *Liberalism without Perfection*, Chs. 5–10. See, in addition, Burton Dreben, 'On Rawls and Political Liberalism', in *The Cambridge Companion to Rawls*, edited by Samuel Freeman (Cambridge: Cambridge University Press, 2003).

[15] For this objection to Gerald Gaus's conception of public justification, see Jonathan Quong, 'What is the Point of Public Reason?', *Philosophical Studies* 170 (2014): 545–553.

other citizens' entitlement to a fair share of resources to pursue their own distinctive ends.

3.2 Parents and Children: A Parallel Case

What are the implications of liberal anti-perfectionism for the upbringing of children and, in particular, what parents are permitted to do to or for their children? I'll defend the view that the idea of public reason outlined above applies to parents with respect to their treatment of their children, because the relationship between parent and child resembles the relationship between government and citizen in relevant ways.

Like most citizens, children do not choose the families or other societal institutions into which they are born; their parents' conduct has significant effects on their life chances and the values they adopt; and their parents sometimes force them to do various things and exercise coercion over them. Some of these facts are not immutable. True, the environment in which at least young children are raised must remain non-voluntary from the point of view of the child, because young children lack the cognitive wherewithal to be able to make informed decisions to enter or exit different environments of upbringing. Inevitably, young children are allocated to live under the custody of others by nature or social institutions. But we could arrange families and other institutions so that how parents act does not have profound consequences for the life of the child; and, assuming that a small number of parents retain a role in raising children, we could limit their rights to exercise force and coercion over their child with respect to how she dresses, what she eats, where she lives, with whom she has relationships, and her other daily activities.

Nevertheless, for various reasons concerning the developmental needs of children, which I discuss in further detail later (§6.1), the institution of the family characterized, among other things, by parents' enjoyment of authority and the right to exercise coercion over their children is a requirement of a just society.[16] Children need to be brought up by parents or guardians who have the authority to direct their lives, sometimes by force or coercion. Thus, the similarities between the state-citizen relationship and the parent-child relationship with respect to the presence of profound effects and the exercise of

---

[16] For a particularly detailed and nuanced elaboration of this argument, see Harry Brighouse and Adam Swift, *Family Values: The Ethics of Parent-Child* Relationships (Princeton, NJ: Princeton University Press, 2014), Ch. 3.

coercion are not merely happenstance; they are stable features of a just society that we have reason to promote and support.[17]

At first sight, then, if the ideal of independence requires us to justify and arrange unchosen coercive political arrangements so that they can be affirmed by citizens whatever the particular religious and ethical ends they endorse, the activities of parents should be similarly constrained. In short, parental anti-perfectionism appears to be a required extension of the reasons that support political anti-perfectionism. If sound, this argument establishes that parents should educate their child according to the demands of public reason rather than the comprehensive reasons that apply to their choice of how they live their own religious and ethical lives.

An obvious objection to the parallel case argument described above is that there is a morally relevant difference between the relationship between adult citizens and the state, on the one hand, and that between young children and parents, on the other. Adults reflectively endorse their religious convictions. If a state required or promoted worship it would impose on citizens rules that go against *their reasoned convictions*. However, unlike a mature citizen whose reasoned convictions operate as principled constraints on how the state can legitimately act and justify its laws, the young child lacks the properties—appropriately formed beliefs—that would make her convictions morally relevant in that way. The exercise of parental power need not, therefore, be regulated by ideals and principles that are acceptable to the child; parents are off the hook with respect to the anti-perfectionist restraint that characterizes political morality.[18]

The response to this objection is that it is mistaken to claim that the child cannot reject the ideals that govern her childhood on the basis of morally relevant—reasoned—convictions. True, she cannot offer that kind of rejection as a young child. Nevertheless, she can object to them in the right way when she becomes an adult and evaluates her upbringing *ex post*. She

---

[17] Blain Neufeld and Gordon Davis offer an extended discussion of whether the family falls within the purview of a theory of justice, and they question the view I defend here and in *JLU*. See their 'Civic Respect, Civic Education, and the Family', *Educational Philosophy and Theory* 42 (2010): 94–111, particularly at 103–107. They argue that the requirement to offer public reasons for one's actions does not apply to parents, because it does not apply to institutions that can be maintained non-coercively. Here I respond to this line of criticism by observing that, even if they are right that only coercively maintained relationships are governed by public reason, parents remain bound by public reason because there are child-centred reasons why parents ought to have rights to exercise force and coercion over their children. I should also stress that this does not mean that I accept their view that the presence of coercion is necessary for the applicability of public reason. At least some non-coercive institutions that are profoundly influential and manipulative should also be regulated by the ideal of public reason.

[18] For a statement of this objection, see Lecce, 'How Political is the Personal?', 34–35.

is capable of rejecting the ideals and principles that guide her upbringing *retrospectively*.[19]

When evaluating *ex ante* how a child ought to be raised—that is, before their child has developed the mental powers to give or withhold morally relevant endorsement—we must accept that the child might retrospectively reject any upbringing the aims of which are given by a particular comprehensive view. The explanation of this fact appeals again to Rawls's observation of the 'burdens of judgement': disagreement about comprehensive matters is an inevitable consequence of our forming beliefs and desires under free institutions.

Accordingly, in brief, the argument for *parental* anti-perfectionism is roughly as follows.

1. Parents have a weighty reason to raise their child by reference to reasons that, consistently with regarding herself as a free and equal person, she cannot retrospectively reject.
2. Parents know that their child might (reasonably) retrospectively reject any education that is justified by reference to particular comprehensive reasons.
3. There are adequate ways of raising the child that are justified on the basis of 'public reasons', reasons given by the claims of 'free and equal persons', that, by hypothesis, are not rejected by free and equal—that is, reasonable—adults.
4. Therefore, parents have a weighty *ex ante* reason to raise their child according to the demands of public, but not comprehensive, reasons.

Let me make some comments about this argument and various objections that might be raised against it. (1) is the major normative premise that animates the argument from self-rule for parental anti-perfectionism and the thought that parents are under a duty to provide their child with an upbringing that is not justified on the basis of ideals that might be rejected by the child later in life. Given its importance, I'll consider this premise and objections to it in the next section.

The second premise in the argument states a non-normative fact, but its precise meaning turns on how we understand '*might* retrospectively reject' comprehensive reasons. Different interpretations are possible. It could mean

---

[19] The idea that the moral permissibility of a particular kind of upbringing might turn on the child's retrospective endorsement is noted by Samantha Brennan and Robert Noggle in their 'The Moral Status of Children: Children's Rights, Parents' Rights, and Family Justice', *Social Theory and Practice* 23 (1997): 1–26, at 4.

'logically possible retrospectively to reject', or 'it is consistent with the laws of nature that she might reject the comprehensive ideals that governed her upbringing', 'there is a chance that she will reject them', or 'it is reasonably likely that she will reject them'. For now, I'll settle on the last interpretation: retrospective rejection of an upbringing that relies on a particular comprehensive ideal is reasonably likely.

The third premise is a claim about the adequacy of an upbringing governed by public reason. I have already offered some defence of the adequacy of an upbringing that is defended by reference to public reasons—reasons such as our status as free and equal and our interests in leading just and independent lives (§2.1) and will offer further remarks later (§5.4). But it is important, here, to note the importance of the claim that a conception of upbringing and education informed by public reason is an adequate upbringing. For if that were not the case it is hard to see how parental anti-perfectionism can be justified. If the only alternative to an independence-violating education informed by comprehensive reasons were an inadequate education based on public reasons, it would hard to choose between the two views. But I do not believe that we face such a hard choice, because, when carefully elaborated, the kind of education that is supported by public reasons is adequate and, indeed, attractive.

The conclusion of my argument is a claim about parents' (*ex ante*) reasons, that is, their reasons for action before they know what particular comprehensive ends their child will go on to follow in her adult life. Of course, if time travel were possible, parents might come to know what religious ends their child will go on to pursue in adulthood and tailor the upbringing they provide so that it does not rely on religious views that she later rejects.[20] But in the absence of such knowledge, to respect their child's entitlement to an upbringing regulated by ideals and principles that she cannot retrospectively reject, they must raise their child according to the demands of public reason and exclude any educational aims given by comprehensive reasons.

One objection to my argument for parental anti-perfectionism appeals to the idea of 'self-justifying paternalism'.[21] Imagine parents who raise their child as a Christian. Not only do they make their child practise a Christian lifestyle, they also cultivate her allegiance to Christianity by inculcating in her Christian

---

[20] I put to one side the objection that such parental conduct might violate the child's entitlement to pursue her own ends, which I discussed in §2.4.

[21] The notion of 'self-justifying paternalism' is elaborated by Archard, *Children: Rights and Childhood*, 81. It is also deployed by Andrée-Anne Cormier in criticism of my use of retrospective rejection in *JLU*: 'On the Permissibility of Shaping Children's Values', *Critical Review of International Social and Political Philosophy* 21 (2018): 333–350, at 342.

convictions. On reaching adulthood, their child looks back and endorses the Christian upbringing she received and the ethical ideals that motivated her parents. What are we to say of such a person: has her independence, understood by reference to the Rawlsian idea of political autonomy, been violated?

Before we answer that question directly, it is important to note that this illustrative counter-example to parental anti-perfectionism is, in one way, misleading because it overlooks certain other features of a liberal upbringing. One moral requirement of parents is that they educate their child so that she can reflect on and revise her comprehensive ends, which forbids parents to educate their child in particular ways. For example, it would be impermissible for them to give their child a drug that inhibited her powers of ethical reflection, or to shield her from exposure to the different comprehensive practices that attract adherents in society. The second premise of my argument trades on Rawls's account of 'the burdens of judgement' to suggest that an individual who is able and free to deliberate about religious and ethical ends might come to endorse one of many different kinds of comprehensive view and that would remain the case even if they were brought up in accordance with a particular religious doctrine. The idea that we can perfectly predict adults' beliefs and ambitions on the basis of the upbringing and education they received is mistaken, at least if we also assume that individuals are also given the wherewithal to form and revise their own comprehensive views.

But to return to the normative issue: do parents violate their child's independence if they raise her as a Christian and she goes on later to endorse the Christian reasons that guided her upbringing? It might seem that the answer is 'no'. In this example, independence is satisfied, it appears, because the individual in question fully endorses the ideals that governed her childhood. The second premise in my argument does not claim that it is impossible to respect the child's independence by giving her an upbringing guided by religious reasons. Rather it claims that, if they gave her such an upbringing alongside an education that developed her powers of rational thought, it is reasonably likely that that upbringing will retrospectively be rejected by their child.

Two further considerations support parental anti-perfectionism. First, the imagined case under discussion considers particular parents and particular children. But we might question whether our conception of parenting should be determined by such special considerations. We might instead favour a conception of parental morality that protects children's independence in general and offer an account of the reasons that inform parenting that takes into account the fact that parents are more or less able to predict or influence the future comprehensive views of their children. On this view, we favour moral rules that both apply to parents in general and protect every child's claim to self-rule across their lives—a conception of parenting that is capable of having society-wide applicability. Given that many parents are not adept in shaping their child's comprehensive values in a way that is sensitive to the comprehensive ideals to which she will become committed in adulthood, an anti-perfectionist conception of parenting, which excludes comprehensive ideals as parental reasons, is warranted.

Second, the ideal of political autonomy supports anti-perfectionist parenting even if we assume, as the self-justifying paternalism objection does, that our conception of parenting should be tailored to the circumstances of different families. For even if, as in the case under discussion, an individual comes to endorse the ideals and rules that constrained her childhood, her parents could not have known that that would be the case. Given the burdens of judgement under conditions of freedom, there is always a significant probability that, when she develops her own perspective on religious or ethical matters, a child will retrospectively reject any comprehensive ideal that informed her parents' choices. Thus, if they raise her as a Christian, parents would expose their child to the risk that she will retrospectively reject the ideals that inform her upbringing. If there is an attractive conception of parenting that avoids the risk that a child's political autonomy is violated, parents are duty-bound not to impose such a risk on her. For these reasons then, we ought to prefer an anti-perfectionist conception of parenting, which is designed to avoid such a risk.

3.3 Alleged Asymmetries

No doubt, many will baulk at the suggestion that parental morality should be responsive to public reasons rather than reasons given by comprehensive views concerning religion or the good life. They might claim that my reply to the objection that political autonomy does not apply to the relationship between parents and children is too quick. The general form of that objection asserts that there are relevant differences between the government/citizen relationship compared to that between parents and their children that render anti-perfectionism appropriate for the former but not the latter.

I have considered one version of the objection, which claims that whereas adults' ethical convictions operate as principled moral constraints such that principles of political morality must be elaborated and defended in a manner that cannot reasonably be rejected by free and equal citizens, it is *impossible* for children's views to operate in the same way, because young children's views are insufficiently well formed for us to have reason to respect them. The objection is mistaken, I argued, because in the normal course of a life children will become mature adults who hold the right kind of convictions and ambitions that warrant respect. Children are wronged by being subjected to an upbringing justified by reference to ideals they might later reject.[22]

Nevertheless, the inapplicability objection might be revised in various ways. I consider three variants of the objection. First, some have claimed that an individual's *retrospective* rejection of the principles that governed her upbringing is not relevant from a moral point of view; only *current* reasoned rejection is morally relevant. Second, it might be claimed that because the requirement of public reason is a specification of equal citizenship, it is inapplicable to the relationship between parents/adults and children since those relationships are characterized by unequal authority and power. And, finally, I consider the view that it is inappropriate to regulate interactions between adults and children by reference to public reason because the affection and intimacy that ought to characterize family life make such regulation unnecessary or damaging.

Is retrospective rejection morally problematic?

I have argued that an individual's independence is violated if she retrospectively rejects the ideals that informed the upbringing she received, for in that case part of her life is governed by moral principles she disowns—she is alienated from her childhood. What gives her rejection moral relevance is the fact that her views are formed in the right way. She exercises the capacity to think rationally for herself, to develop her own convictions, and to affirm a lifestyle on the basis of her deliberation on the alternatives available in society. She is capable of setting her own ends, and possession of that capacity justifies a claim against others to be free to set and pursue her ends; an entitlement to various freedoms—of conscience, expression, and association—so that others do not interfere with her choice and pursuit of the ends she sets herself. Where common enforced rules are required, independence understood as deliberating about and choosing the ends one pursues is impossible. But independence in the sense of being self-governing, rather than being governed by

---

[22] I ignore cases in which human children do not develop into individuals capable of accepting or rejecting their upbringing in a manner that calls for respect.

others, remains possible: we can regard ourselves as self-governing if the rules in question serve our interest in setting and pursuing our own ends and do not impose on us ethical ends that we reject.

Recall that my argument is that the reasonable rejection that condemns the enforcement of a rule can be given after the fact of the enforcement. An individual's independence is violated if she is made to follow a rule that presupposes, or is defended by an appeal to, claims about religion or ethics she later rejects. But some might object to that further step in the argument. According to this objection, independence is violated if, but only if, the enforced rules go against one's *current* reasonable convictions. What matters is that an individual is not made to follow rules or serve ideals that she rejects *here and now*. Others' constraining her when she does not currently have informed and reasoned convictions is not problematic from the point of view of her independence. I'll call this the *present rejection view*. Is the present rejection view more or less attractive than the retrospective rejection view that I have advanced?

The present rejection view might seem appealing because it captures the thought that it is bad for an individual to experience others' taking charge of her life, making her pursue ideals and goods that she believes are unworthy of pursuit. But the badness of the experience of being pushed about in these ways is insufficient to establish the present rejection view as better than the retrospective rejection view. The latter merely picks out a sufficient condition for the moral wrongness of enforcing ethical ideals. It can also allow that the experience of being made to follow ideals that currently animate one's life is a reason not to enforce religious ideals; indeed, we might regard present rejection as an aggravating factor that tells more forcefully against enforcement: that it is a greater violation of a person's independence if she is made to follow ideals that she currently reasonably rejects than if she is made to follow ideals that she subsequently rejects.[23] All I need for my argument is that later rejection renders the (earlier) enforcement wrongful.

The present rejection view must, therefore, establish that it is *only* the *current* rejection of an ethical end that gives us a weighty reason of independence against its enforcement. Perhaps it might be argued that an individual can be wronged only if she suffers a bad or unwanted experience, and an individual's future rejection of an ethical ideal does not count as an experience or as a bad experience. However, it is unlikely that this argument would support the

---

[23] Parfit holds that the respective weights of reasons given by present, past, and future consent differ. See *On What Matters*, Sec. 27.

present rejection view, for the simple reason that an individual's later rejection is often accompanied by an experience, the acknowledgement that ideals she now rejects were imposed upon her earlier in her life, and it is not clear why that experience would not count as bad or morally concerning in the relevant sense. But, in any event, the normative premise of the argument is hard to believe, because there are countless ways in which an individual can be wronged that do not refer to the quality of her experiences. An individual is wronged when her posthumous body is used in ways that do not respect her dignity or wishes: Achilles wronged Hector by dragging his posthumous body behind his Chariot in full view of his father and the people of Troy; a committed atheist is wronged if she is given a Christian burial.

A more direct reply to the present rejection view appeals to the fact that it seems attractive to extend our moral concerns about the imposition of rejected ethical ideals beyond cases in which the rejection is current. There are many cases in which an individual might be wronged by being treated in a particular way notwithstanding the fact that she presently neither accepts nor rejects the treatment in question.

Nose Job. Alan is unconscious following an accident and is undergoing an operation on his head to save his life. The surgeon notices that his nose might be a more attractive shape and fixes that as well.

It is clear that the doctor who performs the nose job wrongs Alan. Suppose that everyone knows that Alan's stable view when conscious is that his nose is the finest. If so, the fact that he does not presently give or withhold consent to an operation on his nose, because he is incapable of doing so, does not give the surgeon license to alter his appearance. She ought not to perform the nose job if, given the choice, he *would* reject the operation. Similarly, if an individual would have opposed this before he became demented, his carers may not involve him in religious worship when he becomes demented. The present rejection view is a counter-intuitive conception of what we owe to those who lose their ability to choose for themselves authentically.

Advocates of the present rejection view might respond that *Nose Job* does not show that their view is mistaken, because we might think that Alan does currently reject the operation even if he cannot express his rejection; the several publicly verifiable statements in which Alan waxed lyrical about the excellence of his nose is sufficient evidence of his current view. But suppose that Alan had not at any point in his life prior to his accident expressed any views about his nose—perhaps he has never formed any considered views about the matter. Would that make a difference? On the present rejection view, it seems that it would, because it would then be implausible to hold that Alan currently rejects the operation. However, our intuitive reaction remains that the surgeon is not morally permitted to improve the shape of his nose in this case. One explanation of that intuitive reaction is that Alan's post-operation rejection or endorsement of his new nose has moral relevance as well as his current rejection/endorsement, and we are not confident that Alan will accept as appropriate the operation he received.

For these reasons the present rejection view fails to exhaust the independence-respecting features of morality. True, a person's present rejection of ethical ideals that she is made to follow is sufficient for her independence to be violated, and that is a weighty reason against making her follow them. But, as we have seen, the further claim that independence is violated only when the treatment goes against one's current reasoned convictions does not seem plausible.

Critics of the retrospective rejection view might turn to a different view: the *present capacity view*. This view holds that it is wrong to impose ethical ends on a person who has the *capacity* to set her own ends in the right way, but not always wrong to set ends for individuals who lack that capacity. Although they do not appear to offer an argument for this view, Bou-Habib and Olsaretti entertain the present capacity view when they write 'we could think that, unless someone has the capacity to be self-determining, or to set goals for oneself, then there is no value in respecting her independence'.[24] If sound, this view would explain why anti-perfectionism applies to adults but not to young children.

The present capacity view is more plausible than the present rejection view, because it is consistent with our intuitive reaction to *Nose Job*, that it is morally impermissible to change the shape of Alan's nose. For, although, as an unconscious patient Alan does not presently accept or reject the nasal operation, he has the capacity to decide for himself the value of differently shaped noses, even though he cannot currently exercise that capacity.

Nevertheless, significant problems for the present capacity view arise in posthumous treatment cases. These problems are evident if we believe that death marks the end of one's possession of the capacity for self-determination. If so, then it is difficult to see how the present capacity view can account for

---

[24] Bou-Habib and Olsaretti, 'Autonomy and Children's Well-Being', 23. For a similar view, see Cormier, 'On the Permissibility of Shaping Children's Values', 340–341.

there being independence-based reasons to respect people's wishes for how their bodies and personal property are treated after they die.

Perhaps the critique of my appeal to the moral relevance of retrospective rejection should be further revised to assert that it is morally impermissible to set someone else's ends when that person (a) has expressed a reasoned decision about how she would like to be treated (e.g. in the event of death or loss of consciousness) or (b) has the capacity to set her own ends. Call this unwieldy conception the *present/past rejection or present capacity view*. Such a view purports to explain our reaction to both posthumous treatment cases and to cases like *Nose Job*. But it claims that parents may permissibly set ends for their child because children both lack the capacity to set their own ends and have never exercised such a capacity in the past.

Evidently, this is a possible view. It cites two sufficient conditions that make others' setting of a person's ends morally impermissible—(a) the person's present or past independent decision, and (b) her present capacity to set her own ends. Like the present rejection view, however, this view has not yet established that there is not a third sufficient condition for the wrongness of setting another's ends—her retrospective rejection. Furthermore, it leaves itself open to the suggestion that retrospective rejection is morally problematic, because it accepts that a person's independence might be violated even when she is not currently capable of choosing for herself. It violates independence if a person is treated in ways that go against her settled convictions about the ethical aims that ought to regulate her life or how she is treated when incompetent to choose for herself—when seriously demented or dead, for example. The present/past rejection or present capacity views pick out as relevant for independence only present or past facts about the person. I claim that future ethical convictions about how one's life ought to go are also relevant. An individual can be wronged by being treated in ways that go against her considered comprehensive convictions, and this is possible when others' treatment of her occurs before she has acquired a considered comprehensive perspective as well as after she has lost it. In both past treatment and future treatment cases, free and equal individuals have a moral claim to be treated according to norms that do not go against their considered convictions. The imposition on them of comprehensive conceptions that they reject before losing the capacity to decide for themselves, or might reject when they later acquire that capacity, are violations of their claim to political autonomy.

Public reason and equal citizenship

My argument is that the ideal of independence justifies extending the idea of public reason to parental conduct. Parents ought to enable their child to develop and exercise a sense of justice and morality and the capacity to set, revise, and pursue her own ethical goals. However, reasons given by particular comprehensive ideals—conceptions of upbringing and education that rest on views about how individuals ought to exercise their entitlements to lead good lives for themselves—should be disregarded for the sake of the child's independence.

One objection to this conception of upbringing is that it extends the idea of public reason beyond its proper remit. According to this objection, public reason is an interpretation of what it means for equal citizens to reason together and thereby govern themselves collectively. A democratic political community is one that includes every citizen who has the capacity to participate within the process of setting policy and the law. Such a community is inclusive in a further way: it insists that the law should be the product of citizens' reasoning together on the basis of ideals they share—what Joshua Cohen calls inclusivity in 'the space of reasons'.[25] Public reason is the tool to achieve such inclusivity, because it consists of the set of reasons that are accepted by free and equal citizens, and it sets aside reasons given by comprehensive doctrines that, in a religiously diverse society, are not recognized as reasons by everyone.

> [D]emocracy is not simply about ensuring political rights and representing interests, but is also in part about reasoning together, on a common ground that we appropriately expect others to occupy. Suppose we find something compelling in the idea of a public reason of democracy. Then we will think that exclusion from the space of reasons is a kind of civic exclusion, and a matter of democratic concern.[26]

The endorsement of a particular religion by the political community would serve to exclude those who reject that religion from the democratic process: given reasonable pluralism, we cannot reasonably expect every citizen

---

[25] Joshua Cohen, 'Establishment, Exclusion, and Democracy's Public Reason', in *Reasons and Recognition: Essays on the Philosophy of T. M. Scanlon*, edited by Jay Wallace, Rahul Kumar, and Samuel Freeman (New York: Oxford University Press, 2011). For related views, see Lister, *Public Reason and Political Community*; R. J. Leland, 'Civic Friendship, Public Reason', *Philosophy and Public Affairs* 47 (2019): 72–103.

[26] Cohen, 'Establishment, Exclusion, and Democracy's Public Reason', 261.

to agree with that ethical view and, therefore, we cannot treat the political deliberation as exhibiting 'reasoning together'. Those favouring the endorsement of the religion by the political community would, thereby, treat the dissenters as 'outsiders' to the reasoning process—to make the point vivid, we might imagine the dissenters not even understanding the propositions that the believers affirm.

To the extent that the ideal of public reason is justified by its role in ensuring that we reason together as equals there is an evident problem in extending its reach to govern parental conduct. The relationship between parents and children, at least young children, is marked by the absence of reasoning together. Unlike the democratic relationship in which every citizen has the right to exercise her capacity to participate as an equal in deciding the law, it is undesirable for the rules that govern the relationship between parents and children to be the product of a deliberative process in which children participate as equals. Young children do not satisfy the relevant capability threshold to qualify for the right to participate in the process of collective self-government, because their beliefs are often ill informed and ill thought out. If the ideal of public reason is applicable only to citizens' reasoning in the project of democratic self-government, its extension to regulate the conduct of parents is unwarranted.[27]

In reply, I agree that the idea of public reason and its restriction on the reasons that might be invoked to justify coercive rules is necessary for democratic self-government, but it does not follow that it is relevant only as a characterization of the democratic ideal. Consider emergency situations in which we have decisive reason to suspend normal democratic politics, such as certain wartime situations in which it is not possible or desirable to deliberate together about what the law should be. Suppose, then, that government by a ruling body that is relatively free of democratic scrutiny by the citizenry were temporarily appropriate to defend the long-term survival of the polity. According to the strong claim, which asserts that it serves only as a characterization of the democratic ideal, public reason would lose its relevance when democratic politics are suspended in that way. But that view seems implausible because it fails to recognize the different ways in which individuals might be excluded or alienated from the political process. No doubt, individuals can be excluded from the process of reasoning together. But they can also be alienated politically by being constrained by laws that are justified by religious ideals that they reject or cannot make sense of, and that kind of alienation remains relevant

---

[27] For a statement of this objection, see Christina Cameron, 'Clayton on Comprehensive Enrolment', *The Journal of Political Philosophy* 20 (2012): 341–352, at 343.

even when it is impossible or undesirable for those who are subject to the law to participate in the law-making process. Public reason is not rendered irrelevant by the inability of children to reason together as equals with their parents.[28]

Does affection make public reason unnecessary?

The third alleged asymmetry between the political and the parental that I discuss, and return to later, claims that it would be a mistake to apply liberal public reason to the relationship between parents and children because parents display, or ought to display, love and affection for their children, and such emotions are inconsistent with the kind of impartiality demanded by the detached impartial norms demanded by public reason. The value of familial love and affection, the argument goes, overrides or cancels the need for public reason.

Before looking at a particular objection of this kind, it is worth reminding ourselves of the central features of public reason as I am using it, to dispel certain misconceptions. In the first place, recall that public reason has positive and negative aspects. Its positive aspects are drawn from, among other things, the needs and interests of citizens in virtue of their interest in developing and deploying a sense of justice and the ability to frame for themselves and to pursue their own view of what it means to live a good life. That part of public reason gives us an agenda for deciding how children ought to be brought up—how parents and others ought to educate children, for example. Its negative aspect picks out as excluded within politics—and, I claim, parenting—certain ideals that are relevant in other parts of one's life. Comprehensive ideals about religion and how to live a good life are excluded reasons when acting politically or in one's capacity as a parent.

Second, note that public reason might be expressed differently by different institutions. For example, the public reasons that apply to judges are different to those that apply to soldiers. The role of a judge in a court of law demands the development and expression of legal understanding, interpretive skill, and virtues such as impartiality and appropriate sensitivity to the situation of particular witnesses, defendants, and victims. From soldiers we demand appropriate fidelity to the command structure in which she works, a

---

[28] I might be even more concessive. I might accept that the full realization of public reason demands people to reason together as equals in the law-making process. It is consistent with this view to claim that the exclusion of non-public reasons is appropriate when the sharing of political power is impossible or undesirable. Thus, an entitlement to be treated according to norms justified by reference to public reason is not conditional upon the possession of the capacity to reason together with others.

sense of camaraderie, courage, and strategic initiative. It is not the case that the requirements of public reason apply in the same way across different roles. Accordingly, the positive aspects of public reason need to be tailored to fit the division of labour between the different basic institutions of society.

With these qualifications in mind, let me address just one affection-based objection—I address others in §6.1. The objection argues that public reason applies only when it is necessary to resolve competing claims, which makes it appropriate for political morality, but inapplicable to the family in which parents rightly take their interests to coincide, rather than to be in conflict, with those of their child. This objection is reminiscent of a particular communitarian critique of liberal political philosophy, which asserts that justice is a remedial virtue, a second-best that is warranted only when concern, community, or common purpose is lacking between people.[29] Even if communitarians are wrong about the possibility of achieving a *political* community in which citizens express solidaristic concern for each other, rather than assert claims that conflict and compete with those of others, we might nonetheless agree with them that we should aspire to maintain families in which communal attachment and altruistic concern make the need for principles to resolve conflicting claims unnecessary.[30]

The argument from self-rule for parental anti-perfectionism takes seriously the fact that affective or intimate family life plays a distinctive role within the basic structure of society. The question we face is how the nature of those relationships should be understood and, in particular, whether they render parental anti-perfectionism redundant—the objection under consideration suggests that they do. However, the critique is not convincing because there are moral constraints on the kinds of altruistic concern that individuals are morally permitted to impose on others.

Suppose that the love and affection we believe that families ought to exhibit also characterized the relationship between citizens. Would that make a difference to the case for political anti-perfectionism? No. Consider a society with a majority of Christian altruists who display as much love, affection, and concern to strangers as they do to their children. Nevertheless, such Christians are not morally permitted to use the state to pursue their mission of saving souls—to

---

[29] See Michael Sandel, *Liberalism and the Limits of Justice* (Cambridge: Cambridge University Press, 1982).
[30] Rawls himself seems to accept this view of the family to some extent when he writes that 'the personal and the familial ... are affectional ... in ways the political is not', and he takes that fact to mean that public reason applies indirectly, rather than directly, to family matters. Rawls, *Political Liberalism*, 137. See also Rawls, 'The Idea of Public Reason Revisited', §5.

78 INDEPENDENCE FOR CHILDREN

use tax receipts to encourage conversion to Christianity, for example. The ideal of political autonomy, which requires citizens to be in a position to endorse the principles that constrain them and the reasons given for those principles, places a moral constraint on the kind of concern that altruists are permitted to display in their capacity as political agents. So, even if individuals' interests are bound up with how others fare, or they are thoroughgoing altruists, it does not follow that the constraints of public reason are unnecessary.[31] And, by extension, the fact that parents should display love, intimacy, and affection for their child does not render anti-perfectionism redundant.

3.4 Some Misconceptions

I have discussed objections to the argument from self-rule that try to establish that there are morally relevant differences between the state-citizen and parent-child relationships, which suggest that respect for independence is a political, but not a parental, requirement. Many other objections might be raised against this argument for parental anti-perfectionism, some of which I discuss later. I finish this chapter by itemizing some possible misinterpretations that might lead us to prematurely reject independence for children.[32]

Retrospective rejection

First, it is important to clarify the role of retrospective rejection in the argument for parental anti-perfectionism. On one reading of retrospective rejection, the moral permissibility of parents' conduct always *turns on* whether the upbringing and education they propose to give to their child will later be rejected or accepted by her when she has the capacity to form her own considered views about ethics and religion. If she later rejects it then the proposed

---

[31] Interestingly, the good Samaritan story told by Luke (10:29–37) involves the Samaritan giving help in the form of providing Rawlsian primary goods—money, transport, shelter, and health care—rather than goods that are defined by reference to a particular religion. The Samaritan did not, for example, exploit the victim's vulnerability by including him in religious practices that were rejected as idol-worshipping apostasy by Jews at that time. Our reaction to his conduct might be different had he done so.

[32] My selection of possible interpretations is informed by others' critical discussions of parental anti-perfectionism as I presented the view in *JLU*. I shall not examine whether what I call misconceptions involve misinterpretations of the view presented in that book. Although I believe that certain critics' objections rest on misreadings, it is entirely understandable if others are not terribly interested in such exegetical matters.

upbringing violates her independence; if she later accepts it then it doesn't violate it. On this view the child's later retrospective acceptance or rejection is the only basis on which we might permissibly decide how to educate her.[33]

That is a misreading of the argument. As I hope the preceding discussion has established, retrospective rejection plays a limited role in my argument for parental anti-perfectionism. It is invoked to rebut an objection that might be raised against the argument that children cannot be wronged in the way citizens are wronged when they are subjected to principles that they reasonably reject. The objection is that whereas adults have appropriately formed convictions about religion and what it means to live well, which render their rejection of the principles and institutions that constrain them morally relevant, because children—at least young children—lack stable and reflectively formed convictions of that kind, parents are off the hook with respect to the requirement that the upbringing they provide must be defended on the basis of ideals and arguments that cannot be rejected by reasonable persons. The possibility of appropriately rejecting the principles that guide one's upbringing retrospectively, when one is mature, answers the objection that purports to give parents an escape route from the requirements of public reason.

Retrospective endorsement is not, then, the primary or only justificatory basis for deciding how children should be raised. Indeed, the liberal anti-perfectionist ideal, which emphasizes the importance of people's endorsement of their upbringing, is nested within a larger conception that demands that we treat each other as free and equal. That status is constituted by having an interest in being educated in such a way that one can form, revise, and rationally pursue ambitions concerning religion and living well, for example, and an interest in being educated to have a sense of justice.

We can imagine an educational regime operating with the aim of developing free and equal citizens so understood but which is in fact rejected by some adults who, for various reasons, have developed views that deny the importance of freedom and equality. For example, many people hold racist views that lead them to reject educational institutions that try to encourage children to treat everyone with equal concern and respect. If retrospective endorsement were the only principle in play then an educational regime that encouraged tolerance and anti-discrimination would wrong those who go on to be racists in adulthood.

---

[33] For this interpretation, see Dennis Arjo, 'Public Reason and Child Rearing: What's a Liberal Parent to Do?', *Journal of Philosophy of Education* 48 (2014): 370–384, at 374–377.

But this misunderstands the argument. The value of individuals' endorsement of the rules that constrain them is limited to certain cases. That thought is captured in the idea that the rejection must be 'reasonable'. To illustrate: suppose that I know that if Amy walked across an unstable bridge she would cause Bryn, who is admiring the view from the bridge, to fall off and die or suffer a serious injury. Assume in addition that, although I cannot communicate with her, I can prevent Amy from walking across the bridge. In this case, I am morally permitted—indeed, morally required—to prevent Amy from crossing the bridge. Does the rightness of my action turn on whether Amy will, after the fact, accept that it was right to have been prevented for the sake of Bryn? (Suppose I know that Amy regards Welsh people, like Bryn, as inferior and I am, therefore, certain that she would object to being prevented from crossing the bridge just for his sake. Should that give me pause?) No. Amy has an enforceable duty not to cause harm to others that justifies my preventing her from crossing the bridge. Whether she later accepts or rejects my constraining her is irrelevant.

Any plausible conception of the ideal of cooperation between free and equal persons includes a conception of the several enforceable duties that apply to us and also the interests that we have regardless of our endorsement, some of which I set out in §2.2.[34] But it is worth highlighting the fact that liberal anti-perfectionist parenting has these features to rebut objections that proceed as if the only basis for determining a child's education is whether she will later accept or reject that education. If the ideals of freedom and equality are taken seriously, then parents and adults are morally required to educate children to develop and deploy a sense of justice and the various faculties to deliberate rationally. The validity of those requirements does not depend on the anticipated future endorsement of the individuals who are so educated.

Is retrospective rejection redundant?

If what I have said is right, then a different objection might be raised—the redundancy objection, I'll call it. If I accept that an education is not rendered morally impermissible just in virtue of being rejected by the individual who was subjected to it, then retrospective rejection plays no role in the argument. All that matters is whether the education in question is appropriate according to standards that make no essential reference to what the person being

---

[34] See also *JLU*, Ch. 4, for a more complete account of an education for a sense of justice.

educated values or will value later in life—what Steven Wall calls a 'correctness-based justification'.[35]

But that objection rests on a different misconception. Accepting the view that retrospective rejection does not always render one's education illegitimate does not imply that it never does. Consider as an analogue Rawls's conception of political liberalism: we need not treat as problematic for the adoption of a particular set of principles of justice the fact that racists would not endorse them; but the rejection of proposed principles by people who are motivated by due concern and respect for other citizens *is* a reason not to adopt such principles.

Similarly, the argument from self-rule objects to treating as reasons for upbringing ethical or religious ideals that, as free and equal persons, children might later reject. Since we have to hand an education that serves their interests in becoming free and equal, we should be content with that. A conception of upbringing that goes further by being informed by a particular view about what a successful life consists in—even supposing that those views are entirely sound—would threaten to violate individuals' political autonomy by subjecting them to an upbringing they might later reject. For those who later reject these views and an upbringing informed by them, part of their lives— their childhoods—would be governed by principles that, on the basis of their mature reflection, they reject as nonsensical, misguided, or damaging.

So the redundancy objection fails. Retrospective rejection has a role to play in justifying the exclusion of comprehensive ideals within a conception of upbringing even if with respect to other issues concerning how children are raised—those that engage our interests in freedom and equality—its presence or absence is irrelevant.

The paralysis objection

A different objection rests on a similar misconception. The objection asserts that retrospective rejection renders any kind of parenting impermissible. Permissible parenting is impossible, the argument goes, because however she is educated, an individual might later object to the education they have received. True, the objection accepts, adults who received an upbringing guided by the value of their holding particular religious convictions, for example,

---

[35] Steven Wall, 'Is Public Justification Self-Defeating', *American Philosophical Quarterly* 39 (2002): 385–394. For this objection to my view, see Arjo, 'Public Reason and Child Rearing', 378–379.

might object to having been so directed; but it is also the case that those who were not given an upbringing premised on the value of that religion might now object because they believe that their lives would have gone better had they received a religiously informed education.[36] In short, the criterion of reasonable rejection seems to condemn an anti-perfectionist upbringing as much as one in which the child is enrolled into a particular ethical or religious conception.[37]

In reply, it is worth reiterating that anti-perfectionism focuses on the *reasons* that inform how we ought to act. A person is not wronged merely in virtue of objecting to being constrained in a particular way. If those constraints are supported by relevant non-excluded reasons, then the fact that she objects to them does not affect their justifiability. As noted above, the kind of retrospective rejection that counts is rejection by individuals who acknowledge a commitment to the ideals of freedom and equality and the interests that correspond to those ideals. We have, then, a basis for an education that cannot reasonably be rejected, where 'reasonableness' is understood in terms of those commitments. In this view, parents and educators are required to bring children up to have a sense of justice and possess deliberative capacities so that they can form and pursue religious or ethical conceptions that grip them as right. Such an education is the core of an education suitable for free and equal persons. If they followed those requirements, the question would arise whether parents might have any further reasons for action—to encourage their children to follow a particular religious view or to ensure that their children's lifetime preference-satisfaction is maximized, for example. Because treating controversial religious or ethical ideals as reasons for parental action might retrospectively be rejected by their adult children, these reasons should be excluded as bases for elaborating a conception of parental morality for the sake of respecting children's political autonomy.

Is this reply sufficient? After all, there might be several ways of getting children to be free and equal persons. Consider, for instance, different kinds of schooling that are capable of developing a sense of justice and children's deliberative capacities, such as homeschooling, comprehensive or integrated schooling, and selective schooling. Suppose that these different regimes of

---

[36] For this objection, see Arjo, 'Public Reason and Child Rearing', 378. For a similar objection, see Andrew Franklin-Hall, 'What Parents May Teach Their Children: A Defense of Perfectionism in Childrearing', *Social Theory and Practice* 45 (2019): 371–396, at 383.

[37] Note that if this objection is sound, then it serves as an objection to political anti-perfectionism as well as parental anti-perfectionism. For an individual might reject the laws that constrain her life if they are justified by appeal to a particular religious doctrine she cannot understand or does not accept; similarly, she might reject political principles that are not informed by the religious doctrine she accepts. If the idea of reasonable rejection produces paralysis with respect to parenting, then it also seems to produce paralysis for political liberalism more generally.

schooling performed the task of satisfying the interests of free and equal persons equally well. Still, they have further features—more or less integration between the sexes and different social classes, for example—that might retrospectively be rejected by individuals in later life. If so, the paralysis objection is given new life because whichever schooling regime is chosen brings with it the possibility of retrospective rejection by the children affected by it, or so the argument might go.

Reply: retrospective rejection is reasonable only if it is consistent with the ideal of free and equal citizenship. Accordingly, individuals must recognize that they need an education that gives them the intellectual and motivational wherewithal to act justly and reflectively form and pursue their own goals. If several kinds of schooling satisfied those demands without jeopardizing other legitimate goals, but one must be selected, then we would need a fair procedure for choosing between the options. Under these circumstances it would not be reasonable for a person to complain that her schooling did not give her the opportunity to be educated with boys (or, conversely, that it mandated coeducation). She should acknowledge that a schooling regime had to be adopted and the particular regime that governed her education was fairly chosen on the basis of public reason among the set of regimes that were fit for purpose. Her personal preference for an alternative kind of schooling could be achieved only by bypassing the fair procedure for selecting among the suitable alternatives.

Just another comprehensive doctrine?

I turn, finally, to the objection that my argument from self-rule for an anti-perfectionist upbringing is incoherent because it collapses into a particular (liberal) comprehensive doctrine that might be rejected by reasonable persons. Before I rehearse the objection, it is worth recalling the distinction between public and comprehensive reasons. Public reasons, I have stipulated, are reasons that are acceptable to free and equal persons, and include, for example, an education that enables individuals to set their own ends and to respect others' claims to do the same in the way I have described. Comprehensive reasons guide us in living well according to some well worked out conception of human flourishing and our place in the universe.

Dennis Arjo argues that an education governed by public reason assumes that 'children qua children have no intrinsic need of or right to religious beliefs and practices, the authoritative texts or teachings of a faith, or the rituals, ceremonies and rites of passage they ground', which assumes 'the truth of a comprehensive doctrine, namely liberalism as a full-blown comprehensive account of a good life'.[38] The comprehensive liberal account of the good life he has in mind is not fully specified, but it seems to have at least the following feature: that children are not harmed if their parents do not initiate them into religious practices.

First, it is worth noticing that if Arjo is right then his argument brings into question not only publicly justifiable education as I have theorized it, but also political liberalism more generally. Political liberals, like Rawls, claim that the political community is under a duty to ensure that children receive an adequate education. Refusing to engage in disputes about comprehensive ethical matters, the political liberal state, as Rawls understands it, allows parents to bring their child up according to their own comprehensive convictions.[39] In this way, it permits parents not to educate their child according to a religious doctrine. If political liberals regard such as education as adequate, and educational adequacy must rest on an account of what is necessary for children to lead good lives, then it seems that, in allowing parents to provide a non-religious upbringing, the political liberal educational policy thereby assumes the truth of a particular comprehensive doctrine, namely, that children can lead good lives without religious belief or practise.

But, more fundamentally, it is not the case that liberal anti-perfectionist education I have outlined assumes that one can live well without religious belief or practise. Rather, it rests on the judgement that an education informed by public reason attends adequately to children's needs as free and equal persons and respects their claims to self-government. It is quite compatible with this conception to hold that people's lives, including children's lives, go worse to the extent that they lack religious commitment and practise. Nevertheless, it adds that the ideal of political autonomy, which supports the exclusion of controversial comprehensive reasons from a conception of upbringing, means that children might not receive an upbringing that is ethically best for them. On this view, an adequate education should not be equated with an education that necessarily maximally promotes the ethical interests of their child: it follows Rawls's insistence that we should not appeal to 'the whole truth'. Arjo's claim that my argument collapses into a comprehensively liberal account of education rests on the assumption that parents ought to give their children what they need to have good lives.[40] But that assumption is not shared by political liberals or those who advocate an anti-perfectionist upbringing. There is, then, no collapse into comprehensive liberalism.

---

[38] Arjo, 'Public Reason and Child Rearing', 381.
[39] Rawls, *Political Liberalism*, 199–200.
[40] Arjo, 'Public Reason and Child Rearing', 381.

4
The Attitudinal Requirement

4.1 Enrolment and Intention

One feature of independence for children is that it requires parents to display a particular attitude towards their child: when deliberating about how to raise her, parents ought to exclude from their set of aims certain goals that they strive to fulfil in their non-parental lives. For example, suppose they have a reason to worship a particular god. That reason may inform their decisions about how they live their own lives, but they should exclude that reason when it comes to raising their child. They are permitted to be guided by their belief that God should be honoured in their own lives and for that reason devote time for regular acts of worship, but they may not be guided by that reason in what they make their child do.

To see this more concretely, consider the nature of religious or ethical *enrolment* of children, which involves parents' making their child act in ways that realize their (the parents') objective that her conduct conforms to particular religious standards. Many parents believe that part of their role is to ensure that their child is raised in a way that brings her beliefs and actions closer to the truth about ethics and religion. That might include intentionally shaping her beliefs and desires such that she comes to appreciate the merits of the religious conception in question; it can also involve intentionally constraining her activities so that she conforms to the demands of the doctrine—preventing her from acting in ways that are sinful, for example, even before she has any well-formed beliefs about the nature of sin or which actions are sinful. In these ways, then, enrolment involves parents' making their child serve—honour or promote—particular religious ends.

Independence for children is hostile to that kind of intentional activity. It claims that parents wrong their child when they make her serve or participate in controversial religious ends. But notice that the claim that *enrolment* is morally impermissible goes beyond the conclusion that follows from the argument from self-rule. For, if sound, that argument establishes only that reasons that are relevant for certain kinds of conduct—how one lives one's own life—are excluded when determining appropriate conduct in other contexts, particularly, how to exercise political and, I argue, parental power. In the roles of citizen or parent, it is *public* reasons that determine how we ought to act. However, that position is consistent with parents' acting on their religious or ethical beliefs provided that the actions they perform are actions that are required or permitted by public reason. Public reason tells us what actions individuals ought to perform in a certain domain, but individuals can perform those actions for a variety of motives, some of which may be religious. To take a well-known example, Martin Luther King and his followers did more than most to promote the public reason ideals of liberty and equality by challenging racial discrimination and campaigning for civil rights for all, but he and many of his supporters were motivated by religious convictions.[1] A similar view is available regarding children's upbringing. It could be that children are entitled to an upbringing that develops their moral capacities and enables them to adopt, reflect upon, and rationally pursue a particular view of religion or ethics. Parents might be successful in satisfying those requirements even if they are motivated by religious convictions.

Even if independence for children said nothing about the kinds of attitudes or intentions parents should have as parents, its claims about the reasons that do and do not apply to the role of parent would remain significant. That is because the exclusion of comprehensive reasons makes a difference to the range of acts that are permissible and impermissible. If the truth of Christianity is an excluded reason, then it is hard to see how one can justify making one's child perform a daily act of worship. Similarly, if atheism is excluded as a reason, it is hard to believe that parents are justified in preventing their child from developing an understanding of a range of different religious views.

Nevertheless, the conception of upbringing I am defending goes further by claiming that the moral permissibility of parental conduct sometimes depends on the reasons that motivate parents to act as they do. Consider this case:

Sunday Schooling. Two sets of parents are deciding whether to accept an invitation to send their child to a Christian Sunday school run by the local church. The Athertons are atheists, but observing that their child, Arthur, is already exposed to atheist norms as a side effect of living within their family, they decide to introduce him to a different ethical perspective—one involving religion. So, they accept the invitation. The Booths are Christians who accept the invitation to send their child, Beth, to the Sunday school because they

---

[1] Rawls discusses King's use of religious arguments for civil rights in *Political Liberalism*, 247–251.

want her to learn and practise the Gospel as a child and make it more likely that she will continue as a Christian in adulthood.

In *Sunday Schooling* there are two notable differences between the Athertons and the Booths. First, there are differences in the non-motivational facts of the case. The Athertons are atheists and the Booths are believers. It could be that this difference makes a difference to how Arthur and Beth ought, respectively, to be educated. Suppose it were valuable for the development of the child's own independent judgement about which ethical practices to pursue to have some schooling that challenges the norms to which one is inevitably exposed within the family setting. In that case, the Athertons would act as they should by sending their child to Sunday School; the Booths would act as they shouldn't, because their sending Beth to the School would reinforce, rather than challenge, the ethical ideas exhibited in the home.

The second difference is that the Athertons and Booths are motivated by different reasons. The reasons that motivate the Athertons are public reasons. Specifically, they do not have an ethical plan for Arthur; their aim is simply to educate him such that he is in a position to make informed decisions about comprehensive matters for himself and to honour his duties to others. By contrast, the Booths are motivated by their religious convictions. They want Beth to practise Christian worship as a child and they want to maximize the likelihood of her remaining a Christian throughout her life by using the available opportunities to reinforce the Christian beliefs and desires they foster within the home environment.

In this chapter, it is the second difference, the difference of motive or intention, that is our focus. Given the parental anti-perfectionist position I have elaborated and defended, is it morally problematic that the reasons that motivate the Booths are ethical or religious in nature? I believe that it is, but to explain and defend that conviction I must draw certain distinctions to clarify the different ways in which attitudes might be morally relevant and engage with some recent writing on the relationship between intentions and moral permissibility.

It is important, first, to notice that *Sunday Schooling* is not a good case to test whether intentions have fundamental relevance for judging the permissibility of parents' actions, because our reaction to it might be explained by the first difference—the non-motivational facts of the case. If we think that the Athertons act permissibly, but the Booths do not, that reaction might be explained by the fact that by sending Arthur to Sunday School the Athertons provide their child with a different perspective on religion whereas the Booths fail to provide that for Beth. That explanation leaves open the question of whether the difference in the putative reasons that motivate the respective parents has fundamental relevance in considering the case. To test that intuition, we need a case in which two sets of parents make the same choice, and the effects on their respective children are the same, but their motivations differ. So, recall the case of *Local Schooling*:

> *Local Schooling.* The Carters and the Dixons are two sets of Christians who hold Christian convictions. They send their respective children to the local Christian school. The Carters send their child, Carly, to that school because it is the local school. They would send her to the school even if it were a school that did not favour any particular religious or ethical doctrine. The Dixons send their child, Dan, to the school because the school's ethos is supportive of Christian values. Were it not supportive in that way, they would send Dan to a different school.

To make it a case to assess the moral relevance of the reasons that motivate parents, let us suppose that sending Carly and Dan to this particular school is consistent with public reason. Suppose there are good reasons for this school to exist and, in this case, for both Carly and Dan to attend the local school: for example, sending them there is supported by environmental reasons—their carbon footprint is significantly lighter if they walk to school rather than travel by car, bus, or train. Still, does the fact that the Dixons send their child to the local school for religious reasons render their decision morally impermissible? In this case, the facts of the case are the same. The Carters and Dixons are both Christian parents who propose to send their children to a school that tends to promote Christian values. The only difference between the two sets of parents is the reason that motivates them—whereas the Carters set aside their Christian views when deciding how to school Carly, the Dixons act from religious reasons.

4.2 Independence and the Trolley Problem

If, as I believe, the Dixons wrong Dan by sending him to the local school, what kind of wrong do they commit? To answer that question, it is helpful to consider how we ought to address a different problem that has received considerable attention in moral philosophy, the so-called *Trolley Problem*.[2] That

---

[2] The original case was presented by Philippa Foot in her 'The Problem of Abortion and the Doctrine of the Double Effect', *Oxford Review* 5 (1967): 5–15. The literature on the different variants of the cases I discuss is vast. See, for example, F. M. Kamm's, *The Trolley Problem Mysteries*, ed. Eric Rakowski

problem concerns how to explain many people's considered reaction to the following pair of hypothetical cases:

Trolley. There is an out-of-control trolley (tram) that, absent human interference, will kill five people who are on its track. The driver, Alice, can divert the trolley, which will prevent the five from being killed. Unfortunately, there is a single person, Bob, on other track who will be killed as a result.

Bridge. There is an out-of-control trolley that, unless it is stopped, will kill five people who happen to be on its track. Candani knows that the only way to stop the trolley is to push Declan off the bridge onto the track. His body will stop the trolley, but he will be killed as a result.

Most people's intuitive reaction to this pair of cases is that, while Alice is morally permitted to save the five by diverting the trolley, Candani is not permitted to save the five by using Declan's body to stop the trolley. Granted, in both cases five are saved and one is killed. But it is the way in which the killing happens that makes the decisive moral difference.

If we accept that there is a moral difference between *Trolley* and *Bridge*, we need to identify how best to characterize and explain that difference. Several answers have been offered, but I focus on what I believe is the most plausible account, which is articulated by Victor Tadros who draws on and develops Warren Quinn's conception of the doctrine of double effect.[3] First, Tadros notes that certain actions are morally optional in the sense that an individual is neither morally forbidden from performing them nor morally required to perform them. Second, he claims that with respect to morally optional actions, individuals are entitled to decide for themselves how to act.

> [P]eople are entitled to determine for themselves which ends to pursue, even if their ends are not the most valuable ends considered impartially. There are

(New York: Oxford University Press, 2016), which also includes important discussions by Thomson, Hurka, and Kagan.

[3] Warren Quinn, 'Actions, Intentions and Consequences: The Doctrine of Double Effect', reprinted in his *Morality and Action* (Cambridge: Cambridge University Press, 1993); Victor Tadros, *The Ends of Harm: The Moral Foundations of Criminal Law* (Oxford: Oxford University Press, 2011), Pt. II, and his 'Wrongful Intentions without Closeness', *Philosophy and Public Affairs* 43 (2015): 52–74. Prominent alternative answers to the questions raised by these cases focus on the differences in the causal facts that obtain in the different cases (e.g. Kamm, *The Trolley Problem Mysteries*) or who it is that is in a position to act to save the five (e.g. Judith Jarvis Thomson, 'Turning the Trolley', *Philosophy and Public Affairs* 36 (2008): 359–374).

some ends that must not be pursued, and there are circumstances in which the only thing to do is also impartially best. But the fact that some end is impartially best does not in and of itself give rise to a duty to pursue it.[4]

In the context of the Trolley Problem, 'impartially best' means saving the greater number: the five rather than the one. It rests on the assumption that the loss of one life is impartially better than the loss of five, which is plausible: no one's life counts more than anyone else's; because each life counts for one, the loss of fewer lives is better than the loss of more, other things being equal. Nevertheless, Tadros plausibly claims that we are sometimes morally permitted to act in ways that depart from what is impartially best. Note, in addition, that the 'best' outcome might be described without reference to the goods and bads that several people enjoy; it might make reference to the goods enjoyed by a single person. For example, when deciding whether to learn to play the piano or the ukulele, suppose that, all things considered, it is better for me to take up the ukulele. This might be for various reasons: it might be that I have a weighty reason to perfect my abilities at an instrument I can accomplish more with and, given the unusual smallness of my hands, I will be able to master the ukulele to a much greater degree than the piano. Still, although it would be better for me if I chose the ukulele—I have decisive prudential or self-regarding reasons to do so—I would not be doing anything *morally* wrong by taking up the piano instead. And given that I am not morally required to take up the ukulele, whether I choose it or the piano is something I am entitled to decide for myself.

The second part of Tadros's argument is an account of what the entitlement to set one's own ends implies for our duties to other end-setters. He claims that 'it is normally wrong to compel a person to serve an end that the person lacks a duty to serve'.[5] In the cases that interest him, such as *Trolley* and *Bridge*, the actions of Alice and Candani are harmful to Bob and Declan respectively. Notwithstanding the harm that Bob suffers when she diverts the trolley, Alice's action is morally permissible; by contrast, Candani's pushing Declan off the bridge to stop the trolley is impermissible. One morally significant difference is that Candani's action involves compelling Declan to serve a particular end, the saving of the five, that he lacks a moral duty to serve. It is reasonably uncontroversial to claim that Declan lacks such a duty. To see this, note that the duty in question would be for Declan to jump off the bridge to his certain death to stop

---

[4] Tadros, 'Wrongful Intentions without Closeness', 65.
[5] Tadros, 'Wrongful Intentions without Closeness', 66.

the trolley from killing the five, or to agree to being pushed off the bridge if he cannot bring himself to jump. Declan has no such duty. Since that is the case, if it is normally wrong to compel a person to serve an end that he is not duty-bound to serve, it is wrong for Candani to push Declan.

By contrast, by diverting the trolley Alice does not compel Bob to serve an end he lacks a duty to serve. In *Trolley*, it is not part of Alice's plan to use Bob; indeed, she would prefer him not to be on the track so that he is not killed. While it is true that Bob is killed, his being killed by the trolley is a *side effect* of Alice's plan to save the five. She does not use him as an instrument to achieve the goal of saving the five as Candani does Declan.

I think that Tadros is right that the best solution to the Trolley Problem appeals to individuals' entitlements to set their own ends and the moral wrongness of others' compelling them to serve morally optional ends. The question we confront is whether his account can be deployed as an argument against the religious enrolment of children. I think it can.

4.3 The Comprehensive Enrolment of Children

There appear to be two important differences between the *Bridge* case and the religious enrolment of children by their parents. The first is that in *Bridge* we suppose that Declan has his own ends and Candani makes him serve ends that he would not willingly serve and has no duty to serve. By contrast in *Local Schooling*, at least when he is young, Dan does not have any ends of his own that he is prevented from pursuing. The second difference is that Declan is *harmed* whereas many children who are enroled into valuable religious or ethical traditions are *benefitted* by that enrolment, because the child is encouraged to practise and develop a commitment to valuable ethical activities. For these two reasons, it is not obvious that the objection to using or intentionally affecting people is as pressing in enrolment cases as in the *Bridge* case. The critic might highlight these differences and argue that the case against the religious enrolment of children gains no support from Tadros's solution to the Trolley Problem.

The first difference need not detain us for long. If the argument from self-rule is successful, the fact that an individual will have well-formed ends later in life, even if she does not presently possess them, is sufficient to be regarded as an end-setter. Such individuals are wronged if they are made to serve ethical or religious ends they might retrospectively reject. In *Bridge*, Bob has his own ends, and it is morally permissible for those ends not to include saving the greater number. For that reason, it is morally wrong for Candani to make him serve that end without his endorsement. Would things be any different if Bob were a child? No. The young Bob will have ends, which may permissibly depart from the goal of saving the five, and he might reasonably retrospectively reject any morally optional end Candani might make him serve. For that reason, she may not incorporate him into any plan that he is morally permitted to refuse to serve, including saving the greater number.[6]

The objection based on the second difference needs a fuller reply. So, let us first deepen our understanding of the Trolley Problem and, particularly, *Bridge*, to gauge whether parallels with religious enrolment can be drawn. In both *Trolley* and *Bridge* one agent *harms* another in the course of pursuing the impartially best outcome, saving the five. As we have seen, the way in which the individual is harmed is morally relevant. Whereas the harm Bob suffers is a side-effect harm, Declan incurs his harm as a product of being compelled to serve Candani's goal of saving the five, a goal that he is morally permitted to refuse to pursue. In other cases, however, it would seem that it is permissible to push the individual off the bridge. Consider the following case:

> *Glancing Blow.* This is the same case as *Bridge*, except that Effie is capable of pushing Frank in such a way that there is not a full impact collision between him and the trolley. The glancing blow is sufficient to stop the trolley and save the five. But Frank would suffer minor injuries—some bruising to his shoulder.

Unlike *Bridge*, it seems that Effie is permitted to push Frank in *Glancing Blow*. That is because Frank has a duty to serve the end of saving the five at the cost

---

[6] There is a further question here. If religious enrolment is impermissible for children who will in due course develop the capacity to choose for themselves, is it also impermissible in the case of children beset by cognitive impairments that prevent them from developing the capacities required to live an independent life? We might hold that the ideal of independence rules out enrolment when individuals are incapable of endorsing or rejecting the activity in question for only those who either have possessed the capacity to make autonomous judgements in the past or will possess it in the future. On this view, seriously cognitively impaired children who can never be capable of setting their own ends in the right way may be cared for in a way that makes them follow a particular religious view. There would be no independence-based objection to doing so, because, by hypothesis, these individuals can never determine these matters for themselves. On another view, it might be claimed that the duty not to set children's ends extends to those who will never be capable of living independently. Those who hold this view would find it objectionable for parents to baptize their child or include her within religious ceremonies even if she could never freely form judgements about the desirability of that inclusion. But this position needs to offer a conception of how we ought to relate to non-human animals that are relevantly like cognitively impaired humans. If it is wrong to enrol such humans into ethical practices, is it also wrong to keep a cat as a pet or train a dog to herd sheep?

of a mildly bruised shoulder.[7] It is wrong to make another serve an end if she lacks a duty to serve it. That principle does not apply in the case of *Glancing Blow*, because in that case Frank is duty-bound to incur the stipulated harm to save the five.[8]

Some of the cases that concern us in this book are ones in which parents propose to *benefit* their child by enrolling her into particular ethical practices. To be sure, this is not true of all instances of comprehensive enrolment. In some cases, the practices into which the child is enrolled do not benefit her, because she is made to worship false gods or made to participate in practices that are not worthwhile. But there are also countless instances of beneficial enrolment, as when parents make their child participate in activities that are worth pursuing.

It might be thought that even though it is wrong to compel individuals to *incur harms* to serve ends they are not morally required to serve, it is not wrong to compel individuals to *enjoy benefits* by serving ends that they are not morally required to serve. On this view, there is something special about worsening another's situation that needs justifying. Worsening another's situation as a side effect of averting greater harms to others—the *Trolley* case—can, as we have seen, sometimes be justified by appeal to saving the greater number; worsening another's situation by making him serve ends he lacks a duty to serve—the *Bridge* case—is normally morally impermissible.

An extreme version of this view holds that it is never wrong to compel an individual to serve an end she lacks a duty to serve whenever doing so would benefit her. However, we should reject this version of the view, because it would permit too much interference in our lives. An individual who, knowing

---

[7] Some might reject this claim. They might say that Frank lacks an enforceable duty to incur that amount of harm to save the five. Indeed, some would argue that Declan or Frank lacks an enforceable duty to incur *any* amount of harm to save the five. That extreme view is implausible. Individuals have a duty to incur a certain level of cost to promote impartially good outcomes or to prevent impartially bad outcomes.

[8] To add a further layer of detail to these cases, we might draw a distinction between enforceable and non-enforceable duties. In the cases above we are discussing enforceable duties, duties that others are permitted to coerce individuals into performing. But there are non-enforceable duties, moral duties that we have, which it is not permissible for others to coerce us into performing. For example, suppose that I have a duty to help my mother hang a picture on her wall. It is plausible to believe that this duty is not enforceable: it would not be permissible for others, including my mother, to threaten to harm me if I fail to hang her picture. We might add that some duties are duties to perform actions willingly or off one's own bat, so to speak—the duty to hang my mother's pictures might be an example of such a duty. In these cases, when an individual's duty to serve an end is unenforceable it is generally not permissible for others to make her serve those ends, even though she has a duty to serve them. That may be because compelling service is self-defeating. If to fulfil the duty I have is to perform the required action voluntarily, others' compelling the relevant act is inconsistent with my fulfilment of the duty. Or it might be that others' coercing me to perform a duty is not justified for some other reason. In these cases, it may be that it would be morally wrong to compel me to serve an end even though I have a non-enforceable duty to pursue it.

my culinary tastes and the menu of a particular restaurant, would choose a better meal for me than I would myself is not permitted unilaterally to choose the dishes I am to eat. I am entitled to choose for myself even if I would choose less well; she has the right to select my food only if I agree to that arrangement.

A more modest claim is that an individual's reason not to make me serve a particular end is less weighty if she makes me better off than if she makes me worse off. There is some truth in this view, which can be seen by revisiting *Glancing Blow*. In that case, because the harm that Frank incurs is minor, it is reasonable to suppose that he has a duty to incur that level of harm in the service of saving the five and, therefore, it is not wrong for Effie to push him off the bridge. Since the moral permissibility of Effie's pushing him turns on whether Frank has a duty to bear the level of harm Effie proposes to inflict on him for the greater good, if Effie proposed to use Frank to save the five by compelling him to perform actions that benefit him, then it would seem that he would have even less reason to object to Effie's use of him. If he is morally required to take on a certain level of harm to save the five, he is, *a fortiori*, morally required to benefit himself if that were necessary to save the five.

There is, then, truth in the general proposition that our reason not to compel an individual to enjoy a benefit in the service of an end is less weighty than our reason not to compel him to incur a harm to that end. Nonetheless, enrolment may remain morally impermissible. *Trolley Problem* cases ask us to identify the moral considerations that are relevant in deciding *conflicts of interest*— between saving the life of the one or the lives of the five—on the assumption that we have a general reason to save people's lives. The claim that it is generally good to live and bad to die is uncontroversial and, accordingly, we have a clear sense of how to operationalize the principle that it wrongs an individual to make her serve an end that she lacks a duty to serve, because our sense of the conditions under which an individual is duty-bound to incur a harm for the sake of another person is reasonably clear. Among the considerations that we ought to weigh to determine whether Declan or Frank has a duty to serve the end of saving the five by stopping the trolley with his body are the costs and benefits for him and the five of his not doing so and the moral permission individuals enjoy to serve their own interests rather than the good impartially considered. Understanding the principle in the case of parent-child relationships is not so clear.

I have argued that a particular conception of independence is an attractive moral principle. As Tadros conceives it, the principle is that it is generally morally wrong to compel an individual to serve an end that she lacks a duty to serve. That account requires us to make judgements about the duties that individuals are under. For parents' ethical or religious enrolment of their children to be permissible, it seems that we need to establish that the child has a duty to serve the end in question. If she does, then her parents do not wrong her by making her pursue or serve that conception of the good. If she lacks such a duty, then it appears that her parents wrong her by making her follow it. So let me make a few comments about the duties we have.

In the first place, it is important to note that this account is premised on the idea that our duties are distinct from our decisive reasons for action. By 'reasons for action' I simply mean considerations that count in favour of the act in question. If, taking into account all the relevant considerations, one has a *decisive* reason to perform a particular action A then there is a sense in which one ought to A: there are no relevant considerations that defeat the considerations in favour of doing A. But our duties are different from our decisive reasons for action. To see this, return to the example of whether I ought to play the ukulele rather than the piano. Given the considerations cited earlier—including the weighty considerations of the good of accomplishment and the smallness of my hands—I have a decisive reason to choose to play the ukulele. Still, I do not have a duty to choose the ukulele. I would not be acting morally wrongly if I took up the piano. Our duties, then, cannot be read off from our decisive reasons for action.

This observation has significant implications for what parents are permitted to do to their children, if we accept what we can call the *no compelled service principle*. For it brings into question the simple argument that very many parents deploy to justify the enrolment of their child into a particular religious practice. The putative justification is that the child's participation in the comprehensive practice is good for her. But that justification wrongly trades on the assumption that it is permissible to make an individual pursue a goal if that goal is, all things considered, good for her or, in the language of reasons, if she has a decisive reason to pursue the goal. The ukulele case shows that to be mistaken. It would be wrong for others to compel me to give up the piano to perfect my ukulele skills because, although I would benefit from doing so, I lack a moral duty to take up the ukulele, and it is wrong for others to make me pursue goals that I lack a moral duty to pursue. Similarly, the mere fact that the child's ethical life would go better by worshipping in a particular way, say, does not mean that she has a duty to worship. If it is wrong for others to make individuals who are capable of setting their own ends serve ends—in this case a particular deity—that they lack a duty to serve, then it would appear that parents who make their child serve a particular comprehensive end fall foul of the no compelled service principle. That principle objects to others' compelling an individual to serve goals that benefit her as well as goals that involve her incurring harms.

4.4 Intentions and Permissible Parenting

I have argued that in *Local Schooling* the Dixons wrong Dan by sending him to the local school for religious reasons. Their decision to send him to that school is motivated by a particular objective, that he develops a commitment to Christian values. They make him do something—attend a particular school—to achieve a certain objective, namely, that he becomes attracted to a particular faith. Because Dan is not duty-bound to pursue that particular faith, the Dixons wrong him by making him go to that particular school in order to realize that objective.

Should the Dixons, then, not send Dan to the local school? Should they be prevented by others or the state from sending him there? No. They should send him to that school, but for different reasons. Although they wrong Dan when they make him attend that school with the wrong intention, they act permissibly—indeed, perhaps as morally required—when they make him attend it because it provides an appropriate educational experience with fewer environmental costs compared to other schools. So, they should send him to the local school. In addition, others should not prevent the Dixons from sending him to the local school. Perhaps they should take steps to try to get them to change the Dixons' motivation so that their sending Dan to the school does not involve wrongdoing. But that does not imply that others should prevent Dan from attending the school when his parents send him to it with the wrong motivation: as Tadros says, 'it is sometimes permissible to achieve our good goals by failing to prevent a wrongful action'.[9]

Some might wonder if there is any point in describing the Dixons' school choice as morally impermissible or wrongful if we accept that they should continue to send Dan to the local school. But that worry is unwarranted. It is a stable feature of morality that certain duties apply if we do wrong but do not normally apply if no wrong has been committed. When a person has committed a wrongful action, she ought to apologize for what she did and, perhaps, compensate the person she has wronged. On the analysis I have offered,

---

[9] Tadros, *The Ends of Harm*, 161.

because the Dixons wrong Dan by making him serve religious ideals he might later reasonably reject, they owe him an apology, or at least the acknowledgement that they could have parented him better. Perhaps they should also compensate him in some way. In addition, others might be justified in interfering in the Dixons' choices. Even if we should not prevent the Dixons from sending Dan to the local school for the reasons given above, perhaps we should try to change their motivations so that their conduct is more respectful of Dan's entitlement to set his own ends in life and political autonomy. They might be morally permitted, at least in principle, to force the Dixons to attend parenting classes that encourage them to exclude their religious motivations in their role as parents. If the Dixons did not commit any wrong by sending Dan to the local school it would seem odd for Dan or others on his behalf to demand an apology from them, or to believe that intervention to change their beliefs or desires would be appropriate.

Plainly, in these matters we need to proceed with caution, particularly when we are designing the education policy of a political community. It might be that when *they* deliberate about how to raise their child, parents should acknowledge that ethical and religious enrolment is morally impermissible. But it does not follow that the political community should investigate parents' motives or try to change them when they do wrong by acting from wrongful intentions. There are good reasons for believing that those kinds of surveillance and interference would give too much and the wrong kind of power to state officials. And, given present technology, we lack the means to forcibly shape other people's motivations in any reliably non-clumsy way: interventions to improve people's motivations might have other harmful effects that we have greater reason to avoid compared to the wrongs parents commit in virtue of making the child pursue their religious commitments.[10]

Even if the government should be wary about trying to change parents' motivations, it might take steps to reduce their opportunity to wrong their child by making her follow their religious doctrine. It might do so by disallowing religious schools or, more generally, schools whose ethos and teaching aim to serve particular controversial religious or ethical views. In the case of *Local Schooling*, I supposed that the existence of schools that are in fact supportive of particular religious doctrines is supported by public reasons. But that assumption might be challenged. If it is wrong for parents to enrol their child into a particular religion, for example, then there might be weighty reasons for the

---

[10] Tadros makes related remarks about the relationship between intentions and criminal law. See Tadros, *The Ends of Harm*, 164–166.

government to prohibit or, at least, not to fund schools that facilitate religious enrolment. I consider those issues in Chapter 7.

In the account I have offered, parents who engage in enrolment activities wrong their child even if the educational choices they make are ones that they ought to make for different reasons. But the view that the moral permissibility of an action can depend on the agent's intentions is controversial and, indeed, rejected by several prominent moral philosophers. For example, building on Judith Jarvis Thomson's argument, T. M. Scanlon argues that the reasons that motivate the agent are generally irrelevant to the moral permissibility of her actions. Scanlon distinguishes between (i) assessing whether a particular action is morally required, morally permissible, or morally forbidden, and (ii) evaluating the individual who performs the action in question. Scanlon himself claims that, putting aside certain special cases, the reasons that motivate individuals are not relevant to the assessment of whether a particular action is morally permissible.[11] To illustrate the claim that an individual's motivating reasons are not relevant in an assessment of the moral permissibility of his action, consider Thomson's example of a doctor who, motivated by his hatred for his patient, gives her a lethal dose of morphine.[12] The doctor shows himself to be a morally bad person and, as Scanlon notes, we might offer the more limited objection that the doctor is open to criticism because he fails to recognize the moral reasons that are relevant to his interaction with this particular patient.[13] Nevertheless, the question of the moral permissibility of giving a lethal dose of morphine is an entirely independent matter. Whether or not it is permissible depends on whether there are reasons to give the morphine. It might be that assisted dying is the right course of action, which in this case satisfies rather than goes against the patient's interests. For example, perhaps the patient is terminally ill, will die in the next few days anyway, is in a state of agony such that she would be better off dead, and, after a free and informed deliberation, has requested assistance in dying. The case for assisted dying would need to take into account further facts, such as whether the practice violates the sanctity or sacredness of human life, for example. But suppose that when all the relevant considerations are taken into account, giving the lethal dose is the right action to perform. If that is the case, then the doctor's giving the lethal dose is morally permissible, even if it is also the case that he is

---

[11] T. M. Scanlon, *Moral Dimensions: Permissibility, Meaning, Blame* (Cambridge, MA: Harvard University Press, 2008).
[12] Judith Jarvis Thomson, 'Physician-Assisted Suicide: Two Moral Arguments', *Ethics* 109 (1999): 497–518, at 516.
[13] Scanlon, *Moral Dimensions*, 21–23.

open to criticism for reasoning in the wrong way or for performing the actions for the wrong reasons.

On the Thomson/Scanlon view of moral permissibility, in *Local Schooling* both the Carters and Dixons act morally permissibly. True, the Dixons are open to criticism because they failed to appreciate the reasons that are relevant to their decision, in particular, that the fact that their child would receive a Christianity-promoting education at the local school does not count as a reason for them to choose that school. Nevertheless, although their reasoning is suspect, their choice is morally permissible, because when the reasons that are relevant are given due weight, they support the permissibility of sending one's child to the local school in this case.

Scanlon's conception of moral permissibility seems to be a threat to the view I have articulated, namely, that the Dixons act impermissibly because they make Dan participate in securing an outcome that he is not morally required to pursue: their sending Dan to the school could be permissible, and it would be if the reasons that motivated them were those that motivated the Carters. But as things stand, their sending Dan to the school is impermissible.

It might seem that there is no real disagreement between followers of Scanlon who might, in this case, say that the Dixons act permissibly but they are open to criticism, and those who say that Dixons act impermissibly by sending Dan to the school to cultivate his Christianity, but they would act permissibly if they sent him there for good environmental/educational reasons. The suspicion that there is no real disagreement here might be supported by the thought that the apparent dispute is explained by the different items that are the focus of the two views with respect to questions of moral permissibility and the thought that this choice is merely a matter of preference. A *narrow* focus might identify an action without reference to the aim that explains why the agent performs the action. Given this focus, in *Trolley* the action is 'switching the points', in *Bridge* it is 'pushing Declan onto the track', and in *Local Schooling* it is 'sending one's child to this particular school'. If narrowly conceived actions are our focus, then the aims that motivate the agent are rendered irrelevant to the question of permissibility. This irrelevance is effected by stipulation. The agent's motivating reasons cannot be relevant because the question is whether there are reasons that make the narrowly defined actions morally permissible or not, which, by stipulation, makes no reference to the agent's aims.

But we might have a *wide* focus when describing an action. With such a focus, an action is characterized by particular acts that the agent performs for certain reasons and, in the present case, to achieve certain outcomes. For example, the agent might have certain goals and the acts she proposes to perform are instrumental to the realization of those goals, as when an individual buys a packet of crisps to serve her goal of inexpensively abating her hunger or satisfying her desire for salt; or when the agent's behaviour might be regarded as appropriate in itself, such as when an individual applauds a great musical or sporting performance because she believes that she has a decisive reason to respond to admirable performances of that kind in that way.

Are there any normative consequences that follow from having a wide rather than a narrow focus? If not, are there other reasons to have the wide or narrow focus? As we have seen, one argument in favour of the wide focus that treats permissibility as sensitive to the agent's motivating reasons appeals to the idea that morally impermissible acts have normative implications: agents become *liable* to certain kinds of interference, but only when they act impermissibly. For example, their liability to interference might make it morally permissible for others to prevent them from performing the action in question, or to impose penalties or punishments on the agent, or to exact compensation for those they have acted impermissibly towards. For example, consider the example of racist selection again. The racist selector's actions are morally impermissible, and he is liable to others' interference: his employer or other authorities may prevent him from taking admissions decisions, he may be sacked or punished, and perhaps he may owe compensation to the individuals whose applications he dismissed because of his prejudice. But recall the case we discussed earlier:

Racist rejection of the unqualified. Alan is a racist admissions tutor. He rejects all black applicants. In fact, in this case, none of the black applicants he rejects would have been offered a place had their applications been evaluated according to the right criteria for deciding between candidates.

If a narrow focus on Alan's action is taken, which considers only his decision to accept or reject applicants, then his actions might be morally permissible.[14] Moreover, if it is the case that only impermissible acts make the agent liable to others' responding to him by preventing him from acting, imposing disciplinary measures on him, or requiring him to compensate his victim and so on, then it seems that Alan may not be liable to such responses; the reasons in play—the right selection criteria that cite, say, academic merit as a necessary condition for acceptance—require that these applicants are not offered a place

---

[14] In this case, we need to assume that not only does Alan not refuse admission to any qualified candidate, there is no risk of Alan doing so. We need to imagine this, because as I argued earlier it is often morally impermissible to act (in the narrow sense of the acting) in a way that risks injustice.

to study. But surely this is mistaken, because it is clear that Alan is liable to responses of the kind mentioned above. So, the narrow focus that considers possible acts in isolation from the agent's motivating reasons gets the wrong result in these cases.

In reply, an advocate of the narrow focus might argue that the claims about liability on which the objection rests are mistaken. 'Alan is liable to interference in virtue of the way he deliberated about black candidates' applications', the advocate might say, 'and, therefore, the fact that he acted permissibly does not make it morally wrong for others to intervene in the ways mentioned. He acted permissibly because he did not refuse to accept anyone who merited acceptance and did not accept anyone who did not merit acceptance. But he is nevertheless liable to being sacked and to pay compensation to the black candidates whose applications he rejected for the wrong reasons.'

It seems, then, that the normative judgements that are justified by the wide focus on the agent's motivating reasons as well as her behaviour can also be justified within a view that considers the permissibility of actions with a narrow focus, provided, that is, that those who have a narrow focus recognize that an agent is liable to various kinds of interference even if she acts permissibly. It appears, then, that the disagreement about what we ought to focus on does not necessarily generate interesting differences with respect to how we ought to act towards those whose motivations or intentions are wrongful.

If the right normative conclusions can be justified with either a narrow or a wide focus, are there other reasons to prefer a wide focus when assessing moral permissibility rather than a narrow focus? It might be thought that the wide focus is a more accurate description of the moral terrain. For example, characterizing moral permissibility without reference to the agent's motivating reasons makes it difficult to explain why pushing Declan in *Bridge* is impermissible while switching the trolley in Trolley is permissible. And there are other cases where reference to the agent's intentions seems necessary to explain why her conduct is morally wrong. There are reasons for believing that appealing to the non-derivative relevance of intentions gives us the best account of inchoate wrongs—attempts to do wrong—for example.[15]

To be sure, I have merely summarized the view that it is often morally wrong to incorporate other people into one's plans. Indeed, many alternative conceptions have been developed, ones that seek to explain moral wrongness without reference to the agent's aims. Rather than offering a more thorough

---

[15] See Victor Tadros, *Wrongs and Crimes* (Oxford: Oxford University Press, 2016), Ch. 16. See also his discussion of his 'poisoned pipe' case in *The Ends of Harm*, 159–160.

examination of this dispute to support the position I believe to be right, I finish on a more concessive note. Suppose I am mistaken about the relevance of intentions for moral permissibility. Still, that does not let parents off the hook, because there are, as we have seen, reasons to believe that they ought to satisfy the attitudinal (non-enrolment) requirement even if it is not relevant in evaluating the permissibility of their school choice. Even if the Dixons act morally permissibly by sending Dan to the local school, they make a moral mistake by reasoning in the wrong way, because they fail to exclude the goal of cultivating Christian sympathies in their child as a reason for parental action. And, consequently, they are liable to incur various burdens and responses by others. They may have a duty to apologize to and to compensate Dan for reasoning wrongly; others might be permitted to criticize, blame, or, perhaps, punish them. These responses are left open even if we accept that they acted permissibly by sending Dan to the local school.

4.5 Non-Parental Influences on Children

Norvin Richards has raised an objection to my argument that parents wrong their child when they *intentionally* cultivate her commitment to a particular conception of the good. He notes that if parents desist from raising their child according to a particular religion or ethical view, the child will inevitably develop such an allegiance as she grows up. She will come to have commitments that are not embraced on the basis of rational reflection but which reflect the environment in which she lives: 'The parents can only have played a role in the values she acquired at this time that was going to be played by *something* outside the child's autonomous self'.[16] For example, the child might imbibe the religious or ethical values of other children or the adults she encounters in her daily activities. The objection, then, is that parents do not wrong their child when they raise her in line with the values and practices of a particular conception of the good, because, whether or not they do so, their child will develop a non-self-determined allegiance to particular ethical or religious views. If it is inevitable that the child will acquire particular comprehensive convictions, then why is it wrong for parents to shape them rather than leave the shaping to happenstance or other agents? Are not parents responsible for their child's

---

[16] Norvin Richards, 'Raising a Child with Respect', *Journal of Applied Philosophy* 35 (2018): 90–104, at 92.

coming to embrace particular comprehensive values whether or not they intentionally cultivate them?[17]

In reply, it is worth emphasizing two different activities that are included under the umbrella term 'enrolment'. First, enrolment can take the form of coercing or manipulating an individual to perform the normal activities that comprise an ethical conception—to worship, for example. Alternatively, it might take the form of shaping the child's beliefs and desires so that she develops a commitment to follow a particular conception.

Richards' objection is levelled at the second element of enrolment, the shaping of the child's beliefs and desires. His claim is that the intentional parental shaping of the child's ethical conception is permissible because some kind of belief-shaping is inevitable. I address that criticism below. But it is important to emphasize that the claim that enrolment is inevitable is not plausible if it is applied to the first element of enrolment—required performance. It is not true that if parents refuse to make their child worship or perform the expected activities of a particular conception of the good, then someone else would step in and make the child perform the same or other activities. Being made to conform to ethical or religious rites and activities by others is entirely avoidable. Even if Richards' argument, which trades on the assumption of the inevitability of enrolment, succeeds with respect to value-shaping, it appears not to touch the argument that parents are not permitted intentionally to force their child to participate in religious worship.

To be clear, I am not arguing that it is always morally impermissible to make a child perform the rites or activities of a particular religion or ethical conception. Independence for children insists that it is impermissible to set another's ends for them; children should be allowed in due course to decide for themselves what ethical or religious activities to follow. Worship or performance that is required to teach the child about the details of a conception of the good, or what the conception is like 'from the inside', might be justified.[18] The aim of such activity is not usurpatory—to make ethical or religious choices for the child given her lack of capacity to choose for herself—but educational. Of course, it will be a matter of interpretation whether requiring performance

---

[17] For a similar objection, see Johannes Giesinger, 'Parental Education and Public Reason: Why Comprehensive Enrolment is Justified', *Theory and Research in Education* 11 (2013): 269–279, at 275; Franklin-Hall, 'What Parents May Teach Their Children', 381–383; Fowler, *Liberalism, Childhood and Justice*, 129.

[18] T. H. McLaughlin makes much of the idea that religious participation might sometimes be necessary for religious understanding. See his 'Parental Rights and the Religious Upbringing of Children', *Journal of Philosophy of Education* 18 (1984): 75–83.

counts as educational or usurpatory. Although some required performance might be required to be educated about the character of certain conceptions of the good, it is hard to believe that requiring the child to perform the same activities every day for their entire childhood can be justified on educational grounds.

Turning to the issue of the shaping of convictions, it is worth distinguishing between two ways in which children might acquire ethical convictions in the absence of rational reflection on their part. First, there are cases in which agents other than parents try to influence the child's ethical or religious convictions. Second, it might be that the child develops allegiances merely by observing how others live their lives and wanting to imitate or emulate them without anyone's trying to enrol them—in a way that involves no intentional shaping by anyone. Let us consider these two possibilities separately.

With respect to the distinction between parents' and other agents' cultivation of commitment, there seem to be certain morally relevant differences, but also certain similarities. First, the similarities. If it is wrong for parents to raise their young child with the aim of cultivating in her a commitment to a particular religious tradition, then surely it is wrong for others to do the same. The fact that parents hold custodial rights with respect to the child is not a morally relevant difference. Independence for children rests on the thought that no one is entitled to set others' ends. In the case of adults, acting on the aim of cultivating allegiance to a particular religion is permissible, because it is consistent with everyone's making reasoned and informed decisions about how to live. Where an individual is temporarily incapable of making informed decisions, but has had or will have that capacity, independence supports others' not taking advantage of her vulnerability to take charge of her life. That applies as much to particularly persuasive or charismatic teachers or strangers as it does to parents. On this basis, then, independence for children condemns much of the advertising industry's activities towards the young.

Still, as I have argued, there is a relevant difference between parents and others with respect to their respective degree of influence over children's fledgling ethical commitments. It does not seem objectionable in principle, for example, for several representatives of different conceptions of the good to visit schools as *ethical exemplars*, to explain what they take to be the attractions of their respective ethical views. Pupils might be exposed to representatives of different reasonable religious views or conceptions in which artistic, scientific, or sporting success are central to a good life. There seem to be sound educational reasons for such education to be offered to pupils if they are to understand what it is like to be committed to a particular conception as well as the beliefs and values that constitute it. Because she is exposed to several religious and ethical belief systems, the child's imaginative horizons are not dominated by a single option. Such an education seems to conform to the independence agenda. Of course, there are many further questions to be addressed here. We should not allow exposure to different comprehensive conceptions to become a kind of competition in which adherents of different conceptions vie with each other to capture the child's attention. And teachers need to guard against the possibility that children will be bewildered by the sheer diversity of ethical possibilities, which can lead to anxiety and confusion. The limited point I want to make is that in a regime of exposure suitably described, we might be more worried about parents' taking on the role of ethical exemplar, because they typically enjoy de facto inspirational authority or are in a privileged position to shape their child's convictions.[19]

I finish this discussion of intentional shaping with a tentative thought. Notwithstanding the differences between parents and other agents, it should be clear that the ideal of independence permits, indeed supports, exposing children to controversial ethical views so that they have the informational and deliberative bases for making their own decisions about ethical and religious matters. But we might distinguish two kinds of educational regime that perform this service. In the first—call it the *no attempt regime*—every agent acts with the intention of presenting her own convictions as an example of how one might lead one's life, but no agent has it as her aim to get young children to adopt her view. Representatives of different comprehensive views see themselves as bearing witness to a particular ethical conception, but they let their conception speak for itself: they merely explain and exhibit their comprehensive doctrine and the reasons for their affirmation of it. In the second—call it the *plural attempt regime*—every advocate's aim is to encourage the pupil to endorse their respective conception, but the child's upbringing is structured to ensure that she is exposed in an appropriate way to many different views, with no advocates having privileged access to the child's developing convictions. In the plural attempt regime, there is an institutional fix, a kind of moral division of labour, to ensure that no conviction shaper is in a privileged position to capture the child's mind: the child's opportunity to decide for herself in due course is preserved.[20]

---

[19] For the idea of inspirational authority see Raz, *The Morality of Freedom*, 31–35.
[20] For a view that is similar to the one I describe as the plural attempt regime, albeit with additional constraints regarding the tools advocates use to attract children to their conceptions, see Anca Gheaus, 'Enabling Children to Learn from Religions Whilst Respecting Their Rights: Against Monopolies of Influence', *Journal of Philosophy of Education* 58 (2024): 120–127.

In the face of a choice between these two ways of cultivating the child's understanding of different conceptions of the good and her capacity to reflect on and decide between them, we ought to adopt the *no attempt* regime. Individuals are entitled to set their own ethical ends so that they can view themselves as self-ruling individuals over the course of their lives. As I have elaborated it in this chapter, that entitlement generates a requirement that we do not attempt to use or perfect children according to our view of what is best when they are morally permitted to refuse to serve those aims. It is disrespectful to individuals to have this as our aim even when we know—as in the case of the plural attempt regime—that our attempt to accomplish that goal will not succeed. The attempt to violate children's independence is morally wrong even if the attempt is never successful. If that is right, then the moral prohibition on the intentional cultivation of children's ethical convictions applies to everyone. That does not mean that we cannot *hope* that children will develop an allegiance to rewarding or virtuous lifestyles, only that we must not act on the aim of bringing it about.

Finally, what about influences that cannot be explained by the intentional shaping of others? Suppose that a child develops an allegiance to a particular view of the good life because she discovers that she has a particular aptitude to music, which develops into an interest in playing musical instruments and participating in musical activities? If the child is young, these will not, by hypothesis, be commitments that are developed on the basis of careful rational reflection of the alternatives. Is it any more respectful of her independence to allow her to form provisional allegiances to ethical or religious ideas in this way, rather than by being encouraged to do so by others?

I think it is. Of course, how parents and others ought to respond to the fact that a child has formed an allegiance to a particular conception of the good needs working out. Given the aims of encouraging individuals to have the wherewithal to form, revise, and pursue a conception of the good and to be attentive to the claims of others, it is not obvious that parents ought to facilitate the child's pursuit of her conception in an unqualified way, at least when she is young. There are complicated questions about how much parents ought to defer to their child's preferences in their educational decisions for her at different stages of childhood and youth, some of which we have already discussed (§2.4). Nevertheless, here we are considering the more abstract question of whether it makes a moral difference if the child's acquisition of a set of comprehensive orientations is explained by the fact that this is the motivating ambition of another agent, given that the alternative to being shaped by others is being shaped by nature or happenstance.

Independence for children holds that there is a relevant moral difference. This is unsurprising, because the ideal of independence is partly constituted by a view of how agents ought to regard and treat other agents or, in our case, individuals who will develop into agents. Ethical and religious reasons should be excluded because, given reasonable pluralism, they are reasons that are not universally shared. It follows, then, that parents and others involved in the child's upbringing ought not to treat the fact that certain religious or ethical ideals are sound as reasons to shape a child one way or another. Because nature or happenstance are not, by hypothesis, governed by reasons there cannot be a moral objection to these processes—following Rawls, we can say that they are 'neither just nor unjust'.[21] Of course, questions remain about how parents and teachers ought to respond to the fact that children's values and desires are affected in various ways by different kinds of influence. Still, the basic moral difference between being shaped by agents and being influenced by biology or happenstance is clear.

---

[21] John Rawls, *A Theory of Justice*, rev. edn (Cambridge, MA: Harvard University Press, 1999), 87.

5
Ethics and Children's Interests

I have argued that, when elaborated properly, the political ideal that individuals should endorse the rules that constrain them supports independence for children. In this chapter, I examine parental morality, and the ideal of independence, by addressing various *ethical* questions. What does living well or having a good life consist in? Is anti-perfectionist parenting good or bad for children according to the best account of living well or human flourishing? And are there limits to the ideal of independence such that the comprehensive enrolment of children is justified in some cases?

There are several reasons for engaging with ethics. First, a popular view among the public and in some academic circles is that there are no right or wrong answers when it comes to ethics. It might be thought that this view supports independence for children, or at least an account of childrearing that resembles it. Because it is no better for children to become Christians rather than atheists, for instance, parents should not enrol their child into either comprehensive practice; or so the argument might go. In §5.1, I explain why sceptical or subjectivist conceptions of ethics do not support independence for children and suggest that they are, in any event, implausible ethical views.

Second, we might wonder whether anti-perfectionist parenting is bad for children according to the best account of ethics. In other words, if they followed the moral conception I have defended would parents diminish their child's opportunity to live well or to have a good life? The question needs addressing, because very many hold that parents have weighty reasons to help their children live well. Some argue that our living well is helped, rather hindered, by being enrolled into religious or ethical practices. If they are right, we need to address whether anti-perfectionist parenting can be sustained in light of the costs children bear in living less good lives than they might.

Third, recently, the ethical interests of children have received considerable philosophical attention. One prominent debate is whether, all things considered, childhood is bad for us—a predicament, as it were—or a period of human life that is good for us because it affords us opportunities to enjoy distinctive goods that are unavailable or more difficult to realize in adulthood. If there are various special 'goods of childhood' that independence for children cannot accommodate, then that might be a reason to worry about the view I have defended.

It is important, first, to remind ourselves how our subject matter is demarcated. The term 'ethics' is used in different ways. When some people discuss ethical issues, they focus on certain fundamental *moral* issues that address how we ought to treat others. However, we are operating with a restricted understanding of 'ethics' as referring to questions about what is good for an individual, or the nature of a life well lived. Of course, one view is that acting morally contributes to the success of a life, ethically speaking. Notwithstanding that truth, however, what it means to live well might be distinct, at least to some extent, from acting morally. It is commonly thought that the life of an individual whose conduct complies with sound moral principles can go more or less well—that an ethically successful life is not exhausted by moral probity, even though that might be necessary for, or contribute to, such a life.

The arguments under consideration in this chapter are those that purport to show that the right conception of human well-being or living well either supports or is in tension with the ideal independence for children. Our question is this: once we understand the truth about ethical matters, are we led to embrace, or should we be concerned about, the view that parents ought not enrol their child into a particular religious practice by, for example, encouraging her to adopt particular comprehensive beliefs or desires?

First, it is worth recalling that, as I have presented it, independence for children does not appeal to ethical considerations (see §3.2). If we are morally required to have an anti-perfectionist approach to parenting, then it follows that we are morally required to set ethical considerations aside. Just as Christian parents must set aside the Christian beliefs that guide their own life choices when deciding how to raise their child, parents must also exclude their ethical beliefs and may not appeal to the truth about what it means to live a good life. To the extent that parents' conduct is informed by ethical considerations, then, it violates their child's independence. For that reason, the idea that there is an ethical argument for independence for children is incoherent.

However, it is also worth noting that there might be ethical arguments for a conception of parenting that is similar to independence for children as I have presented it; for parents to refrain from enrolling their children into particular comprehensive doctrines, for example. These arguments do not require the exclusion of ethical and religious ideals as required by respect for individuals' independence. Rather they proceed by arguing that the best account of what it means to live well or to have a good life requires non-enrolment. In other words, the best account of what it means to live well might, when fully elaborated, require parents to disregard the truth about some or all ethical matters when raising their children, or at least not to impart that truth to their children. The Muggletonians discussed earlier illustrate this possibility (see §2.3). They believed they had religious reasons not to try to get their children to believe in their god, because failure to convince them would condemn their children to eternal damnation. Even if we reject the extraordinary views of the Muggletonians, it might be that, on the best account of our ethical interests, parental refusal to enrol their children into particular religious or ethical practices is the best way to ensure that children live ethically successful lives. What I call the dignity argument for children's independence has this feature. It claims that although parents ought to aim to improve children's lives by providing them with certain capacities, they ought to disregard certain other ethical truths when raising their children.

5.1 Appeals to Ethical Scepticism and Subjectivism

Before trying to identify the most promising ethical argument for independence for children, I want to rehearse arguments made by others that explain why ethical scepticism and ethical subjectivism lack the resources to defend the ideal of independence. First, consider ethical scepticism, the claim that there are no right or wrong ways of living, nothing right about the thought that individuals can live better or worse lives or can have reasons to pursue certain goals with respect to religion or occupation rather than others. Is that view sound? If so, does it support independence for children? I shall tackle these questions in reverse order.

First, it is important to be clear about the nature of the sceptic's claim, because several different sceptical positions have been defended. To simplify the discussion, I consider the argument as it is presented by so-called error sceptics who do not deny that, according to the way we understand their meaning, moral or ethical statements purport to describe some reality; these sceptics simply deny that any such statements are true, because there are no ethical or moral facts in virtue of which such statements are true.[1] For example, the statement that one's life goes better if one lives an active life rather than watching television all day, every day, is false. The statement would be true if it were an

---

[1] For a famous elaboration and defence of error scepticism about ethics and morality, see J. L. Mackie, *Ethics: Inventing Right and Wrong* (Harmondsworth: Penguin Books, 1977), Ch. 1.

ethical fact that active lives are better for us than passive ones. But because there are no ethical facts, we must conclude that the statement is false, as is every ethical proposition.

Ethical scepticism might be thought to support something like ethical independence on the grounds that scepticism rebuts certain arguments that deny ethical independence. Consider a particular kind of parental perfectionist argument that starts with a set of claims about what is best for an individual—that her life would literally go better if it involved the active pursuit of musical or sporting success, say, rather than the passive consumption of soap operas. On the basis of an account of what makes people's lives go better or better lived the perfectionist might claim that it is sometimes possible for parents to improve their child's life by encouraging her to be active. That encouragement might take different forms. They might coerce her to engage in active pursuits, penalize her if they see her making the wrong choices about worthwhile activities, or incentivize her to pursue goals requiring her active participation. The parental perfectionist claims that parents are sometimes morally permitted to use some such levers to improve their child's well-being. However, one key premise of the perfectionist argument we are considering is that it is literally true that active lives are better than inactive ones. If ethical scepticism is true, that fundamental ethical premise is false. We have no reason to interfere in people's lives to make them pursue more active lifestyles, the sceptic insists, because it is not true that active lives are better than inactive ones. Of course, because no ethical claims are true, neither is it the case that inactive lives are better than active ones. But, crucially, parents are not justified in interfering in their child's life when the justification for doing so is to improve her well-being.

Ethical scepticism might, then, be thought to support ethical independence by showing that those who believe they ought to benefit others by shaping their ethical choices, such as parents who seek to benefit their child by directing her to certain ethical standards, lack a sound justification for so doing. But this would be a Pyrrhic victory for those who object to the ethical enrolment of children. To see why, let us draw a distinction between *global* and *local* normative scepticism. According to *global* normative scepticism, there are no true statements about how we ought to act, whether the 'ought' refers to purely ethical matters about how one ought to live one's own life or also to moral matters that concern how one ought to treat other individuals. According to *local* normative scepticism, there are true statements about only certain normative matters. The particular kind of local scepticism I'll consider claims that, although there are some true propositions about what we owe to each other, there are no true claims about what a successful life consists in. Either version of the scepticism view runs into difficulty when defending the claim that parents ought not to comprehensively enrol their children.

First, consider global normative scepticism, which holds that no ethical or moral statement is true. If that were sound, then the ideal of independence—a claim about what we owe to each other—would be false. The ideal claims that it is morally impermissible to make children follow a particular conception of human flourishing they might reject as an adult. Scepticism about the soundness of any moral or ethical claim implies that it is not true that we ought to respect others' independence. The claim that we are morally required to act in ways that are inconsistent with the ideal of independence is also untrue. But it is of no comfort to the advocate of independence to be told that her opponent's view is as wrong as her own. Global normative scepticism is inconsistent with the truth of independence for children.[2]

Now consider local scepticism and, specifically, *ethical* scepticism. According to this view, although there are moral truths, there are no truths about how we ought to live our lives, no reasons that ought to guide us in deciding how to use our moral options—whether we should adopt and practise a religion, which occupations or leisure pursuits would benefit particular individuals, and so on. There are at least two problems with using ethical scepticism as an argument against comprehensive enrolment. First, it is entirely unclear how the falsity of every claim that a certain ethical lifestyle is better than others supports the moral conclusion that individuals ought to be free to decide ethical matters for themselves. That moral claim might be independently sound, but its soundness cannot be given any argumentative support from the observation that there are no ethical truths, because the absence of ethical truth has no implications for what morality requires of us. Granted, we can use the absence of ethical truth as a minor premise in an argument for ethical independence. Suppose, for example, there were an argument that established that if there are no right or wrong ways of living then the political community ought not to interfere in individuals' ethical choices. In that case, given the fundamental moral premise that ethical independence ought to be respected *if there are no ethical truths*, the soundness of ethical scepticism would support the ideal of independence. But, crucially, ethical scepticism would not give us any reason to endorse the major moral premise that independence ought to be respected if there are no ethical truths. That is unsurprising, because local ethical

---

[2] See Raz, 'Liberalism, Scepticism, and Democracy', in his *Ethics in the Public Domain* (Oxford: Oxford University Press, 1995), which offers a compendious rejection of sceptical defences of toleration to which I am indebted in this section.

scepticism is a claim about ethical matters and remains silent on issues concerning morality.

The second problem with local ethical scepticism is that it is unclear whether the distinction on which it rests—between moral statements, some of which are true, and ethical statements, all of which are false—withstands scrutiny. That scrutiny starts with our own moral and ethical experience. It is hard to believe that although we have beliefs about how we ought to act to make our own lives a success and about how we ought to treat others, only some of the latter are true; hard to believe because our confidence in our normative judgements does not track the distinction between ethics and morality. Indeed, some have more confidence in their ethical judgements than they do in their judgements about morality or political morality.

The view that we ought to be more sceptical about our ethics than our morality is certainly not intuitive and requires a justification, but it is not obvious how such a justification can get going. Ethical and moral judgements share many features, not least the fact that they include normative judgements about how individuals ought to act. It is true that there are certain dissimilarities: whereas moral judgements largely concern how one ought to treat others, ethical judgements sometimes concern how one ought to act in cases where all of the available options are morally permissible. But it is unclear how that difference gives us reason to be sceptical about ethics and only ethics.

Thus, neither global nor local scepticism supports the ideal of ethical independence. If there is an *ethical* argument against the comprehensive enrolment of children, it must be a non-sceptical argument that appeals to the soundness of a particular conception of what makes for a good life or what it means to live well.

Before proceeding to consider other ethical defences of independence it is worth pausing briefly to assess ethical scepticism as a *critique* of ethical independence. The nature of the critique is evident if we consider global normative scepticism, the view that every moral and ethical claim is false, because there are no moral or ethical facts, nothing to be discovered. If global normative scepticism were true, then the ideal of independence would indeed be unsound, but then so would every ideal that propounds principles of how we ought to act. Many thousands of pages have been written about global normative scepticism, and I shall not attempt to review the different positions within the debate. I content myself with following others in casting doubt on global normative scepticism with the following, controversial, consideration. Global normative scepticism is hard to believe because if it were true everything would be morally permissible, at least on one way of understanding permissibility. If it is not true that we are morally required to let the individual decide the shape of her own ethical life, and it is also not true that we are morally required to interfere in her ethical life, then we are free to interfere or not as we choose in the sense that whether we interfere or refuse to interfere we contravene no sound moral principle or ideal.[3] But, if that is right and global normative scepticism is correct, then the scope of our moral freedom generalizes to include every possible action; there is no sound moral principle that prohibits the torture and killing of innocent vulnerable individuals, for example. If you have read this far, I take it that you have already rejected such a view.[4]

Let us now turn to ethical subjectivism. Sometimes, when people claim that there is no right or wrong when it comes to ethics what they really mean is that what is good for an individual is wholly determined by reference to what she values or prefers. Strictly speaking, according to subjectivism, the claim that there is no ethical right or wrong turns out to mistaken, because subjectivism holds that it is literally bad for an individual if her preferences go unsatisfied, and it holds that her well-being is enhanced to the extent that her preferences are satisfied. But, importantly, subjectivism holds that there is no *content-based* standard for evaluating an individual's preferences such that we can say that her life goes badly if she adopts ethical values that fail to meet that standard.

To be sure, some subjectivists hold that there is *a* standard for evaluating people's preferences. They claim that it is better for a person if her *well-formed* preferences are satisfied, by which they mean preferences that are formed in light of the right level of information about the consequences of different activities and developed consciously rather than as an unconscious response to one's environment, and so on.[5] But such standards for discriminating between preferences are purely procedural. Provided the formation of a person's preferences has the right kind of history, how well her life goes is a function of the satisfaction of her preferences irrespective of their content. To use Rawls's famous example, suppose that on the basis of the proper kind of reflection in the right kind of environment, an individual forms the lifetime ambition to cordon off different parts of the grassed world and to count and record the

---

[3] See Dworkin, *Justice for Hedgehogs*, Pt. 1, especially Chs. 2–3. Dworkin argues that error sceptics contradict themselves when they claim that all moral statements are false, because the consequence of global normative scepticism is that we are morally free to perform any action.

[4] Of course, the fact that you reject such a view does not imply that you are right to reject it. Fortunately, alternative non-sceptical accounts are available. See, for example, Dworkin, *Justice for Hedgehogs*, Pt. 1; Parfit, *On What Matters*, Pt. 6; T. M. Scanlon, *Being Realistic About Reasons* (Oxford: Oxford University Press, 2014).

[5] For relevant discussion, see Jon Elster, *Sour Grapes: Studies in the Subversion of Rationality* (Cambridge: Cambridge University Press, 1983); Richard Arneson, 'Liberalism, Distributive Subjectivism, and Equal Opportunity for Welfare', *Philosophy and Public Affairs* 19 (1990): 158–194.

number of blades of grass in each segment. In that unlikely event, subjectivists would regard his life as going well to the extent that he satisfies his grass-counting preferences.[6]

It might be thought that ethical subjectivism supports the ideal of ethical independence. That alleged support is vividly illustrated if we consider paternalistically inspired violations of independence. Consider a community that attempts to improve citizens' well-being by forcing them to conform to a particular religious doctrine. Religious worship, suppose, is mandatory and the law prohibits various activities that contravene the tenets of the religion— drinking alcohol is an historical example. If ethical subjectivism is true, then paternalism so described seems self-defeating. The community aims to act in ways that improve the well-being of its citizens, but, according to subjectivism, the well-being of those forced to pursue a religious ideal that they reject is diminished, not enhanced, by the community's interference; suppose, for example, that the citizens have stable non-religious preferences the satisfaction of which is set back by being forced to pursue religious ideals: they would be better off if others did not interfere with the pursuit of their projects, because their preference-satisfaction would be higher. Subjectivism seems, then, to offer support to the ideal of independence at least when the political community is under an obligation to improve the well-being of its citizens.

There are, however, at least two forceful objections to subjectivist defences of independence. The first highlights cases in which subjectivism and respect for independence diverge in their practical recommendations. Indeed, as a conception of political morality, the claim that the government should enable citizens to satisfy their desires denies the foundational claim of independence, that it is morally wrong to impose one's own ethical judgements on others. The second notes that even if independence followed from it, subjectivism does not justify independence because subjectivism is an unconvincing account of ethics.

To see that ethical independence and a morality animated by subjectivism diverge in their practical recommendations, it is worth introducing an alternative set of accounts of human well-being, objective list views, according to which the criteria for assessing the success of a person's life are independent of her tastes or preferences. On some objective list views, the informed grass counter's life goes badly even if her preferences are fully satisfied, because counting grass is a worthless enterprise and a good life consists in the successful pursuit of worthwhile activities.[7] Now let us assume that it is the government's

---

[6] Rawls, *A Theory of Justice*, 379.
[7] For a nice elaboration of this conception of well-being, see Raz, *The Morality of Freedom*, Ch. 12.

duty to promote the well-being of its citizens. According to ethical subjectivists, the government fulfils its duty when it enables citizens to secure more rather than less preference-satisfaction—we can leave aside complications about whether the government should maximize preference-satisfaction within the community, promote it equally, or distribute it according to some other moral principle. But if the government acted in that way, it would violate independence, because its policies and laws would impose on every citizen a particular conception of what makes for a good life. Those who adhere to some kind of objective list view would be forced to live under rules framed in the service of an ethical ideal they believe to be mistaken. Their independence would be usurped.

To see this concretely, consider Puja who believes that she has a decisive reason to act in ways that happen not to sustain or improve the satisfaction of her preferences. She believes she ought to refuse a medical procedure to remove a cancerous tumour so that she can attend a wedding even though, let us suppose, her overall preference-satisfaction would be better served by having the operation. If well-being is defined in terms of preference-satisfaction, and the government is duty-bound to promote it, then there seems to be a case for forcing Puja to miss the wedding and have the operation. Yet, even without further investigation, the ideal of independence would give Puja the entitlement to decide between the wedding and the operation. She is entitled to act in ways that fail to satisfy her preferences.

There is a more fundamental reason for doubting the appeal to ethical subjectivism. Even if it could be shown that the ideal that individuals should be free to set and pursue their own ends follows or gains support from ethical subjectivism, that would be of little value. For an ethical argument for independence to succeed we need to appeal to the best account of ethics; yet subjectivism is not the most plausible account of human flourishing. In a moment, I'll set out an alternative, more attractive conception of ethics in which living well does not consist in preference-satisfaction. For now, it is sufficient to make the observation that reflection on one's own life as well as those of others gives us countless examples in which it is clear that a person's life would go better if she did not fulfil her desires, because her desires do not track activities that are worthy of pursuit. The grass counter's life goes less well than the lives of others who maintain close friendships, or who realize their potential, or who successfully pursue goals in music, sport, or community service.[8]

---

[8] For a nice critique of desire-satisfaction conceptions of well-being, see Scanlon, *What We Owe to Each Other*, 113–126; Raz, *The Morality of Freedom*, 137–145.

5.2 Living Well, Dignity and Authenticity

We are exploring whether there is a plausible *ethical* defence of a conception of parental morality that is close to independence for children in its implications, a conception that would require parents and other adults to direct their children towards certain moral standards, provide them with the wherewithal to set and pursue their own ends, but refrain from religious and ethical enrolment. And recall that ethics concerns the question of how we live successful lives. Thus, our question is whether parents who enrol their child into a particular religion—including those who sustain an open future for her—improve or worsen the prospects of her living a successful life.

In this section I set out the main features of an attractive conception of ethics developed by Ronald Dworkin, who supports a conception of ethical independence for adults.[9] On his view, the state should not be in the business of judging whether participation in particular religions or pursuing particular goals or relationships is good for people. I explore whether his argument for independence for adults might be extended to support parental anti-perfectionism.

At the outset, Dworkin draws an important distinction between 'living well' and 'having a good life', and he offers some examples to show how the two notions can come apart. We might evaluate the lives of the Medici as being very good in virtue of their contributions to the Italian renaissance and other achievements, as well as their prosperity and relative security, but nonetheless think that they lived poorly because they ignored their responsibility to treat others justly or even humanely. Similarly, one can live well and yet have a bad life. An example is that of morally required sacrifice: an individual who sacrifices her young life to save those of many others lives well because she responds appropriately to the moral reasons in play, but it would be a stretch to say that her life was a good one: it is cut short and the worthwhile plans and projects she formed remain unfulfilled; she would have had a better life if she had ignored her moral responsibilities.

Although one ought to strive for a good life and to live well, Dworkin claims that when there is a conflict between these imperatives the latter takes priority: 'it is ethically irresponsible for you to live less well in order to make your life a better one, and inappropriate for you to take pleasure or pride in your life's goodness when you achieved this at the cost of living badly'.[10] This much

---

[9] See Dworkin, *Justice for Hedgehogs*, Ch. 9.
[10] Dworkin, *Justice for Hedgehogs*, 201–202.

is clear from reflection on the examples of morally required sacrifice and the Medici. And, importantly, the priority of living well applies as much in the third person as it does in the first person. That is, it is not merely that when she reflects on how to live an individual ought to choose to live well even if that comes at the price of having a worse life than she could have; it is also the case that parents ought to raise their child in a way that improves her prospects of living well—to encourage her to recognize and honour her duties to others, for example—even if a different upbringing would, in all likelihood, give her a better life.

But what, more precisely, does living well consist in? Dworkin appeals to the idea of 'dignity'. Living well, he insists, 'means striving to create a good life, but only subject to certain constraints essential to human dignity'.[11] As we have seen, many of the requirements of dignity are moral in nature. Other people have claims on us, and living well consists in respecting or attending to these claims. But dignity also has an ethical component that can be identified independently of the claims of others and which serves to justify and shape our moral duties. There are certain purely ethical principles that we ought to respect when leading our own lives. These principles are not justified by reference to the claims of others, because they apply to us even when we do not interact with others; neither do they necessarily enable us to have better lives. Rather the principles of dignity are fundamental practical imperatives that are constitutive of living well.

The two key ethical principles that comprise Dworkin's interpretation of dignity are 'self-respect' and 'authenticity'. Self-respect obtains when each person treats it as objectively important that her life is well lived. In its ethical dimension, it is a particular attitude the person has towards her own life: that she is faced with the task of living well and she ought to try to make a success of her life. That attitude is warranted because it just is objectively important for each person to live well. On this account, we live without dignity if we don't care about how well we live our lives, or if we regard living well as only subjectively important—important only because we happen to value it. In addition, it is easy to see how the idea of self-respect can be converted into the moral principle of respect for others. If it is objectively important that my life is well lived and there is nothing special about my life compared to others, then we ought to show the same respect for the life of every person.[12]

---

[11] Dworkin, *Justice for Hedgehogs*, 195.
[12] Dworkin, *Justice for Hedgehogs*, 255–260.

For our purposes, it is 'authenticity'—the second principle of dignity—that has most significance. Dworkin understands authenticity as follows:

> Each person has a special, personal responsibility for identifying what counts as success in his own life; he has a personal responsibility to create that life through a coherent narrative or style that he himself endorses.[13]

An authentic life is more than simply an endorsed life or, in other words, a life that accords with one's convictions about what religious goals, career, or relationships are worth pursuing. It also has a historical dimension that requires the individual herself to *identify* and pursue worthwhile goals. What does that mean? Dworkin suggests that it requires 'ethical independence', but not freedom from influence or from natural or social limitations. The goals and projects that are available to us are shaped by history, geography, and how others lead their lives. We do not have access to certain goals or lifestyles unless the corresponding social conventions are in place. More generally, we must frame our lives in the light of the options available to us, and the goals other people pursue generate meaningful options for us: as noted earlier, because of the infrastructure in place, it is easier to become an accomplished piper in Scotland than in England.

Dworkin says that 'indignity lies in usurpation, not limitation'.[14] Because each individual has the duty to identify and pursue what counts as a successful life, she is morally entitled to decide whether to adopt and practise a religion and which other goals and relationships to pursue. The entitlement in question places others under a duty not to coerce or manipulate her into activities that they believe to be valuable. They might try to encourage her to pursue goals that they believe are valuable; if she is their friend, perhaps they should regard themselves as duty-bound to persuade her to reject valueless pursuits in favour of those that are more worthwhile. But it would violate the authenticity dimension of dignity to design someone else's life for her, to take the ethical decisions she has the right and responsibility to take for herself.[15]

---

[13] Dworkin, *Justice for Hedgehogs*, 204.
[14] Dworkin, *Justice for Hedgehogs*, 212.
[15] Authenticity has a first-personal aspect as well. We lead dignified lives when we ourselves take up the challenge of identifying and pursuing valuable goals, rather than following what others do for fear of criticism or because we can't be bothered to take the time to evaluate the different goals available to us. Leading an authentic life is an achievement that requires each of us to take up the challenge of living well. It is a fragile good, because it can easily be usurped by others or be lost by our own failings. See Dworkin, *Justice for Hedgehogs*, 212–213.

Thus, for Dworkin, ethical considerations support political anti-perfectionism, at least on one understanding of that idea. The government, he argues, 'must never restrict freedom just because it assumes that one way for people to live their lives—one idea about what lives are most worth living just in themselves—is intrinsically better than another ... In a state that prizes freedom, it must be left to individual citizens, one by one, to decide such questions for themselves, not up to government to impose one view on everyone'.[16] The state must not involve itself in such ethical matters because the political community has a duty to enable its citizens to live well, and their living well requires them to live authentic lives in which they, not the government, identify the kinds of career, leisure activity, relationship, and religion, if any, are worthy of pursuit, and to pursue those that they believe to be valuable. If the government were to impose a particular religion on its citizens by enacting laws that require its observance, or by taxing them in order to promote its adoption, it would usurp its citizens entitlement to live authentically and, therefore, well. In either case, it would be making them serve particular conceptions of what makes for a good life and, thereby, deny them opportunities or resources that they might use to identify and pursue their own conception of the good.[17]

Dworkin's account of authenticity is nested within a more general performative conception of living well. Living well is, he argues, 'adverbial, not adjectival'. It consists in a particular performance—'a rising to the challenge of having a life to lead'.[18] A life well lived has a particular history in which the individual performs successfully. On this view, just as the production of a great piece of art has objective value even when the art is destroyed before anyone gets to view it, an individual can live well without having a positive impact on the world. Self-respect and authenticity are two necessary properties of a life with the right kind of history. Of course, an individual's life can be more or less successful, depending on whether she selects for herself goals and projects that are worth pursuing—the life of Rawls's grass counter is not as good as it might be, for example—and whether she realizes her goals. Nevertheless, since living well is an achievement, a life lacks dignity if it is performed by someone else.[19]

---

[16] Ronald Dworkin, *Religion without God* (Cambridge, MA: Harvard University Press, 2013), 130.
[17] Dworkin's conception of dignity is an example of a partially self-effacing account of ethics: an ethical account that supports political actors disregarding certain ethical truths. Since to live well each of us must identify certain ethical truths ourselves, it would be self-defeating for political actors who care about how well we live to adopt and promote concrete religious or ethical goals as a means of improving our lives. For further discussion of self-effacing theories in morality and ethics, see Parfit, *Reasons and Persons*, Ch. 1.
[18] Dworkin, *Justice for Hedgehogs*, 197.
[19] See Dworkin, *Justice for Hedgehogs*, 195–199.

What are the implications of respect for dignity for parents? Before exploring an account that favours independence for children, consider the view that Dworkin's conception of ethics supports the liberal consensus. Using Dworkin's distinction, it would appear that children, at least young children, cannot live well, because they lack the capacities the successful exercise of which are constitutive of living well; but their lives can go better or worse in virtue of having or lacking valuable experiences or activities. Young children lack the power to live authentically, for example, because they cannot appreciate that it is their responsibility to identify the ethical or religious goals that are worth pursuing, and they lack the mental resources systematically to pursue those that match their considered convictions about what is valuable. It seems, then, that on Dworkin's view children cannot live well.[20] However, children can have better or worse lives as children and their lives go better if they engage in practices that have value. If so, then surely it is the duty of adults to force or manipulate children into valuable activities if enrolment does not jeopardize their taking responsibility for their own lives when they have the intellectual power to do so. An open future for them must be protected, but within that constraint parents may, perhaps should, use their power over their child to ensure that her childhood is a good one.

If something like that interpretation is right, then there is an asymmetry between what ethics prescribes for children and adults, respectively. Adults can live well or poorly: they are capable of adverbial success—of making authentic decisions—which takes priority over living in a way that merely happens to be good for them. Young children lack the capacities that make living well and living poorly possibilities. Nevertheless, their lives can go better or worse in virtue of being provided with opportunities that enhance their developmental interests and the non-developmental quality of their childhood.

I want to propose the different view that the authenticity requirement of dignity raises concerns about the comprehensive enrolment of children. I do not deny that very young children lack the capacities that make it possible for them to take responsibility for the decisions that make their lives go better or worse. Nevertheless, that fact does not imply that parents cannot act in ways

---

[20] See Dworkin's brief remarks about children in the context of issues of moral responsibility: 'Living well is a matter of making the right decisions; how well we have lived is a matter of how far we did that. But not every decision counts: *we do not count what we did before we gained the capacities the responsibility system makes prominent*—the capacity to form true beliefs and to match our decisions to our values—or (if we are later in a position too identify these) decisions we made while we had lost those capacities'. See Dworkin, *Justice for Hedgehogs*, 226, emphasis added.

that compromise their dignity. To see this, we need to probe the nature of dignity a little more.

Dworkin argues that maximizing the chance of having a good life is of secondary importance—less worthy of choice—compared to living well.[21] He offers an account of living well that involves the individual herself, rather than other people, making the decisions that determine the goals and relationships she pursues. Thus, authenticity is constituted by two conditions. First, each individual takes responsibility for making decisions, and how well she lives depends on an evaluation of the rightness of her decisions. But, second, authenticity has an interpersonal dimension: it involves others' not making decisions about religion, occupations, and sexuality for her. In cases involving adults, others might do that in several ways. They might manipulate the environment so that it is more likely that she decides to pursue activities that they believe to be worthwhile; for example, they might deliberately increase the costs of the choices they believe lack value, or subsidize those they think valuable, or they might use nudges to get her unreflectively to make the choices they want her to make. These third-party interventions are inconsistent with respect for an individual's dignity; usurpations of that kind mean that other people are living her life, at least in part.

Similarly, while a young child cannot make the kind of decisions that are apt for ethical appraisal, her dignity is compromised by others' taking charge of her life. As with adults, there are many ways of doing so. Parents might narrow their child's exposure to lifestyles they believe will be bad or unrewarding for her to pursue. Such shielding is compatible with enabling her to understand an adequate range of options between which she might choose as she matures, but it is nevertheless a form of usurpation. Or they might trade on the fact that the religious or ethical commitments into which children are habituated tend to be resistant to change later in life; they might try to leverage influence over the choices their child makes as an adult by encouraging her to develop particular commitments as a child. Some accounts of ethics, which operate without an appreciation of the requirement of authenticity, insist that these kinds of manipulation are consistent with the child's exercising agency as an adult.[22] That is no doubt true: the manipulated child may become capable of reflecting and choosing between a range of options. But her dignity is nevertheless compromised by others' shaping her life choices in accordance with their own ethical convictions. If we are attracted to Dworkin's account of dignity, then, there is a

---

[21] Dworkin, *Justice for Hedgehogs*, 199.
[22] See, for example, Fowler, *Liberalism, Childhood and Justice*, Ch. 7 and 124–125.

plausible basis for extending his dignity-based argument for anti-perfectionist political morality to the treatment of children by their parents and other adults.

5.3 Self-Rule and Dignity Arguments Compared

No doubt the dignity argument for parental anti-perfectionism, which extends Dworkin's account of living well to children, needs further development and defence. My modest aim has been to show that while certain ethical defences of independence for children are unconvincing, the ideal can draw support from Dworkin's remarks about what it means to live a dignified life.

In the next section, I shall consider certain conceptions of children's ethical interests that represent challenges to the ideal of independence for children. Prior to that, however, I want to consider the relationship between the dignity argument and the appeal to self-rule I set out in Chapter 3 and to explain why I do not rely on this ethical argument for the ideal of independence for children. First, it is important to recognize that even if Dworkin's account supports the moral principle that it is wrong for parents or adults to enrol children into particular religious or concrete ethical views, it does so by appeal to a controversial set of ethical claims about the centrality of authenticity to human dignity. That ethical view goes against the views of many people, such as those who believe that living well consists in devotion to God within a supportive religious community, or those who resist Dworkin's thought that living well always takes priority over maximizing the chances of having a good life. Those attracted to independence for children in virtue of the political ideal of individual self-rule seek to provide an argument for their view that is more ecumenical and less wedded to particular views about ethics over which there is considerable disagreement. As we discussed above (§3.3), they believe that we ought to run with arguments that are inclusive in what Cohen calls 'the space of reasons'. According to the argument from self-rule, it is important for reasonable individuals to endorse the moral and political rules that constrain their actions *and the foundational ideals that justify those rules*. Given the inevitability of disagreement about the nature of living well and human flourishing, a rich ethical argument of the kind Dworkin offers is unsuited to delivering the political autonomy that political liberals prize.[23]

---

[23] For further elaboration of Rawlsian worries about Dworkin's ethical defence of liberal institutions, see my 'Liberal Equality: Political not Erinaceous', *Critical Review of International Social and Political Philosophy* 19 (2016): 416–433.

For this reason, the political argument for children's independence proceeds on the basis of a more parsimonious set of claims about individuals' entitlements. It does not claim that our lives are best lived or go best when parents refrain from enrolling their child into particular ethical or religious traditions. Rather it appeals to the ideal of the free and equal person who has an interest in developing and exercising a sense of justice, on the one hand, and in being able to determine the shape of her own ethical life, on the other. With respect to a sense of justice, for example, the argument from self-rule need not rest on the claim that it is ethically good for an individual to exercise a sound sense of political morality—though it is not inconsistent with that view. It might, instead, claim that we have certain duties of justice to others and that a certain kind of moral education enables us to fulfil those duties and maintain political autonomy. And with respect to the capacity to reflect on, revise, and rationally pursue a particular ethical conception, the argument need not rest on the further claim that the development and exercise of that capacity enhances enables individuals to live better lives—though, again, it is not inconsistent with that view. Rather, it might simply offer the ideal of living an independent life as fitting or appropriate for persons, such as most humans, who are capable of living self-governing lives.

The reason political liberals resist appealing to further claims about what it means to live well or to have a good life is that to do so would introduce a deeper foundation for its moral and political principles that might reasonably be rejected. There is a weighty reason to avoid such defences of moral principles, because respect for individuals' political autonomy requires them not to be constrained by principles motivated by ideals they reasonably reject.

Nevertheless, there are reasons for highlighting the fact that many of the features of independence for children gain support from a particular conception of ethics. First, it is valuable to show that the principles of parenting that follow from the argument from self-rule do not jeopardize the fulfilment of children's ethical interests. If there were a serious tension between respect for children's independence and their living well, then we would have to investigate further the weight of the reasons for complying with its concern to find principles of parenting that no one can reasonably reject. If, alternatively, the ideal of independence for children is congruent with parenting that serves their child's interest in living well, then we might avoid further examination of the importance of the foundational ideals that motivate political liberalism, for in that case there would be a marriage of the demands of respect (the self-rule argument) and concern (the ethical argument).[24]

---

[24] The thought that we should establish that there is congruence between complying with justice and the fulfilment of individuals' ethical interests is Rawls's. See *A Theory of Justice*, Pt. 3.

Second, it is valuable to have ethical arguments for children's independence expressed in the public domain. An individual's articulation of ethical reasons for children's independence in civil society and political forums, whether these be the dignity-based considerations reviewed above or other arguments that follow from religious premises, is valuable because it gives everyone assurance that her respect for their independence is secure and expressed in good faith. Others can see that she is committed to refraining from enrolling her child into a particular religion and that she has further reasons grounded in her ethical convictions for observing the same moral constraint. In that way, ethical arguments for independence for children might play a role within public discourse, even if they do not feature in the official political doctrine that governs society.[25]

Finally, there is a more mundane, rhetorical, reason to put the dignity argument on the table. Those unpersuaded by the argument from self-rule for children's independence might be attracted to the ideal for ethical reasons. It is strategically shrewd to build a case for a conception of upbringing that can be endorsed not only by those who believe that parental morality is sensitive to the kinds of political concerns expressed earlier, but also by those who think that questions about upbringing are importantly different from political questions and should be theorized by reference to what is best for the child. If there are ethical reasons for independence as well as the argument from self-rule, then the case against the religious and ethical enrolment of children is likely to have more traction in public discussion.

5.4 Does Anti-Perfectionist Parenting Harm Children?

Having explored the idea that independence for children might receive support from within ethics, I now put that thought to one side and consider several objections that might be raised against the ideal itself. In the next chapter, I discuss objections that claim that independence for children jeopardizes valuable family life or that it should be rejected because it is too burdensome for parents. In the remainder of this chapter, I respond to objections that might be raised on behalf of children. The headline complaint here is that

---

[25] Here I trade on Rawls's remarks concerning what he calls 'the wide view of public political culture' where he introduces the 'proviso': ethical arguments 'may be introduced in public political discussion at any time, provided that in due course proper political reasons—and not reasons solely given by comprehensive doctrines—are presented that are sufficient to support whatever the comprehensive doctrines introduced are said to support'. John Rawls, 'The Idea of Public Reason Revisited', in his *Collected Papers* (Cambridge, MA: Harvard University Press, 1999), 591.

independence-respecting parenting makes children's lives go worse than they would go if parents followed a different view, and it should be rejected for that reason.

Let me first distinguish this set of objections from a different kind of response to independence for children. Many people deny that anti-perfectionist childrearing is morally required because there are countless ways of enrolling children into comprehensive practices that do not harm them in the sense of preventing them from having a good life. Suppose, for example, that a child's parents are committed to particular ethical goals and projects that give their lives genuine meaning and fulfilment. They decide to encourage their child to follow their goals. Suppose, in addition, that they equip their child with the wherewithal to reflect on and rationally pursue her own conception of the good as an adult and provide her with an upbringing that fosters her sense of justice. It might be argued that such an upbringing does not harm the child and, for that reason, is a morally permissible one.

As should now be clear, there is more to morality than 'do no harm'. We have a moral claim to set our own ends even when our doing so causes us more harm than if someone else were to choose our goals and projects for us. Moreover, when others exercise authority over us, they should do so on terms that are acceptable to us as free and equal persons. I have argued that we have a moral claim to endorse the constraints we live under, a claim that applies retrospectively to how children are treated by their parents. If these arguments are sound, then it is not enough for critics to note that children are not harmed by several types of parenting that flout the requirements of independence, because the ideal of independence objects to certain instances of harmless wrongdoing, at least where harm is cashed out purely in terms of well-being.[26] Indeed, one of the aims of this book is to invite those interested in matters concerning children to abandon the fixation with whether various social policies harm or benefit children that is characteristic of so much writing about children and education, and to embrace a richer array of moral considerations.

Harm-based objections to independence for children must, therefore, do more than merely note that children's well-being would not be set back by disregarding the ideal. They must make the stronger claim that respecting independence is bad for the child and, furthermore, that parents are under a moral duty to promote their child's well-being, a duty that defeats their reasons

---

[26] For nice discussions of the general point, see Arthur Ripstein, 'Beyond the Harm Principle', *Philosophy and Public Affairs* 34 (2006): 215–245, and his *Force and Freedom: Kant's Legal and Political Philosophy* (Cambridge, MA: Harvard University Press, 2009), particularly Ch. 2.

to respect her independence. So let us review some objections to independence for children that make this stronger claim, that independence is bad for children.

We might distinguish between three *harm to children* objections to the ideal of independence. Some claim that anti-perfectionist parenting is *bad for children's development*. Because parents are not permitted to enrol their child into a particular religion, for example, the child will not develop the right kind of understanding of the rich meaning of religious commitment that can be gained only from being immersed within a set of religious practices. Children will be left directionless, the argument goes, and not develop a sense of commitment to a project, which is a necessary feature of leading an independent life. This objection suggests that independence for children is incoherent, because parental anti-perfectionism does not provide children with the necessary preparation for them to live independently as adults.[27] A different version of the developmental harm objection asserts that the development of a sense of justice involves children learning to appreciate *why* they ought to treat others with concern and respect, and seeing how acting morally relates to living a good life. Since anti-perfectionist parents refrain from engaging with such comprehensive issues, the moral education they offer their child is inadequate. Again, the argument is that anti-perfectionism is inconsistent with children's having an upbringing that gives them what they need to become just citizens.[28]

A second version of objection is not that anti-perfectionist childrearing serves our interests as independent adults less well than a regime that permits religious enrolment; rather, it fails to serve us *as children*. Childhood should not be theorized simply as preparation for adulthood. The child's enjoyment of certain goods—uninhibited, imaginative, and adventurous play and discovery, for example—makes her childhood go well irrespective of whether those goods also prepare her well for life as a free and equal adult. However, because these goods, what Colin Macleod calls the 'intrinsic goods of childhood',[29] are not universally valued and, indeed, might be rejected by one's child when she reaches adulthood, it appears impermissible to enable one's child to

---

[27] For this kind of view, see Giesinger, 'Parental Education and Public Reason', 273–275. The background claims on the basis of which the objection draws its strength are discussed by McLaughlin, 'Parental Rights and the Religious Upbringing of Children'; Eamonn Callan, 'Autonomy, Child-Reading and Good Lives', in *The Moral and Political Status of Children*, edited by David Archard and Colin Macleod.
[28] For this objection, see Franklin-Hall, 'What Parents May Teach Their Children', 379–381.
[29] Macleod, 'Primary Goods, Capabilities and Children', in *Measuring Justice: Primary Goods and Capabilities*, edited by Harry Brighouse and Ingrid Robeyns (Cambridge: Cambridge University Press, 2010).

enjoy them in an anti-perfectionist conception. If that is the case, then parental anti-perfectionism condemns too much, because it does not permit parents to offer their child a childhood in which she can experience and partake in the activities that are particularly valuable for the young.

Finally, some object that anti-perfectionist parenting is bad for the child's life *as a whole*. It might be that our upbringing equips us with the wherewithal to live a just and reflective life, and affords us the opportunity to experience the right goods of childhood, but nevertheless fails to instil beliefs and habits that are conducive to our long-term flourishing. The background of this perfectionist objection is that parents should impart to their children the qualities that tend to enhance their well-being over the course of their lives; the proper role of parents is to act in ways that promote rather than neglect their children's long-term flourishing.[30]

In response to the first set of objections, that children of anti-perfectionist parents suffer developmental harm, it is worth noting that although anti-perfectionist childrearing forbids comprehensive enrolment and immersion, it allows, indeed requires, moral enrolment. The acquisition of a sense of justice requires an upbringing in an intimate family and relevant associations that enable the child to cultivate an appropriate understanding of morality and justice, and to acquire the motivation to comply with their demands. That can be viewed as developing a sense of commitment to particular moral ideals, a sense of permissible and impermissible conduct, and fitting attitudes towards moral success or failure. To the extent that the objection is premised on the claim that parental anti-perfectionism leaves individuals incapable of understanding fully what it means seriously and responsibly to pursue goals, the moral and political demands of liberal citizenship give assurance that this kind of orientation to life will not be lost. Religious enrolment is, therefore, unnecessary to give individuals an understanding of what it means to adopt, reflect on, and execute plans, because that understanding is provided via the development of a sense of justice.[31]

Does parental anti-perfectionism, however, make the pursuit of certain conceptions of the good impossible or considerably harder on the grounds that a full appreciation of those conceptions requires full immersion into their traditions, rites, and values when young? Perhaps there are certain conceptions

---

[30] For the most thorough elaboration of this view, see Fowler, *Liberalism, Childhood and Justice*, particularly Ch. 11.

[31] For a discussion of the importance of the idea of learning what it means to pursue a personal project, see Monika Betzler, 'Enhancing the Capacity for Autonomy: What Parents Owe Their Children to Make Their Lives Go Well', in *The Nature of Children's Well-Being*, edited by Bagattini and Macleod.

of the good that cannot be fully appreciated and pursued unless individuals become initiated to them when very young. Perhaps musicianship is a case in point. Many of the great composers and musicians of the past and present were made to practise an instrument as a very young child. It could be true that one's musicality is not as well developed as it might be if one is not introduced to it at a young age when the child's brain is undergoing rapid development and she is acquiring habits and abilities that become second-nature to her.

Nevertheless, these facts speak in favour of age-appropriate introductions to comprehensive pursuits, not a parental permission comprehensively to enrol children. An anti-perfectionist upbringing requires children to learn about various conceptions of the good. Sometimes, as in the case of music, that will take the form of learning a technique and developing the associated virtues of deferred gratification and regular practise. There seems little that is objectionable about such an upbringing. Indeed, independence for children suggests that such opportunities should be provided to every child, not merely those whose parents happen to value the activity in question; those kinds of educational opportunity are integral to the ideal of independence. It draws the line, however, when parents propose to give a single comprehensive view a commanding position with respect to the child's ethical imagination. So, the critic must cite examples of valuable ethical or religious conceptions that the child can appreciate only by being shielded from exposure to other conceptions. I doubt that there are many comprehensive conceptions of that kind. In any event, there is a rich array of valuable comprehensive options that do not have that feature.

Let me briefly turn to the objection that the child's *moral* development is inadequate if it is not accompanied by comprehensive enrolment. Franklin-Hall makes the observation that at some point it is inevitable that the child will ask why she ought to treat others with concern and respect and how moral probity relates to her other beliefs and desire. He argues that these questions can be answered satisfactorily only if the child's moral education is embedded within a comprehensive doctrine on the basis of which she can 'make sense of these things'.[32] A moral education is lacking, he contends, if the child's parents merely impart the right understanding of what we owe to each other whilst refraining from explaining to children the more fundamental religious or philosophical foundations that justify those moral principles.

This argument overlooks the fact that the morality of independence—regarding and treating each other as free and equal—is appropriate for agents

[32] Franklin-Hall, 'What Parents May Teach Their Children', 380.

who hold distinctive and conflicting religious and ethical views. As Rawls remarks, there are diverse comprehensive views, some of which treat moral principles as justified without appealing to deeper comprehensive foundations while others endorse those principles for theological or ethical reasons.[33] It is valuable for the child to come to appreciate that, say, the moral imperative that everyone's independence be promoted and respected is unaffected by changes in one's comprehensive view, and also that the ideal of independence is an ecumenical view in the sense that its moral principles do not gainsay the variety of ethical and religious views that people find attractive. In other words, we want moral education to impart to us an understanding of, and motivation to abide by, the categorical nature of moral demands, but also an appreciation of the compatibility of those demands with a wide variety of comprehensive conceptions. For these reasons, then, anti-perfectionist parents do not harm their child by refusing to ground the moral education they provide within a comprehensive tradition. Indeed, it appears that they impart to her a more resilient moral sensibility compared to one that is dependent on a comprehensive doctrine she might well abandon later in life.

The second objection, that anti-perfectionist parenting affords children less good *childhoods* than they might enjoy, appears more threatening. This objection might trade on the thought that theorizing children's advantage in terms of the development of a sense of justice and the wherewithal to live an independent life is incomplete in virtue of not offering a conception of what is good for children as children.[34] It might also draw on the further claim that there are distinctive goods of childhood, that the items that make a individual's life go non-derivatively better or worse *as a child* are different to the things that make her *adult life* go well.[35] The possibility that the child might retrospectively reject any upbringing that is premised on a comprehensive conception that posits certain intrinsic goods of childhood seems to make it impermissible for parents to treat the alleged value of those activities as reasons to encourage their child to participate in them. If so, then the charge is that independence for children restricts parents to providing a dreary or insipid upbringing in which children do not fare well as children. Or it condemns children to a childhood that lacks various items that the young are uniquely or particularly capable of enjoying. While those who endorse the idea that there is an objective list of

---

[33] Rawls, *Political Liberalism*, 154–158.
[34] See, for example, Samantha Brennan, 'The Goods of Childhood and Children's Rights', in *Family-Making: Contemporary Ethical Challenges*, edited by Françoise Baylis and Carolyn Mcleod (Oxford: Oxford University Press, 2014).
[35] See Patrick Tomlin, 'Saplings or Caterpillars: Trying to Understand Children's Well-Being', *Journal of Applied Philosophy* 35 (2018): 29–46.

goods that are non-derivatively good for children disagree somewhat about what is on the list, it might include some or all of the following: a certain kind of play—imaginative, uninhibited, adventurous, more or less unstructured, and carefree play or discovery; innocence regarding sexuality; the exercise of one's capacity to imagine and be awed; the creation of different possible worlds including magical ones that violate the laws of nature.[36]

In reply, people disagree profoundly about issues concerning what makes children's lives go well and, indeed, whether childhood is a period of life that would best be skipped if we had the technology to do so. Still, childhood is a fact of life, and we need moral principles to regulate it. So, suppose that the advocates of special childhood goods are right that there are certain kinds of activity that enhance the goodness of children's lives as children. Does that pose a problem for parental anti-perfectionism, which eschews reliance on a conception of human flourishing?

In answering that question, I'll assume that there are certain types of activity that are appealing to us as children but which we might find disagreeable as adults. Consider, for example, an individual who loves uninhibited dance as a young child but who, as an adult, develops puritanical convictions that condemn dance as ungodly. Should parents support their child's desire to dance knowing that she might retrospectively reject its value? I believe they should. Two reasons speak in favour of doing so. First, in virtue of its focus on the reasons that motivate parents, the non-enrolment requirement treats the intention/foresight distinction as morally relevant. Parents who allow their young child to engage in uninhibited dance knowing that she might later develop puritanical convictions that condemn the activity do not thereby wrong their child. Even if the child's later rejection of the activities she pursues in childhood were foreseeable, that would not be sufficient to render her parents' conduct illegitimate. Anti-perfectionist childrearing objects to parenting that tries to shape the child's life in accordance with a particular comprehensive doctrine, not indiscriminately to any upbringing that happens to involve the

---

[36] For discussions of the value of childhood, whether childhood is bad for children, and whether our ethical interests as children differ from those we have as adults—in addition to those cited above—see Tamar Schapiro, 'What Is a Child?', *Ethics* 109 (1999): 715–738; Anca Gheaus, 'The "Intrinsic Goods of Childhood" and the Just Society', and Colin Macleod, 'Agency, Authority and the Vulnerability of Children', both of which appear in *The Nature of Children's Well-Being*, edited by Bagattini and Macleod; Sarah Hannan, 'Why Childhood is Bad for Children', *Journal of Applied Philosophy* 35 (2018): 11–28; Patrick Tomlin, 'The Value of Childhood', and Anthony Skelton 'Children and Well-Being', both of which appear in *The Routledge Handbook of the Philosophy of Childhood and Children*, edited by Anca Gheaus, Gideon Calder, and Jurgen Wispelaere (London: Routledge, 2019); Andrée-Anne Cormier and Mauro Rossi, 'Is Children's Wellbeing Different from Adults' Wellbeing', *Canadian Journal of Philosophy* 49 (2019): 1146–1168; Daniel Weinstock, 'On the Complementarity of the Ages of Life', *Journal of Applied Philosophy* 35 (2018): 47–59; and Fowler, *Liberalism, Childhood and Justice*, Ch. 4.

child's engaging in activities that she may retrospectively reject. Second, as we have seen, the child has a moral claim to pursue her enthusiasms at least if they are compatible with fulfilment of her developmental interests in acquiring the capacities to live independently and justly (§2.4). For these reasons, parents do not act wrongly by facilitating their child's childhood desires, notwithstanding the fact that the child might come later to regret the choices they made when young. An adult child who, when looking at a photograph of herself as a child says to her parent 'I can't believe you let me choose that hair cut!', does not make a valid complaint.

Suppose, then, that the child is introduced to a range of different activities, including different kinds of sport, music, art, and literature. Part of the justification of that exposure appeals to the child's interest in developing a sense of justice and having the wherewithal to lead an independent life. However, it is also the case that living within the particular background culture of a free society makes it inevitable that the child will experience a variety of those activities. Suppose, in addition, that her parents notice that their child is attracted to a certain activity and face the decision of whether to facilitate or encourage her pursuit of it. Of course, they will take various considerations into account, such as the nature and strength of the child's preferences, whether her pursuit of that activity needs to be balanced against other developmental considerations, risks to her psychological well-being (if the activity in question has a significant competitive element, for example), and so on. But in this story there need be no violation of the non-enrolment constraint, because it is the child's preferences and her developmental needs that determine the shape of her childhood.

Anti-perfectionist childrearing is compatible with parenting that delivers the goods that some take to be distinctively good for children: a childhood involving adventure, play, and creativity. True, it does not justify such parenting on the grounds that it enhances the well-being of children. It is not obvious, however, how many of the intrinsic goods of childhood are lost in virtue of the impermissibility of enrolment. It appears that many of these goods—carefree, imaginative, and uninhibited play, for example—are goods that young children choose to pursue without any parental guidance, at least when they are given a rich exposure to alternative activities. To the extent that that is the case, parents need only facilitate their pursuit and, perhaps, share their child's enthusiasms. The imposition of ends is not required.

Finally, let me turn to discuss the objection that parental anti-perfectionism diminishes the child's life as a whole; it makes parental neglect of their child's well-being a moral requirement. For an illustration of the concern, consider the dispute about the teaching of Darwinian evolution as science. The public debate about that issue is whether the science curriculum in schools ought to give students the opportunity to learn about creationist or intelligent design (ID) theories as alternatives to Darwinian natural history. It appears to some that anti-perfectionist liberals who neither affirm nor deny the truth of particular religious conceptions of the world or universe must be committed to the view that public money should not be used to promote a sectarian irreligious conception of natural history. Critics insist that this case vividly reveals the counter-intuitive implications of this kind of liberal political morality. Not only are creationism and intelligent design demonstrably false, they claim, a schooling that presents them as genuine alternatives to Darwinian accounts makes a mockery of science education and allows impressionable children to form the belief that scientific understanding can be gained from reading the Bible or some other religious text. Permitting those outcomes is, they insist, detrimental to individuals to the extent that holding veridical beliefs or having knowledge makes their lives go better, and worse for society in virtue of setting back the project of scientific progress, which enhances our collective ability to deal with many pressing problems.

Similar, perhaps stronger, objections of this kind might be raised against parental anti-perfectionism. The critic claims that parents have a weighty reason to attend to their child's interest in leading a flourishing life. Compliance with that reason supports imparting to their child an understanding of the methods and current state of scientific knowledge. Such an understanding is instrumentally beneficial for the child, for it enables her to form her beliefs and desires on the basis of reliable non-normative facts, and it is, for some, a constituent of living well. Since parents have a special and, arguably, very weighty reason to attend to their child's interests, it is surely a dereliction of their duty if they fail to take a stand on important issues such as the dispute between Darwinian and creationist conceptions of biological change. Parental anti-perfectionism does not merely permit parents to offer their child a non-scientific education, it requires parents not to take a stand on the debate between ID and Darwinian evolution as accounts of natural history. In other words, it requires parents not to promote their child's interests. Or so the critic argues.

Parental anti-perfectionists might offer two responses to the charge that their view requires parents to neglect their child's well-being. First, we might soften the objection by pointing out that while parents may not adopt and promote a controversial comprehensive doctrine, such as a particular religious or irreligious doctrine, they are permitted, perhaps morally required, to educate their child according to the requirements of public reason. In the context of the debate about natural history, for example, parents might have weighty reasons stemming from their duty to promote their child's sense of justice to provide an education in science that conforms to well-established standards of scientific inquiry and knowledge. In that way, it might be that parents have reasons other than the promotion of her well-being to encourage their child to adopt certain true or justified beliefs about various matters. To the extent that that is the case, the differences between anti-perfectionist and perfectionist accounts of child-rearing are smaller than they might at first appear and the charge of negligence loses some of its force.

The softening response depends on the soundness of the claim that public reason requires an education that imparts an adequate understanding of biology and natural history, or at least one that denies the assertions of those who advance creationist or ID accounts. That response depends, in turn, on showing that one's responsibilities as a citizen are better fulfilled if one possesses a more accurate understanding of science. I'll not provide a complete justification of that claim here. The prima facie case for it is that citizens are duty bound to attend to the interests of their fellow citizens with respect to health and the environment, for example, and those interests are likely to be more effectively served through public institutions that are responsive to reliable science, just as individuals' interests in securing socioeconomic goods are better served if citizens' deliberative and electoral activity rests on good reasoning and evidence about society and the economy. Anti-perfectionists may take a stand on the soundness of claims that are relevant to our status or conduct as free and equal citizens.

The second response to the negligence claim is to bite some bullets. The softening response goes only so far, and it must be accepted that in some cases anti-perfectionist childrearing does indeed require parents to refrain from promoting their child's long-term flourishing as much as they might. In that respect, parental anti-perfectionism is on a par with its political counterpart, which claims that it is impermissible for citizens to use the legal powers of the state to advance their own well-being and that of other citizens. Parents may hope that their child's life goes well, but respect for her independence limits the extent to which they can legitimately make that happen.

5.5 The Limits of Independence

I have argued that respect for a child's independence requires parents to act in ways that they know may lead to their child flourishing less than she might. But are there any limits to this moral requirement? Objections that appeal to the child's well-being should be taken seriously because it seems that any plausible conception of childrearing must be attentive to the interests of children in avoiding *disastrous* outcomes in terms of their well-being. As with issues concerning respect for adults' choices, it is hard to believe that our reasons to respect children's independence always defeat our reason to protect their well-being.

Consider the official Catholic view of infant baptism, for example. 'Through Baptism we are freed from sin and reborn as sons of God ... Born with a fallen human nature and tainted by original sin, children also have need of the new birth in Baptism to be freed from the power of darkness and brought into the realm of the freedom of the children of God, to which all men are called ... The Church and the parents would deny a child the priceless grace of becoming a child of God were they not to confer Baptism shortly after birth.'[37] Although the *Catechism* states that 'The Lord affirms that Baptism is necessary for salvation', the official view seems to be that baptism is not always required: 'God has bound salvation to the sacrament of Baptism, but he himself is not bound by his sacraments.'[38] This is relevant when children die without having been baptized. In such circumstances, the *Catechism* asserts that 'the Church can only entrust them to the mercy of God' albeit in the reasonable hope that He will be merciful given His concern for children.[39] But worries about children's salvation given the uncertainty surrounding those who die without baptism motivates the Church to declare, 'All the more urgent is the Church's call not to prevent little children coming to Christ through the gift of holy Baptism.'[40]

I have argued that infant baptism is a form of comprehensive enrolment that wrongs the child, because it violates her claim to a life that exhibits self-rule rather than rule by someone else. Nevertheless, the official Catholic view seems to offer a forceful objection to this argument, because it claims that the harm a child suffers by not being enrolled (baptized) is very great, particularly given the exceptionally high stakes involved in her relationship with God. After all, if the Catholic view is right, then not baptizing her risks her eternal salvation.

It should be noted that the *problem of high stakes*, as we might call it, applies to political liberalism quite generally. Rawls asks political actors to appeal to public reasons and to exclude from consideration reasons stemming from

---

[37] *Catechism of the Catholic Church*, par. 1213 and 1250: available at https://www.vatican.va/archive/ccc_css/archive/catechism/p2s2c1a1.htm.
[38] *Catechism*, par. 1257.
[39] *Catechism*, par. 1261.
[40] *Catechism*, par. 1261.

comprehensive doctrines, at least when the two kinds of reason conflict. Yet it is hard to believe that the moral ideals served by public reason—social unity and political autonomy for everyone—weighty though they are, are sufficiently weighty to defeat a moral requirement to prevent individuals from suffering eternal damnation. Rawls considers someone who asserts 'that certain questions are so fundamental that to insure their being rightly settled justifies civil strife. The religious salvation of those holding a particular religion, or indeed the salvation of the whole people, may be said to depend on it.'[41] If the devout person Rawls describes had true beliefs about the requirements of salvation, then she may be right to engage in civil strife; our reasons to secure our own and others' eternal salvation defeat our reasons to protect self-rule for everyone.

The problem of high stakes is not a new one. Since antiquity, it has been a recurring objection to arguments for there being a moral obligation to obey the law. For example, Sophocles' Antigone makes this objection when, while explaining to her uncle, King Creon, why she broke his law instructing her not to bury her brother, she said:

> Of course I did [break the law], It wasn't Zeus, not in the least,
> who made this proclamation—not to me.
> Nor did that Justice, dwelling with the gods
> beneath the earth, ordain such laws for men.
> Nor did I think your edict had such force
> that you, a mere mortal, could override the gods,
> the great unwritten, unshakable traditions.[42]

Similarly, Hobbes acknowledged the problem of high stakes as a difficult issue confronting any argument for justified political authority:

> The most frequent praetext of Sedition and Civill Warre, in Christian common-wealths hath a long time proceeded from a difficulty, not yet sufficiently resolved, of obeying at once both God, and Man . . . It is manifest enough that when a man receiveth two contrary Commands, and knows that one of them is Gods, he ought to obey that, and not the other, though it be the command even of his lawfull Soveraign (whether a Monarch, or a sovereign Assembly) or the command of his Father.[43]

---

[41] Rawls, *Political Liberalism*, 152.
[42] Sophocles, *Antigone*, lines 499–505.
[43] Hobbes, *Leviathan*, 321.

Where do these observations leave political liberalism and my extension of it to parental morality? I think we can say that respect for children's independence is a very weighty moral consideration that is normally decisive with respect to how we ought to act. That is because in the central range of cases, the decision not to enrol a child into particular ethical or religious practices does not have very serious consequences for her well-being. Two reasons explain why that is the case. First, on the basis of another softening response to the objection that independence harms children, an upbringing for independence equips children with various skills and motivations that serve their ethical interests: an education that develops a child's sense of justice also enhances her well-being, because it gives her the intellectual wherewithal to reason well, which enables her to reflect rationally on the various conceptions of the good that are represented within society; to the extent that our well-being or living well is constituted by living authentically, as many conceptions of the good claim, the child is benefitted by being encouraged to understand and explore existing ethical and religious views; and even if well-being does not require authenticity, it is widely acknowledged that, because different individuals are suited to different lifestyles in virtue of their distinctive talents and interests, individuals' well-being is served by being in a position to choose among various lifestyles: the positive requirements of independence-respecting parenting are instrumentally valuable from the point of view of individuals' well-being.[44]

These claims about the side-effect well-being benefits of parents' complying with the demands of independence rest on views about the nature of human flourishing. In particular, they assume that children's ethical interests are served by having a sense of justice and the capacity to reflect on and choose lifestyles they find most attractive. We need, however, to supplement these claims with a further observation to explain fully why comprehensive enrolment is not necessary to avoid serious harm. The further thought is that those conceptions of the good that assert that failure to enrol may be disastrous from the point of view of the child's well-being are mistaken conceptions of the good. This is a claim about the nature of the ethical landscape. Political liberalism's refusal to take a stand on comprehensive matters is appropriate for a world in which it is not true that very high stakes are involved in the choice of one's comprehensive doctrine. If pressed, we must deny that salvation turns

---

[44] These arguments are characteristic of J. S. Mill's comprehensive liberal arguments for autonomy and liberal freedoms in *On Liberty*, in *On Liberty, Utilitarianism and Other Essays*, 2nd edn., ed. Mark Philp (Oxford: Oxford University Press, 2015).

on being within the church.[45] Though I cannot give a full justification of that claim about the ethical universe, which would require extensive engagement with theological controversies, I believe it to be sound. Similarly, the response to parents who acknowledge the pro tanto reasons to respect their child's independence, but propose to baptize her into the Catholic Church out of concern for her salvation, must be to deny their theological views.

In sum, there are limits to independence. In cases where the well-being costs to the child not being enrolled are very high, reasons to respect her independence may be defeated by our reasons to act out of concern for her well-being. Nevertheless, in our world, there may be only a few, or no, cases in which that condition holds, because an upbringing for independence gives us capacities that also serve our well-being and we do not live in a world where the consequences of non-enrolment are disastrous.

---

[45] As Rawls remarks (*Political Liberalism*, 152), '[I]n affirming a political conception of justice we may eventually have to assert at least certain aspects of our own comprehensive religious or philosophical doctrine (by no means necessarily fully comprehensive)'. For further discussion of the problem of high stakes, see my paper with David Stevens, 'When God Commands Disobedience: Political Liberalism and Unreasonable Religions', *Res Publica* 20 (2014): 65–84.

6
Family Values and Parents' Interests

6.1 Familial Intimacy

One prominent set of objections to independence for children is that it lacks the resources to justify forms of family life that are both widely practised and valuable. The family is a vital institution within society, its defenders argue, for both child-centred and adult-centred reasons; its value consists in the production and maintenance of a certain kind of intimacy between parents and their children. If my view is inimical to the right kind of intimacy between parent and child, that would indeed be a weighty reason to reject it.

In this section, I argue that independence for children has the resources to accommodate intimate family life. To be sure, as should now be evident, anti-perfectionist parenting is a radical departure from widely practised forms of parenting, because it requires parents to exclude as a reason for action their own conception of the good when deciding how to raise their child and, instead, proceed on the basis of the public reasons that apply to parenting and education. They may not, for example, enrol their child into a particular conception of religion. Nevertheless, as I'll argue, such a view is quite compatible with the realization of intimacy between parent and child. No doubt, it requires parents to pursue intimacy with their children in a different way compared to those commonly practised. But it is none the worse for that and, indeed, it offers an attractive alternative way of understanding the parental role.

It is worth distinguishing between several different objections to my view that arise from the claim that the family, characterized by a particular kind of relationship between parent and child, is valuable. First, some worry that families cannot be justified within, and should not receive support from, an anti-perfectionist liberal community, because the value of the family can be established only by appealing to a rich conception of human flourishing. A conception of morality that denies itself these religious or ethical reasons is incapable of defending the institution of the family in which a small number of adults care for, and share space and goals with, particular children over the course of their childhood.

A different objection is that the kind of family life independence for children demands is suboptimal from the point of view of parent-child intimacy. There are several criticisms under this heading: it is sometimes claimed that parental anti-perfectionism fails to give parents the opportunity to exercise discretion, to display spontaneity in their relationships with their children, to be themselves by revealing their comprehensive convictions and the projects they hold dear to their children, or to pursue shared goals and projects with their child. Not allowing parents to enrol their children into the religious traditions they affirm, these critics claim, jeopardizes the maintenance of family life as it should be.

Finally, it is worth considering a different kind of criticism. The objections outlined above rest on concerns about the incompatibility between parental anti-perfectionism and valuable family life. If my replies are successful, I will have established that the alleged incompatibility is not borne out. But it might be thought that the compatibility of parental anti-perfectionism and intimate family relationships is more thoroughgoing than I suggest. Some have argued that there is, indeed, a sound anti-perfectionist justification for permitting, perhaps encouraging, parents to get children to share their values, and for parents and children to jointly pursue them. On this view, even if anti-perfectionism in upbringing is sound, its implications for parental conduct are not as radical as I claim them to be. Rather, because intimacy is a public reason in virtue of being helpful for the development of children's critical faculties or a sense of justice, for example, and intimacy requires or permits parents to enrol their child into their religion to facilitate the sharing and joint pursuit of goals, an anti-perfectionist upbringing supports something akin to the liberal consensus in which parents are morally permitted to raise their children according to the values and practices of their religion. Parents may enrol their children into a religion—take their child to church, make them worship and participate in its rites—not because these activities are valuable, but because they enable or constitute the shared pursuit of activities and projects between parents and children. If this objection were sound, then parental anti-perfectionism would be a boring view because its revisionist claim that parents may not enrol children into particular conceptions of the good would be mistaken.[1]

I believe that all of these objections from intimacy can be rebutted. But my discussion is designed not merely to defend a moral view from its critics. It serves an additional purpose: in replying to these concerns about the

---

[1] For this objection, see Cormier, 'On the Permissibility of Shaping Children's Values', 344–345.

relationship between parents and their children, I provide further elaboration of how the ideal of independence for children understands the character of family life and its value.

Before addressing the objections raised above, it is worth clarifying the nature of parent-child intimacy and different reasons for valuing it. Although there are differences of emphasis between different accounts, there is broad consensus about the items that constitute familial intimacy. What Macleod calls the 'affective family' involves 'close, loving relationships characterized by both mutual concern and participation in shared activities and projects'.[2] For Gheaus, intimacy is constituted by, among other things, 'the [child's] experience of caring affection from adults whom the children can trust and love wholeheartedly'.[3] Perhaps the most detailed and nuanced account is provided by Brighouse and Swift, for whom the value of an intimate relationship between parent and child justifies both social policies that support access to family life for both children and adults and a particular conception of the rights parents have to do various things to, for, and with their children.[4]

For Brighouse and Swift, a valuable intimate relationship between parent and child has several distinctive features. The parental role is a fiduciary one in which parents exercise paternalistic control over their child in the service of her developmental and non-developmental needs. The kind of family they defend is one in which a small number of adults, possibly one, raise a child by being a constant and considerable presence in her life, particularly in her childhood but also in her adolescence. Such parents love and give special attention to their child, responding appropriately to her needs on the basis of an unrivalled understanding of her personality so that, over the course of time, she acquires the skills and emotions to be independent and to act justly towards others. Similarly, the child identifies with, loves, and gets to know, her parents. As she becomes able to form beliefs about her parents, parent-child intimacy is constituted by a belief on the part of the young child that her parents have authority over her, which includes their exercising some degree of discretion with respect to what she does and with whom she has relationships, and their acting with some degree of spontaneity. Finally, familial intimacy is constituted by sharing a life in which parents and children share space, reveal themselves ethically to each other, and pursue particular values together.

---

[2] Colin Macleod, 'Liberal Equality and the Affective Family', in *The Moral and Political Status of Children*, edited by Archard and Macleod, 215.

[3] Anca Gheaus, 'Children's Vulnerability and Legitimate Authority Over Children', *Journal of Applied Philosophy* 35 (2018): 60–75, at 66.

[4] Brighouse and Swift, *Family Values*, Pts. 2 and 3.

Brighouse and Swift argue that intimate family life, so understood, is valuable for both children and adults. The child-centred case for intimacy rests on psychological findings concerning the developmental need of children to be attached to particular loving adults who they view as authoritative.[5] But they also argue that occupying the role of parent is a distinctive and vital source of well-being for very many adults; they argue that, provided they would do a sufficiently good job, an adult's interest in having a family life generates a claim to parent even if the child's interest would be better served by being parented by someone else.[6]

With this account of parent-child intimacy in place, let us examine the objections raised above; first, the objection that we cannot account for the value of the family without appealing to a rich conception of what a good life involves, which is inimical to the anti-perfectionist liberal's insistence that we theorize parental morality on the basis of a more limited set of reasons related to our interests in freedom and equality.

It is, of course, true that certain arguments for familial intimacy, like some of Brighouse and Swift's, invoke controversial claims about human well-being: for example, the claim that for many adults, perhaps most, occupying the role of parent is necessary to live a good life.[7] Such a claim is controversial because there are countless people who believe not only that their own lives are better served by avoiding parenthood, but also that childfree lifestyles are generally better for people, or that parenting is certainly not necessary to enjoy a flourishing life. Such people might accept that once an individual takes on the role of parent her well-being depends on how well she fulfils the responsibilities of that role and that the goodness of her life would be diminished if she abandoned it. Nonetheless, that view is compatible with holding that becoming a parent is bad for most adults. Many believe that to be true. Raising children is a costly pursuit in terms of time and money, and it reduces one's opportunity for success in one's occupation and in the pursuit of one's various goals outside work. It is not unheard of for adults who reflect on their life to regret their earlier decision to become a parent and to warn others not to make the same mistake.[8]

---

[5] Brighouse and Swift, *Family Values*, 70–75. They draw on Sue Gerhardt's *Why Love Matters: How Affection Shapes a Baby's Brain* (London: Routledge, 2015).

[6] Brighouse and Swift, *Family Values*, Ch. 4, particularly, 87–97.

[7] In a later article, Brighouse and Swift emphasize the ways in which the child-centred strand of their argument is compatible with an anti-perfectionist account of morality. See their 'Family Values Reconsidered: A Response', *Critical Review of International Social and Political Philosophy* 21 (2018): 385–405, at 389–392.

[8] There is a considerable empirical literature devoted to the question of whether parenthood improves or diminishes one's happiness. For a review of some of this literature, see Thomas Hansen, 'Parenthood and Happiness: A Review of Folk Theories Versus Empirical Evidence', *Social Indicators*

An anti-perfectionist theory of the family does not align itself with either positive or negative assessments of whether parenthood makes one's life go well. How, then, can it defend the value of the family? Perhaps the most straightforward defence is child-centred. Regardless of our views about the morality of procreation, the existence of children with developmental needs, including the need for an intimate relationship with a small number of parents, is a fact of life. More to the point, the fundamental ideals and values that explain the developmental interests of children need not be religious or ethical in character. It is enough to appeal to the interests of individuals viewed as free and equal or, in other words, with the interests set out in the idea of independence. We have interests in developing the relevant capacities, skills, and motivation to develop and pursue a conception of the good and to treat others justly. The psychological facts to which Brighouse and Swift appeal—the child's need to have close and constant carers who act as role models and have authority and discretion over her, and so on—are reasons for familial intimacy in virtue of serving our interest in independence just as much as they are reasons within alternative, comprehensive accounts of human flourishing. An elaborate account of the nature of a good life is not, therefore, required to justify the family.[9]

It is harder for anti-perfectionists to provide a justification of the family that appeals to adults' interests in parenting. Brighouse and Swift build the adult-centred strand of their argument on claims about the unique and non-substitutable ethical value of parenting for those who parent, or at least for those who have parenthood as their goal. In their view, an adult has an ethical interest in parenting that is often sufficient to give her a right to parent, which correlates with various duties on the child they raise and others in society, even when alternative adults would parent better. It is difficult to see how a general right of that kind can be justified without appealing to a reasonably detailed account of what makes one's life go well of the kind they set out and towards which anti-perfectionists must demur.[10] To be sure, there is an anti-perfectionist

---

Research 108 (2012): 29–64. One unfortunate feature of these empirical studies is that their focus is subjective or self-reported well-being. It is unfortunate because those, like Brighouse and Swift, who defend the view that parenthood is good for most adults often operate with an objective, rather than a subjective, conception of well-being. It should also be noted that anti-perfectionists resist attaching any non-instrumental importance to subjective well-being from the point of view of identifying a conception of justice. Some reasons for scepticism about such metrics are set out in my paper with Andrew Williams, 'Distributive Justice and Subjective Health Assessment', in *Measuring Health and Medical Outcomes*, edited by Crispin Jenkinson (London: UCL Press, 1994).

[9] Others have argued that the defence of the family need not rest on a controversial account of human flourishing: most prominently, David Archard in his *The Family: A Liberal Defence* (Basingstoke: Palgrave Macmillan, 2010).

[10] For a similar observation, see Archard, *The Family*, 98. Archard offers a critique of other popular parent-centred arguments for the family that are anti-perfectionist in character but rest on implausible

adult-centred defence of the maintenance of *existing* families, which appeals to parents' interest in not having the children they love taken away from them, which is often devastating because it can destroy one's self-respect, as Rawls understands it: it can shatter one's self-confidence and lead to the belief that one's life is not worth living or that one's goals lack value.[11] Our interest in self-respect carries considerable weight, sufficient weight to defeat the child's claim to be parented by others who would do a marginally better job of raising her. But it should also be noted that this interest remains agnostic on other issues; for example, it does not support giving adults who want to parent an equal claim to adopt a child when they would do a worse job of parenting compared to others. Nevertheless, taking children's and adults' interests into account, it is clear that an anti-perfectionist approach to families has the resources to justify the central range of familial institutions.[12]

I turn now to the different worry that my account cannot be reconciled with familial intimacy because anti-perfectionism requires parents to act in ways that are inimical to the maintenance of families as they should be.[13] Earlier, I distinguished several concerns under this heading. I pick out two. First, some emphasize the value of parents' and children's joint pursuit of goals, projects,

---

claims about justice, such as the view that procreators have a right to parent their offspring in virtue of their investment of labour or their intention to found a family. See Archard, *The Family*, Ch. 3.

[11] See Rawls, *A Theory of Justice*, §67.

[12] Here, I do not offer a detailed account of what has become known as 'the right *to* parent' or the moral principles that regulate the allocation of custody rights over children. Several accounts have been offered: child-centred, parent-centred, and dual interest conceptions. For a compendious survey of the different views within this debate, see Anca Gheaus, 'Biological Parenthood: Gestational, Not Genetic', *Australasian Journal of Philosophy* 96 (2018): 225–240. It is sufficient for my purposes to establish that anti-perfectionism is consistent with support for the institution of the family. In *JLU* (Ch. 2) I defended a dual-interest conception of the allocation of custody over children, but it should be noted that independence for children is also compatible with a wholly child-centred account of the kind defended by Peter Vallentyne, 'The Rights and Duties of Childrearing', *William and Mary Bill of Rights Journal* 11 (2003): 991–1010; and Anca Gheaus, 'The Best Available Parent', *Ethics* 131 (2021): 431–459.

[13] This objection forms part of a larger set of objections that claim that liberal justice jeopardizes familial intimacy. For an early version of a different objection within that set, which focuses on the alleged conflict between the principle of equality of opportunity and the family in Rawls's conception of justice as fairness, see Francis Schrag, 'Justice and the Family', *Inquiry* 19 (1976): 193–208. For other discussions of the distributive aspects of the issue, many of which seek to soften the alleged conflict, see Véronique Munoz-Dardé, 'Is the Family to be Abolished Then?', *Proceedings of the Aristotelian Society* 99 (1999): 37–56; Colin Macleod, 'Liberal Justice and the Affective Family' and 'Parental Responsibilities in an Unjust World', in *Procreation and Parenthood*, edited by David Archard and David Benatar (Oxford: Oxford University Press, 2010); Swift, *How Not to be a Hypocrite*; Archard, *The Family*, Ch. 5; Andrew Mason, *Levelling the Playing Field: The Idea of Equal Opportunity and its Place in Egalitarian Thought* (Oxford: Oxford University Press, 2006); Brighouse and Swift, *Family Values*, Ch. 5; Paul Bou-Habib, 'The Moralised View of Parental Partiality', *Journal of Political Philosophy* 22 (2014): 66–83. I restrict myself here to the objection as it applies particularly to anti-perfectionism and familial intimacy. My discussion of this version of the intimacy objection is compatible with a wide range of accounts of distributive justice.

and enthusiasms, which requires or permits parents to enrol their child into their distinctive religious or ethical practices. Second, some argue that intimacy between parent and child requires parents to be themselves, to act with a considerable degree of discretion and spontaneity, and, importantly, to reveal their comprehensive views to their children.

My main response to these concerns is to show how parental anti-perfectionism is compatible with intimacy, or at least certain elements of it. We might distinguish between different aspects of an intimate parent-child relationship: sharing space; parents' attending to the daily needs of their child; eating together; displays of affection between parent and child; parents' being themselves within the relationship with their child; the joint pursuit of goals, values, and practices; the joint pursuit of projects that are comprehensive in nature; and so on. Even if joint pursuit of the parents' conception of the good is threatened by an anti-perfectionist upbringing, other kinds of intimacy are not. Indeed, there might be more or less extensional equivalence between the kind of intimacy supported by an anti-perfectionist upbringing and the intimacy that some claim is a distinctive form of human good.

Daniel Weinstock argues that intimacy is threatened if parents are not permitted to pursue their religious practices with their child. One of his arguments appeals to the instrumental value of enrolling one's child into one's comprehensive doctrine. As a matter of empirical fact, he claims, for parents to pursue activities with her, their child needs to be introduced to them, become competent in performing them, and enthusiastic about the activity in question. Weinstock argues that, because these attributes are more likely to be imparted by parents who are competent and passionate about the practices their child pursues, intimacy supports parents' sharing their comprehensive commitments with their child.[14]

This argument seems to overlook certain mundane facts about upbringing. Young children like to eat, play, play games with others, build models, solve puzzles, draw pictures, listen to and read stories, communicate their interests and enthusiasms to others, seek approval from others, and so on. There are good public reasons for parents to facilitate these activities and, to the extent that intimacy matters, share these experiences with their child. Notwithstanding their commitment to a particular religion, it is not phenomenologically sound

---

[14] Weinstock, 'How the Interests of Children Limit the Religious Freedom of Parents', 223. For a similar argument see Chris Mills, 'The Case for Restricted Perfectionism in Upbringing', *Social Theory and Practice* 49 (2023): 709–738, at 716–724.

to claim that parents cannot share a range of suitable activities with their young child in the absence of their giving those activities a religious inflection.

In addition, Weinstock assumes that parents must act as exemplars so that their child develops their competence with respect to the goals and practices they pursue, or a secure commitment to certain values. That is clearly sound in some cases. For example, it is vital that children become committed to, and competent in, practices that recognize and treat others as free and equal; it is important for parents to show their children how they should relate to others with concern and respect. But in other cases, it does not matter whether the sharing of a practice also involves competence or reflects the parent's passions. Suppose a child has the ambition to play golf, but her parents have never played. What should the parents do? Make the child play cricket instead, because cricket is more valuable, they appreciate that fact, and play the game well themselves? I do not think so. Perhaps the parents should help her to play golf, learn to swing a club themselves, and try to generate some enthusiasm for it. From the point of view of developing or sustaining intimacy with the child, it does not matter that they cannot pursue the activity competently. Indeed, intimacy can be found in parents' ferrying their child to and from sporting or musical venues and sharing in the joy she experiences from playing games or musical instruments, regardless of whether they are passionate about, or competent in, the activity in question.

Some make a stronger non-instrumental claim, namely, that intimacy is constituted by the sharing and joint pursuit of values.[15] Living in close proximity with one's child and attending to their needs are insufficient, they claim, because intimacy involves having a shared orientation within the world of value. But this does not seem to justify the joint pursuit of a conception of the good life. Even if it is accepted that the sharing of values between parents and child is important—I believe that sometimes it is—it is unclear why it is not enough to share moral and political values, the values the child becomes attracted to, or the activities related to the child's acquisition of her own independent view.[16] With respect to moral values, for example, we might understand independence-respecting parents' explaining how they share and pursue

---

[15] See, for example, Jurgen De Wispelaere and Daniel Weinstock, 'The Grounds and Limits of Parents' Cultural Prerogatives: The Case of Circumcision', in *The Nature of Children's Well-Being*, edited by Bagattini and Macleod.

[16] A related response, which I do not gainsay, is offered by Sarah Hannan and Richard Vernon, who argue that intimate relationships do not require many shared commitments. See their 'Parental Rights: A Role-Based Approach', *Theory and Research in Education* 6 (2008): 173–189, at 176. They make this argument in their review of Ferdinand Shoeman's 'Rights of Children, Rights of Parents, and the Moral Basis of the Family', *Ethics* 91 (1980): 6–19, which has influenced subsequent intimacy-based defences of parents' rights to enrol their children.

commitments with their children in the following terms: 'we stand together for showing concern and respect for others, fighting against injustice and pursuing the gamut of further values and principles that follow from those fundamental principles'. Although it does not permit parents to pursue their comprehensive commitments with their children by enrolling them in their own religious institutions, for example, independence for children preserves a space for parents and children to jointly pursue moral and political goals and their children's current goals.

Brighouse and Swift offer a brief argument that purports to establish that the values of sharing and the joint pursuit of goals and beliefs give parents a moral permission to deliberately shape their child's comprehensive values.[17] They argue that familial intimacy requires some overlap between the parent's and the child's interests and values. For that reason, the parent has a reason 'to increase the likelihood that he and his child will continue to have shared interests'. Their next key argumentative move is to claim that the parent has a right that the shared values and interests be his, at least when the child is young, because, 'it must be the parent who supplies the values' and because 'adults' values are less plastic than children's'.[18]

In reply, it bears repeating that even if we grant that an overlap between the parent's and child's interests and values is constitutive of intimacy, that alone does not support allowing parents to intentionally shape their children's comprehensive convictions. Instead, parents might effect the overlap by sharing sound moral and political values and goals or by sharing the child's emerging enthusiasms. For the reasons given above, it is not true even for young children that their non-moral or non-political interests must be supplied by parents.

The further reason Brighouse and Swift offer for giving 'priority' to parents' values is that they are less 'plastic' than their child's. The argument seems to be that parents lose more by being required to jointly pursue their child's interests and enthusiasms than the child does if she is required to pursue theirs—children are more flexible with respect to the terms on which they can share and jointly pursue interests compared to adults. I postpone a full response to this argument until the next section in which I address parent- and adult-centred objections to independence for children. It is enough for now to observe that anti-perfectionist parenting is not incompatible with the joint pursuit of projects and interests between parents and their children.[19]

[17] Brighouse and Swift, *Family Values*, 155–157.
[18] Brighouse and Swift, *Family Values*, 156.
[19] It should be noted that in a later article, which responds to various criticisms of *Family Values*, Brighouse and Swift express more openness than they do in their book to the view that the kind of parent-child sharing that is central to familial intimacy may not justify a parental moral permission

A different version of the incompatibility objection claims that independence for children requires parents to act like the Muggletonians and hide their comprehensive convictions from their children. For example, Weinstock argues that intimacy is threatened because he believes that an anti-perfectionist upbringing requires parents to pursue their own comprehensive convictions away from their children. Commenting on my conception of anti-perfectionist parenting in *JLU*, he writes:

> Imagine that, convinced of the correctness of arguments of Matthew Clayton, religious parents were to decide to prescind from sharing their religious beliefs with their children, and hired babysitters to look after them while they engaged in religious practices. This would create a separation between parents and children that would clearly be inimical to the development of intimacy.[20]

Brighouse and Swift object to my view for similar reasons. They argue that parents have a right to reveal their values and passions to their child: '[A] close, loving relationship will surely involve parents honestly revealing their enthusiasms and aversions, their sense of what matters in life and what is trivial.'[21] They argue for a moral permission and sometimes, it seems, a moral requirement for parents to reveal their comprehensive commitments to their children on various grounds. As noted above, they believe that an intimate relationship between parent and child must be spontaneous, not involve constant self-monitoring on the part of parents, and be one in which each can be herself as well as get to know the other well.[22] But they go further by arguing that the fact that the child might reject their comprehensive convictions gives parents an intimacy-based reason to disclose their views to ensure that she knows about them in detail; such knowledge helps the child to understand their different point of view, which helps her to sustain a meaningful relationship with them.[23]

In summary, these objections claim that anti-perfectionist parenting requires an unhealthy separation between parent and child or Muggletonian

---

to deliberately shape one's child's comprehensive values. See Brighouse and Swift, 'Family Values Reconsidered: A Response', 392–394. See also Swift's 'Parents' Rights, Children's Religion: A Familial Relationship Goods Approach', *Journal of Practical Ethics* 8 (2020): 30–65.

[20] Weinstock, 'How the Interests of Children Limit the Religious Freedom of Parents', 224.
[21] Brighouse and Swift, *Family Values*, 152; see 170 for their articulation of this specific objection to my earlier statement of parental anti-perfectionism. They also share other critics' views about other aspects of independence for children, which I consider elsewhere.
[22] Brighouse and Swift, *Family Values*, 153–155.
[23] Brighouse and Swift, *Family Values*, 157.

conduct that inhibits parents being themselves because they cannot permissibly reveal their views. There is much to say in response, but before setting out various qualifications it is worth re-emphasizing that parental anti-perfectionism forbids the enrolment of children, such as parents' making their child routinely practise their religious doctrine, for example, or parents' deliberately encouraging their child to share their comprehensive convictions. This prohibition of enrolment does not imply that, as a matter of moral principle, parents are required to pursue their religious commitments in a geographically separate manner or are forbidden from revealing their views to their children. Of course, revealing, even deliberately exposing one's child to, one's religion may lead to her developing a desire to pursue it. That may generate certain concerns from the perspective of independence for children, which will be briefly discussed below. But such side-effect influencing of children's beliefs and desires is, in principle, consistent with parental anti-perfectionism, because it does not involve the intentional transmission of the parents' religious beliefs and there may be sound public reasons for the activities, notwithstanding these side effects.[24]

Should we say, then, that parents are always morally permitted to pursue their religious beliefs in front of their children or to get their child to understand their comprehensive beliefs? Should we make the stronger claim that parents are normally morally *required* to engage in this kind of sharing—would it be morally objectionable for intimacy-based reasons for parents to take a Muggletonian view of religious disclosure, for example? These are complicated issues, the resolution of which turns on developmental psychological facts, but I know of no empirical research that is informed by the ideal of independence for children. Instead, I'll try to offer a guide through this thorny terrain that uses the ideal to raise issues and defend certain conjectures and conditional imperatives.

First, the strong view that parents are morally required to reveal their comprehensive convictions to their children seems too strong: the necessity of parents' doing so does not seem to be phenomenologically borne out. For example, other than realizing and maintaining a valuable family life, the central comprehensive goals of some parents are occupational and can be pursued outside the home environment without their children's participation. That does not mean that they lose intimacy with their children when they return

---

[24] For related sapient remarks about the distinction between being brought up within a particular religion and being exposed to one's parents' religious beliefs and activity, see Eamonn Callan, 'McLaughlin on Parental Rights', *Journal of Philosophy of Education* 19 (1985): 111–118, at 111–112.

home. So let us turn to the view that parents are morally permitted to practise their comprehensive goals within the home in full view of their child, responding with justificatory arguments to her questions about why they do what they do. Such a view seems to be defended by those surveyed above, because for some parents, particularly religious ones, their conception of the good informs everything they do—what they eat, who they associate with, what they wear, and so on. To make them hide these aspects of their lives from their child would be costly for them, because it would deprive them of 'being themselves' and place burdens of self-monitoring on them, and it would jeopardize the mutual understanding between parents and children at the heart of familial intimacy.

There is much that is true in that line of thought and, at some point in the child's upbringing, it tells in favour of a moral permission for parents to expose their child to their religious convictions and pursuits. Whether the permission extends to all of the child's upbringing will turn on certain psychological facts concerning what helps or hinders the child's development into an independent person.

For example, if certain psychological facts hold, non-disclosure would, morally, be the right course of action for parents to follow at least in certain periods of their child's development. Suppose, for example, a child naturally mimics the behaviour and attitudes of her parents. She observes their mannerisms, their accent, and their beliefs and desires about a range of things. Suppose, in addition, that behaviour, beliefs, and desires that are formed in early childhood, particularly those that replicate their parents' attitudes, prove to be sticky in the sense that they are difficult or costly to shake off in later childhood or adulthood. This might be because the child becomes habituated to embrace certain lifestyles, which become her second nature, and she finds it hard to reflect on them in a rational, informed manner; or it might be because her attachment to these ways of living makes it harder for her to pursue other lifestyles even when she reflectively believes these to be better—the feelings of guilt or shame that she experiences in turning her back on the activities she pursued, or beliefs she shared, with her parents from infancy might make it difficult or costly for her to pursue the conception of the good she now reflectively endorses.

I do not know whether these psychological suppositions are true. If they were, then there would be an independence-based concern about parents' revealing their comprehensive convictions and practices to their young children. True, such revelatory activities need not amount to enrolment as I understand it, because parents might not treat these psychological facts alongside the value of religious practise as reasons for revelation—they might not trade on the facts about mimicry and the stickiness of beliefs to get their children to follow their religious doctrine, for example. But the existence of such mechanisms is, nevertheless, worrisome. Like views in the liberal consensus, independence for children is also concerned with offering children an upbringing that enables them to become agents whose lifestyles are responsive to their informed and reflective judgements about ethical value. The side effects of parenting can be as harmful to realizing that end as the intentional shaping of children's lives. Thus, the Muggletonian view might be appropriate for young children.

Still, parents' revelation of their comprehensive views might not inhibit their child's acquisition of the capacities, information, and emotional skills that are central to an independent life. Indeed, there might be something to the thought that, from a suitable age, it is valuable or at least not harmful for the child to witness at close hand what pursuing a conception of the good might look like. If so, revelation is morally permissible. Nevertheless, respecting the child's independence means that parents who reveal their conception of the good should make the child aware—again in an age-appropriate way—that they believe that her life is not theirs to shape. They might say to her: 'We're just your parents. These are our comprehensive values; you will develop your own ethical judgements and goals. Our role is to ensure that you are in a position to reflect on the available alternative conceptions of the good, to make your own choices in life, and to have the relevant capacities to act on them. And we will love and support you regardless of the values you go on to adopt.' One of the features of an attractive conception of *familial* intimacy that is sometimes underemphasized by its advocates is a mutual understanding of the acceptability of differentiated unity: unlike voluntary associations, which are often defined by shared comprehensive values and interests, family members ought to be committed to maintaining special relationships with each other regardless of whether there is a shared orientation or commitment to particular comprehensive values.[25] Parents ought continually to articulate this understanding during their child's childhood and adolescence. If they did so, revealing their comprehensive views might not diminish their child's opportunity to reflect on and pursue her own ethical and religious judgements later in life.[26]

---

[25] Here I agree with Hannan and Vernon, 'Parental Rights', 176–177. For an important paper that discusses the implications of this moral obligation for questions concerning the moral right to parent, see Samantha Brennan and Colin Macleod, 'Fundamentally Incompetent: Homophobia, Religion, and the Right to Parent', in *Procreation, Parenthood, and Educational Rights: Ethical and Philosophical Issues*, edited by Jaime Ahlberg and Michael Cholbi (New York: Routledge, 2017).

[26] In *JLU* (106–109), I argued that considerations of the cost of revising and pursuing one's own conception of the good provide an instrumental argument for the impermissibility of enrolment. Many commentators have offered arguments against that view, including Cameron, 'Clayton on

There is, then, a case for certain kinds of restraint when parents reveal their interests and values to their child, such as the insistence that they communicate their unconditional love for her, frame their revelation by encouraging her to understand that they have no expectation that she will follow them, display respect for her emerging values, and gauge whether their unintentional influences impede the development of capacities that are helpful to her in leading an independent life.

One final question is whether principles requiring these kinds of restraint jeopardize certain other goods of intimacy emphasized by Brighouse and Swift, such as parents' being free to act spontaneously and without excessive self-monitoring. I do not believe they would. This is partly because a certain degree of parental self-monitoring is appropriate and partly because the degree of self-monitoring required by respect for the child's independence is not excessive. With respect to the first point, I agree with Brighouse and Swift that a degree of parental self-monitoring is required. They argue that both children and parents need 'a relationship in which the adult offers love and authority, a complex and emotionally challenging combination of openness and restraint, of spontaneity and self-monitoring, of sharing and withholding'.[27] Parents need to self-monitor not least because their natural impulse is to act in protective ways that might inhibit their child's opportunity to learn how to be independent: motivated by a concern for their child's well-being or their own desire not to lose them, they might prevent her from engaging in activities in which she can experiment and learn from failure, for example.[28]

So, self-monitoring is a parental virtue, but how much? I have set out the kinds of restraint that independence for children requires and the considerable latitude it affords parents with respect to how they organize family life. Brighouse and Swift worry about the loss of two kinds of parental discretion. First, like others, they insist that parents must enjoy legal options: intimacy is jeopardized if parents lack considerable space to make decisions 'unmonitored by other authorities'.[29] Second, even if they are not scrutinized or disciplined by others, parents should not be 'slavish enforcers of an official child-rearing protocol', because children need to see that their parents are authority figures

---

Comprehensive Enrolment', 350–351; Cormier, 'On the Permissibility of Shaping Children's Values', 336–338. The case for independence presented in this book does not rely on the emotional costs argument; but that does not mean that the argument is unsound, particularly if we are mindful of the risks posed by indoctrination. For further discussion, see Callan, 'McLaughlin on Parental Rights'.

[27] Brighouse and Swift, *Family Values*, 93.
[28] Brighouse and Swift, *Family Values*, 90.
[29] Brighouse and Swift, *Family Values*, 120; Archard, *The Family*, 71–74.

who are capable of offering them 'loving guidance' by using their judgement.[30] Both reasons to preserve parental discretion are important. However, they do not give us reasons for extending to parents the moral permission to raise their child with a sense of *in*justice or to inhibit her development of the wherewithal to reflect on and pursue her own judgements. Nor, I submit, do they support parents' having moral options to disrespect their child's claim to independence.

To conclude this section, I turn briefly to the final intimacy-based objection outlined above. According to Cormier, the good of familial intimacy is defensible within an anti-perfectionist liberal view, but, importantly, this includes a parental moral permission to deliberately shape the religious and ethical beliefs of children. Independence for children asserts that every child has an interest in developing the cognitive and emotional capacities to reflect on, choose from, and pursue one of a range of comprehensive options. To satisfy that interest, a child needs to be raised in an intimate family in which parents share and deliberately shape her comprehensive pursuits and values. For that reason, rather than object to comprehensive enrolment, advocates of anti-perfectionism should encourage it for the sake of the child's interest in developing her own religious and ethical perspective.

If that line of reasoning were correct, independence for children would become just another member of the liberal consensus, because its distinctive claim that comprehensive enrolment is morally wrong would not be sustainable. However, my replies to the previous objection also serve as replies to the thought that parental anti-perfectionism supports comprehensive enrolment. Because familial intimacy in the service of the child's developmental interests can be sustained without parents' enrolling their child into their religious or ethical view, the moral objection to comprehensive enrolment is not threatened by an appeal to the value of intimacy.

I have sought to integrate a conception of familial intimacy into my account of independence for children. I have assumed, as others do, that intimacy between parent and child involves some kind of sharing, some kind of mutual understanding, and a degree of spontaneity in their relationship. But the precise details of these relational facts and the degree to which they need to be realized are far from clear. There are different kinds and degrees of sharing, understanding, spontaneity, and the exercise of discretion. I have argued that an intimate family life of the kind described by some, in which parents have reasonably wide-ranging moral permissions with respect to the religious character of their child's life, is not morally required. I have also claimed that

---

[30] Brighouse and Swift, *Family Values*, 72–73.

familial intimacy is compatible with the ideal of independence for children. In pursuit of familial intimacy, parents must recognize their child's moral entitlement to set her own ends; they may not seek to make her follow controversial religious or ethical practices, and they may not intentionally direct her towards controversial comprehensive convictions.

Those moral constraints leave parents with considerable moral space to shape their child's life and share activities with her. They are morally required to mould her convictions to align with the right conception of justice. In addition, they may, in an age-appropriate way and under the proviso of their publicly expressed commitment to her independence-based entitlements, reveal their religious and ethical convictions to their child. Finally, independence for children provides the basis for a different understanding of a shared family life compared to common practice in which parents' interests are given priority. The child has a moral claim to a family that develops her wherewithal to pursue an independent life. As she approaches adulthood, she should have a good understanding of the character of different controversial comprehensive options available within society; she should understand the different kinds of reasoning and evaluation that she might deploy in reflecting on the merits or demerits of different conceptions; she should have the psychological makeup to plan and pursue a distinctive conception and to deal with setbacks in the pursuit of her chosen comprehensive ends. In short, the child needs an upbringing in which she explores the controversial world of religious doctrines and conceptions of the good. That exploration is a great adventure, much of which parents may share with their child by joining her in learning about and trying out different conceptions. Thus, the ideal of independence offers an exhilarating alternative conception of familial intimacy compared to existing accounts, which tend to be too centred on parents' ambitions.

6.2 The Interests and Claims of Parents

Independence for children rejects parentalism, the view that parents enjoy a wide range of moral options with respect to how to raise their child, including the moral permission to give her a religious or non-religious education as they choose and to enrol her into particular comprehensive practices. In this section, I elaborate and defend that rejection by drawing on the arguments of previous chapters and by responding to arguments that have been, or might be, developed by those who defend comprehensive enrolment by an appeal to the interests or moral claims of parents.

At the outset, we need to draw a distinction between a parent-centred conception of parental morality and parent-centred moral arguments about family law. Many existing defences of parental choice have the law as their focus. They defend legal options for parents by arguing that the government is not morally permitted to tell parents how they may raise or educate their child, or why others are morally required not to interfere coercively to restrict how parents raise or educate her. I'll discuss these views later (§7.1). Here, I want to focus on the somewhat neglected question of whether parents enjoy wide-ranging *moral* permissions with respect to their child's upbringing. Plainly, the view that they do enjoy such moral options does not follow from their enjoyment of a moral injunction that protects their choices with respect to their children from interference by others.[31] It is coherent to believe that parents should not be constrained by laws that significantly limit what they can do to, for, or with their child and yet believe that there are very demanding moral requirements that mean that parents' scope for permissible choice in raising their children is negligible or at least more limited than is often assumed. To take a simple case, even if we grant that parents should be legally free to prevent their children from forming relationships with others who have a different ethnicity or whose parents pursue a different religion, it is clear that parents wrong their child if they exercise that legal freedom by always preventing the formation of such relationships. Here, then, I am interested in what parents owe to their children rather than the moral principles that inform whether the political community ought to respect or interfere with parents' choices.

It might be thought that, in virtue of the distinction between questions about the morality of family law and those concerning what parents owe to their children, defences of legal regimes that protect parental choice are of little relevance to the discussion of the moral options that parents enjoy. However, that conclusion is too hasty. Certain justifications of laws that protect parental choice rest on claims that can be extended to provide a putative case for the view that parents enjoy a wide range of moral options. There is a general explanation of why that might be the case. Many advocates of parental moral options worry about the loss of parents' freedom, which is akin to the loss of freedom they incur if the choices available to them are reduced by legal prohibitions. True, moral restrictions do not involve the loss of opportunities *to act* that paradigm cases of legal restrictions involve—they do not involve others'

---

[31] I am indebted to Shelly Kagan for the nice distinctions he draws in *The Limits of Morality* (Oxford: Oxford University Press, 1989), particularly Ch. 6. See also Jeremy Waldron, 'A Right to Do Wrong', *Ethics* 92 (1981): 21–39.

physically preventing us from performing a particular action. Nevertheless, they can involve a diminution of freedom in this sense: moral restrictions reduce our opportunity *to act without incurring (apt) guilt, blame, or liability*.[32] For that reason, at least some of the reasons given in support of a legal regime of parental choice might be promising as justifications of parental moral options that seem attractive, at least prima facie.

I should also note that my discussion of parent-centred objections to independence for children is by no means complete. For instance, I do not consider justifications of wide-ranging parental options that rest on clearly implausible moral foundations, such as the view that morality permits the strong (adults) to subjugate the vulnerable (children), or views that claim that there are differences in moral status between adults and children that explain why children's claims count for less compared to those of adults. And I do not engage with defences that have been refuted by others, such as 'proprietarian' accounts that claim that parents cannot wrong their child because she is their property and, within certain moral constraints, one is morally, as well as legally, permitted to do as one pleases with one's property.[33] Notwithstanding their historical importance and, more worryingly, their contemporary currency, I treat these arguments as non-starters. All the arguments I consider purport to defend parentalism in a way that is consistent with the foundational moral principle that children's interests and claims must be regarded as equal to those of adults.

I consider two kinds of parent-centred arguments for parental moral options. The first appeals to the interests of parents qua parents. When individuals occupy the role of parent they necessarily have a relationship with their child that generates certain special duties towards her. One parent-centred argument for the existence of parental moral options appeals to the costs parents would bear in executing those duties if they were not free to deliberately shape their child's comprehensive convictions or to enrol her into particular religious or ethical practices. Another argument that has this character appeals to their interest in fulfilling the parental role with integrity or in ways that are consistent with their deeply held convictions. A second kind of argument for parental choice appeals to parents qua adults or, in other words, to their non-parental interests. Notwithstanding their role as parents, adults who parent have their own lives to live, and it might be argued that the moral permissibility

---

[32] On this issue I have learned much from Seana Shiffrin's 'Moral Autonomy and Agent-Centred Options', *Analysis* 51 (1991): 244–254.
[33] As with many other issues concerning children and parenting, I am indebted to David Archard's trailblazing work. For his discussion of proprietarian conceptions, see *Children: Rights and Childhood*, 142–145; *The Family*, 44–45.

of pursuing their own conception of the good justifies their raising their child within that conception.

Let us begin by considering Brighouse and Swift's argument for a parental moral option to comprehensively enrol one's child, which I interpret as appealing to the costs parents would incur if such an option did not exist. Recall that their argument is that the sharing and joint pursuit of goals and projects between parents and children is valuable; it is conducive towards an intimate family life, which parents have a duty to provide for their children. For this reason, parents must effect some kind of overlap between the child's interests and values and their own. They then argue that parents are morally permitted to deliberately shape their child's values and interests to align with their own. They provide two reasons. First, they say that, at least when the child is young, 'it must be the parent who supplies the values'. Second, they observe that 'adults' values are less plastic than children's'.[34]

Earlier, I responded to their first argument by observing that even if it is right that parents must supply the values, they can cultivate appropriate independence-respecting shared moral and political values and pursue many activities with their child without enrolling her in their comprehensive doctrine. But what about the plasticity argument? The argument seems to be that parents lose more by being required to jointly pursue their child's interests and enthusiasms than the child does if she is required to pursue theirs. Lacking a firm and reflective commitment to any particular interests and values, the child incurs few opportunity costs by joining her parents in pursuing theirs. By contrast, if parents were not permitted to shape their child's comprehensive values to align them with their own, it may not be possible for them to combine the realization of their own comprehensive ambitions with their intimacy-based duty to pursue activities with their child and, accordingly, their interests would be set back.[35]

It should be clear why I do not find this argument convincing. The frustration of not fulfilling one's ambitions and the associated well-being losses do not enter the picture when we are assessing the moral permissibility of shaping others' convictions or enlisting them in our activities. This is evident in the cases between adults. Consider an adult, Alena, who demands that another adult, Brett, change his plans so that her goals are easier to realize. Perhaps she wants to make a pilgrimage to Lourdes and the journey would be less

---

[34] See Brighouse and Swift, *Family Values*, 155–156. The quoted phrases are from 156.
[35] For an argument in the same vein, see Colin Macleod's defence of a parental 'prerogative of *provisionally privileging* the conception of the good they favour' in his 'Conceptions of Parental Autonomy', at 129. See also 121–122 and 129–131.

expensive if Brett joined her, because they could then drive, which is cheaper than taking public transport. Suppose, in addition, that although Brett has decided to holiday in Ireland he did not give the decision much thought and he would be equally happy taking a trip to Lourdes. Still, it is clear that Brett is not morally required to change his plans and Alena is not morally permitted to coerce or manipulate him into changing them. She can try to persuade him to revise his plans, but she is not permitted to try to change them behind his back.

The fact that Alena's well-being or preference-satisfaction would be increased, without perhaps any diminution of Brett's well-being or preference-satisfaction, does not give Alena a permission to incorporate Brett into her plans. Brett is morally entitled to set his own goals and plans. Others are not permitted to make him conform to decisions that he can reasonably reject. The same claims can be made by a child or her representative in the case set out by Brighouse and Swift.[36]

It might be claimed that the Alena-Brett case would different if they were close friends. In that case, it might be a duty of friendship for Brett to change his plans to diminish the cost of Alena's holiday. Similarly, given that it is in the child's interest to have an intimate relationship with her parents, some might think that the child has a duty of intimacy to go along with her parents' values and interests because of the costs and benefits of the alternatives. If that were so, then parents' requiring the overlap to be on their terms and, for example, manipulating their child into endorsing their values is merely making her do what she would have a moral duty to do if she were reason-responsive and capable of incurring duties.[37]

In reply to this suggestion, note the relevant differences between the friends case and the parent-child case. In the former, the relationship is voluntary. Both parties choose to form and, by not exercising their exit options, to maintain the relationship. Voluntariness can make a difference to the duties of a role, as it does in many jobs and associative memberships, for example. We have the option of taking certain jobs or being part of religious communities that place us under obligations: to exhibit certain virtues or to live by particular standards of conduct. Still, in these cases there are alternative comprehensive options available to us, we choose to enter these roles and associations, and we

---

[36] One difference here is that shaping young children's religious and ethical values is inevitably manipulative in the sense that persuasion is not possible: values and interests cannot be imparted to a young child in a way that involves appropriate reflection and deliberation on the part of the child.

[37] For the thought, albeit in a different context, that interference is morally permissible if it makes a person do what she would have a duty to do if she were able to respond to moral reasons, see Victor Tadros, 'Orwell's Battle with Brittain: Vicarious Liability for Unjust Aggression', *Philosophy and Public Affairs* 42 (2014): 42–77, at 49.

may leave them without detriment to our interest in developing and exercising our key interests in exercising our sense of justice and capacity to pursue our own comprehensive convictions. By contrast, the child's presence in the family is non-voluntary. At the very least, then, the analogy with friendship as an argument for allowing parents to decide the terms of intimacy between them and their child needs further defence. In the light of how our views about duties of friendship rely on the voluntariness of the relationship, it is hard to see the argument succeeding.

Let me turn to a different parent-centred defence of the moral permissibility of comprehensive enrolment: integrity-based or conscientious objections to the account I have elaborated. At the outset, we should note that these moral considerations are usually presented in defence of *legal* permissions or exemptions from generally applicable laws to pursue one's conscience or perceived duties.[38] Indeed, it might be that the appeal to integrity is particularly powerful in identifying legal constraints and options. Nevertheless, the appeal to integrity has also been made in moral philosophy in criticism of theories like consequentialism,[39] and it is that kind of objection I want to discuss here.

The most promising parental integrity objection to independence for children starts with the thought that a conception of morality is implausible if it jeopardizes individuals' integrity. Even if a simple appeal to the costs parents would have to bear if they were not morally free to enrol their children into their comprehensive convictions is insufficient, it might be thought that a moral conception goes awry if it requires parents to act in ways contrary to their deeply held religious or ethical convictions, or perceived moral duties. Consider, for example, parents who believe they have an obligation to both God and their child to raise her in a way that honours God's commands.

---

[38] The most prominent recent defender of parents' rights as conscience rights is Moschella, *To Whom Do Children Belong?*, particularly Ch. 2. A similar argument that appeals to *authentic* parenting is advanced by Scott Altman in his 'Parental Control Rights', in *Philosophical Foundations of Children's and Family Law*, edited by Elizabeth Brake and Lucinda Ferguson (Oxford: Oxford University Press, 2018). There is a vast literature on the legal accommodation of religious practices through the granting of exemptions from generally applicable laws. For integrity-based defences of religious accommodation, see Paul Bou-Habib, 'A Theory of Religious Accommodation', *Journal of Applied Philosophy* 23 (2006): 109–126, and 'The Integrity of Religious Believers', *Critical Review of International Social and Political Philosophy* 22 (2020): 81–93; Martha Nussbaum, *Liberty of Conscience: In Defense of America's Tradition of Religious Equality* (New York: Basic Books, 2008); Cécile Laborde, *Liberalism's Religion* (Cambridge, MA: Harvard University Press, 2017), Ch. 6. For critiques of religious exemptions or integrity-based arguments, see Brian Barry, *Culture and Equality* (Cambridge: Polity, 2001); Dworkin, *Religion without God*, Ch. 3; and my 'Is Ethical Independence Enough?', in *Religion in Liberal Political Philosophy*, edited by Laborde and Bardon.

[39] Most notably by Bernard Williams, 'A Critique of Utilitarianism' in *Utilitarianism: For and Against* (Cambridge: Cambridge University Press, 1973), in which J. J. C. Smart and he debated the plausibility of utilitarianism.

Independence for children requires them to exclude their religious beliefs from consideration when they act as parents. Of course, they are permitted to act in full compliance with their perceived duties in their lives outside their parental role. Nevertheless, they must put their religious convictions aside when reasoning as parents. The objection is that independence for children often alienates parents from their actions and sometimes their most deeply held moral convictions, because it requires many parents to act in ways they believe to be morally wrong, such as failing to bring their child up in their faith.

Before replying to this objection, it is worth reminding ourselves of the reasons that motivate independence for children. The key ideas are that free and equal individuals are morally entitled to set their own ethical and religious ends, they have duties to each other to respect that entitlement, and principles for regulating the exercise of necessary power and authority over others must be ones that are capable of endorsement consistently with everyone regarding each other as having these entitlements. Thus, the ideal of independence generally protects each person's integrity, because it allows her to develop and pursue her deeply held convictions and fulfil her perceived ethical duties. So, unlike certain fully prescriptive moral conceptions, such as certain kinds of consequentialism, which deny the existence of moral options—views that assert that every action is either morally required or morally forbidden—independence for children is consistent with a wide range of moral options.

It draws the line when we consider moral options to impose behaviour or beliefs on others. The ideal of independence polices the boundaries between distinct individuals, as it were, to ensure that everyone's pursuit of her religious convictions and values is protected against manipulative or coercive interference by others.[40] It does so for the same reasons that motivate us to protect opportunities for people to act with integrity. The argument for self-rule is a set of claims about the principles that regulate people's use of power over others: principles must be capable of endorsement by everyone consistently with regarding herself as a free and equal person.

Consider an analogous case concerning political activity. Suppose some regard themselves as under a strict duty to improve the lives of their fellow citizens according to some controversial conception of religion. The political liberal response is to deny such citizens the moral permission to press for

---

[40] In *Justice for Hedgehogs*, 371, Dworkin captures this thought with the metaphor 'of people swimming in their own lanes ... Morality, broadly understood, defines the lanes that separate swimmers. It stipulates when one must cross lanes to help and what constitutes forbidden lane-crossing harm. Ethics governs how one must swim in one's own lane to have swum well'.

legislation that succeeds in realizing their perceived duty. It does so to preserve a political community in which no one is alienated from the rules that constrain her given the fact of comprehensive pluralism. If my earlier arguments concerning parents and children as a parallel case are successful, then the argument generalizes to justify the moral prohibition of the parental enrolment of children into comprehensive practices. In these ways, then, independence for children is consistent with giving individuals the opportunity—and, sometimes perhaps, exemptions from legal rules or moral norms that are otherwise justifiable—to live *their own lives* with integrity. But it rejects the integrity-based argument for permitting individuals (parents) who hold power over another (their child) to make her live her life in accordance with *their* profoundly held convictions.

Although the appeal to integrity appears to be a more threatening objection than the simple appeal to cost, it is subject to the same rebuttal grounded in the distinctive way in which independence for children interprets the separateness of persons. The fact that comprehensive enrolment involves making *others* conform to one's judgements of value or perceived duty transforms the moral case in a way that excludes the costs to the would-be enroller from consideration.

The integrity objection proceeds from a concern to accommodate people's *beliefs* about the duties they are under. A different objection claims that we should theorize the situation on the basis of parents' *real duties*, rather than the duties they believe apply to them. Some religious parents hold this view. They believe that they are morally permitted to raise their child in the faith because God commands them to do so, not because their integrity would be threatened by the moral prohibition of comprehensive enrolment. On this view, independence for children, which denies such a permission, requires parents to flout their duties to God (and, perhaps, their duties to children if God's command is that children have a moral claim against their parents to be brought up in the faith).

Notice, first, that this view appears not to defend the moral option to enrol children or not as parents choose. Advocates of the real duty view claim that parents are under a moral *requirement* to enrol their child in the faith. Still, it is a parent-centred objection to independence that demands a response, because if it is true that parents are under a stringent duty to enrol their child then independence would condemn them to living an immoral, perhaps a gravely sinful, life. For example, some parents believe they are under a strict duty to baptize their child—to wash away her original sin: failure to do so is itself a parental sin.

Here we butt up against the limits of independence once more. As I discussed in connection with attending to the interests of children (§5.5), the ideal of independence is plausible only if we live in a world in which non-enrolment does not have disastrous consequences for children or, in this case, parents. Trading on Rawls's remarks I cited earlier, if a parent proposes to violate her children's independence because it is vastly more important that she honours her duty to God to raise them in the faith, then ultimately we may be forced to deny the religious view she holds.

Earlier I distinguished between two kinds of parent-centred objections to independence for children. I have discussed those that appeal to the interests of adults qua parents. But I suggested that adults who are parents have non-parental interests, interests in realizing goals that have essentially nothing to do with the parenting role they occupy. They have goals or want to pursue relationships with people outside the family who share their comprehensive convictions and have no fundamental desire to involve their child in these activities. Is it permissible for such adults to enrol their child into their religious practices just because that would make it easier for them to pursue their religious commitments?

I am thinking of adults who recognize that they have no moral right to enrol their child into their comprehensive convictions in order to realize their aims *with* their children. Consider two variants:

AILSA: 'I propose to take my children to church, not because it is good for them or because it is valuable for us to pursue comprehensive activities together, but because I have a moral right to pursue my Christian conception of the good outside of my role as parent and taking my children to church, rather than getting someone else to sit with them, is more convenient and less costly.'

BETTY: 'I propose to encourage my children to want to pursue a Christian lifestyle, not because it is good for them or because it is valuable for us to pursue comprehensive activities together, but because I have a moral right to pursue my Christian conception of the good outside of my role as parent. Encouraging them to adopt my beliefs and desires makes it easier for me to pursue my religious interests: for example, they will enable me to overcome my moments of weakness of will in which, without their encouragement, I would fail to honour my commitment to worship.'

Neither Ailsa nor Betty is motivated by reasons of familial intimacy. They do not propose their different ways of treating their children as the right way to share or jointly realize their interest and values; neither are their proposals motivated by a concern for their respective children's well-being. Rather, they are motivated wholly by a concern to diminish the costs of their own pursuit of their non-parental interests and values.

From the point of view of independence for children it is evident that Betty acts wrongly. Her proposal assumes that she is morally permitted to encourage her children to adopt controversial comprehensive values, which violates the requirement to parent on terms that are acceptable to every free and equal person. Indeed, there is a further objection: she proposes to treat her children as a means; she uses them in order to make her plans easier to accomplish by developing their faith in order to help her to overcome her moments of weakness of will.

By contrast, Ailsa does not use her children as a means to pursue her religious ends. Moreover, her conduct does not fall foul of the requirement to raise her according to values and principles that are acceptable to everyone: for instance, she recognizes that she may not enrol her children in her religion. Whether she is compliant with the ideal of independence for children, however, turns on certain further facts about how she raises her children. First, her children are owed an upbringing in which they are exposed to, and form relationships with, a variety of different people who hold different, sometimes competing, conceptions of the good to hers. This requirement is explained by her children's interests in developing a sense of justice and the capacities and understanding that help them consider different alternative lifestyles and comprehensive doctrines and to pursue the distinctive conception that they adopt. Second, Ailsa must provide her children with an environment that does not encourage them to close their minds to alternative conceptions of the good; that would be inimical to developing an independent perspective on religious and ethical matters. We might worry, then, if her children's ethical diet is limited to the religious conception Ailsa affirms. Third, as they develop, Ailsa must display increasing respect for her children's interests and values. The abilities that justify the norm of increasing respect for children's judgement often accompany children's ability to conduct their lives away from their parents, in sport or music clubs for example. For that reason, it might be increasingly less justifiable for Ailsa to make her children join her in attending church, particularly if that interferes with their pursuit of their interests. Still, if these further conditions of an independent upbringing are satisfied, the ideal permits Ailsa to take her children to church because she has a non-parental interest in pursuing her conception, which the ideal of independence respects.

6.3 Independence and Procreation

To finish this chapter on families and parents I turn to an objection that claims that independence for children cannot be right because parental anti-perfectionism generalizes to condemn many instances of *procreation* that are obviously permissible from a moral point of view. Typically, people's reasons for bringing a child into the world are religious or ethical in nature. If religious enrolment is morally wrong, is it not also morally impermissible to create a child because one's religion demands or expects procreation? In both cases, a controversial religious doctrine is imposed on the child, and in both cases the child might, on the basis of her maturely held conception of the good, retrospectively reject the comprehensive reasons that motivated her parents.[41] Under pressure from this objection, advocates of independence for children might be forced to embrace a qualified form of anti-natalism, which holds that very many instances of procreation—those that are motivated by comprehensive convictions—are morally impermissible. But such claims are hard to believe.

The objection is threatening because, as we have seen, independence for children treats the reasons that motivate actions as relevant to their moral permissibility. Indeed, it regards impositions on children, such as making them worship or shaping their beliefs, as morally wrong when they are motivated by ethical and religious beliefs that these children may well reject when they become adults. Since that is the case, it is hard to see why the same objection should not be levelled against procreators who beget children for religious reasons.

Some might be tempted to accept that independence for children must regard it as wrongful for us to procreate for religious reasons or because we believe that it would improve the quality of our own lives, but also to deny that such a view constitutes a reductio of the ideal. After all, the wrongness of religiously motivated procreation would not imply that procreation is always morally impermissible, as extreme anti-natalists argue.[42] For instance, it would remain permissible to beget children for certain reasons, such as the maintenance of a society of free and equal persons over time.

---

[41] I thank Colin Macleod for raising this objection.

[42] The most prominent advocate of anti-natalism is David Benatar. See his *Better Never to Have Been: The Harm of Coming into Existence* (Oxford: Oxford University Press, 2006); 'The Misanthropic Argument for Anti-Natalism', in *Permissible Progeny: The Morality of Procreation and Parenting*, edited by Hannan et al.

However, this response concedes too much to the objection, namely, its claim that the wrongness of comprehensively motivated procreation follows from the wrongness of the comprehensive shaping and enrolment of children. Instead, because of their distinctive properties, procreative decisions do not fall within the ambit of the ideal of independence as straightforwardly as do parenting decisions. Respecting a person's independence is a matter of others' not taking charge of her life by imposing on her their judgements about what counts as a successful life; rather, decisions about what comprehensive goals to pursue should be taken by the person herself on the basis of her own mature convictions about ethics and religion. In the case of the argument from self-rule, the focus concerns the principles that guide the exercise of power and authority over children; the right principles, I have argued, are those that rest on ideals that everyone can share, or that everyone can retrospectively endorse consistently with regarding and treating each other as free and equal. Independence, then, is set of claims about how we are governed; it concerns the moral principles that regulate the shaping of the characteristics of a life.

My reply to the objection that independence for children renders most procreative decisions impermissible is to draw a distinction between others' choosing the comprehensive properties of a child's life and *their deciding the bare fact of her existence*. Independence for children objects to the former, but not the latter. If that reply is right, there is a response to someone whose mature judgement is that it would have been better had they not been created. Such a person lacks an independence-based complaint against her procreative parents for bringing her into existence. Her parents have not chosen the comprehensive attributes of her life and, therefore, they have not violated her independence.

There are certain interesting implications of this account. First, it holds that, even though they must exclude religious reasons when choosing or shaping the characteristics of the children they beget, it is morally permissible for parents to procreate for religious reasons. Many parents procreate because they regard themselves as under a God-given obligation to do so, or to contribute to the maintenance of a religious community, or because it gives them the opportunity for what Macleod calls 'creative self-extension', which consists in expressing 'their own commitment to ideals and ground-projects by passing them on to children'.[43] On my account, it is permissible for individuals to beget children for such reasons, but they should understand that these reasons must be excluded when they become parents who exercise rights over their children.

---

[43] Macleod, 'Parental Responsibilities in an Unjust World', 142.

Reasons that motivate procreation do not carry over to become operative reasons for parents.[44]

Second, the independence view has the virtue that it condemns certain kinds of procreation that many find intuitively objectionable from a moral point of view. The revolution in genetic science has given us the opportunity, and will make it increasingly possible, to choose the genes and, consequently, the phenotypes of the individuals we beget. Moral and political philosophers continue to try to identify the moral and legal principles that ought to regulate our use of genetic technologies.[45] The ideal of independence for children offers a distinctive and attractive perspective within these debates. It insists that procreators are not morally permitted to choose the comprehensive characteristics of children in the process of creating a child. For instance, they may not choose particular genes because those genes make it more likely that their child will be attracted to a particular occupation, religion, gender, sexuality, aesthetic sensibility, and so on. True, there are possible grounds for genetic selection within the ideal that follow from its account of an independent life that is respectful of others' choices; in addition to tackling genetic disease, we might think of 'therapeutic' genetic interventions as those guided by individuals' claims to an independent life, which, among other things, justifies interventions that ensure that children do not lack the capacities set out earlier. However, as should be clear, the idea that parents should have access to a 'genetic supermarket' in which they can choose what comprehensive sort of people their progeny become is anathema to the ideal of independence.[46] In this way, then, anti-perfectionism applies to the selection of the characteristics of one's offspring in procreative decisions as well as childrearing ones.[47]

---

[44] This is much like other cases. A person might have religiously informed reasons to pursue a career in politics or to work as a judge. That is fine, so long as they do not act on their religious convictions when in office.

[45] See, for example, Jonathan Glover, *What Sort of People Should There Be?* (Harmondsworth, Penguin, 1984); David Heyd, *Genethics: Moral Issues in the Creation of People* (Berkeley, CA: University of California Press, 1994); Allen Buchanan et al., *From Chance to Choice: Genetics and Justice* (Cambridge: Cambridge University Press, 2000); John Harris, *Enhancing Evolution: The Ethical Case for Making Better People* (Princeton, NJ: Princeton University Press, 2010); Julian Savulescu and Nick Bostrom, eds., *Human Enhancement* (Oxford: Oxford University Press, 2009).

[46] Robert Nozick, *Anarchy, State and Utopia* (Oxford: Blackwell, 1974), 315; Glover, *What Sort of People Should There Be?*, 45–56. Here I draw on my paper 'Individual Autonomy and Genetic Choice', in *A Companion to Genethics*, edited by Justine Burley and John Harris (Oxford: Blackwell, 2002).

[47] Clearly, I have not provided a complete view of procreative morality. In the first place, the limits of independence suggest that disaster avoidance should be part of a fuller account. That is usually elaborated in terms of the moral requirement that one's progeny has the opportunity to have a life worth living: see Derek Parfit's classic discussion in *Reasons and Persons*, Ch. 16. Second, I do not claim that it is morally impermissible to beget a child who is incapable of living an independent life if that is the only life that procreators can create. Third, I do not examine further questions about the relationship between procreative morality and parental morality. For example, Anca Gheaus argues that genetic selection is more problematic from a moral point of view if those who select the genes are also those who raise the child who is created. See Gheaus, 'Parental Genetic Shaping and Parental Environmental Shaping', *The Philosophical Quarterly* 67 (2017): 263–281.

7
From Parental Morality to Political Morality

I have elaborated and defended independence for children as a conception of *parental* morality. Among other things, we may regard that account as a set of claims about how parents are morally required to exercise the legal options they enjoy with respect to their children. In many countries, parents' legal options are extensive. If the upbringing and education they provide does not fall below a reasonably low standard with respect to satisfying their child's physical, mental, and developmental interests, parents are legally permitted to enrol their child into controversial religious or ethical practices, to prevent her from engaging with people and conceptions of the good that represent alternative ways of living, and to choose the kind of schooling she receives—including the option of homeschooling in many societies. Independence for children serves as a guide to how parents ought to exercise their legal options.

In this chapter I turn from questions about parental morality to those concerning political morality and, specifically, I try to make progress in identifying what legal options with respect to upbringing and education parents should have. If, as I have argued, it is morally wrong for parents to encourage their children to hold controversial religious beliefs, should comprehensive enrolment also be legally prohibited? If we decide that the enrolment of children should be legally permitted in some cases, should the law also allow parents to choose the character of the schools their children attend: should faith schools or schools with a religious character be prohibited or phased out, for example? And what are the more general implications of independence for children for the regulation of educational institutions and parents' engagement with them?

Before addressing these questions, I need to explain more clearly how I understand them. In debates about political morality, it is common to distinguish between 'justice' and 'legitimacy', though frustratingly different writers interpret the distinction in different ways and, consequently, apparent disagreements are really only interlocutors talking past each other. Rather than reviewing the different elaborations of these concepts, I stipulate one way of interpreting the distinction, which will allow me to clarify the particular questions that interest me in this chapter.[1] As I'll understand them, questions about legitimacy concern, first, what representative political institutions like the legislature and the government ought to do, what legislation—in the case of education, what arrangements with respect to schools—they are morally permitted or required to enact and enforce. Second, the issue of political legitimacy concerns the conditions under which individuals have a moral obligation to obey the law and an obligation to support political institutions in other ways, such as by voting or serving on juries, for example.

By contrast, I'll understand *just* political and legal arrangements to be those that are ideal. In a just society, then, the legal rights and duties of citizens and non-citizens are *fully responsive* to their respective moral claims regarding those rights and duties. Consider, for example, the right to freedom of expression. Suppose that citizens ought to have the legal right to express their political and non-political views. Of course, the shape and stringency of that right is controversial, but suppose we have identified the correct interpretation of the legal right to which citizens have a moral claim. We can say that a society's legal arrangements are just to the extent that they match the right to freedom of expression so understood. Laws that give citizens fewer rights to express their views, and in some cases laws that give individuals more rights to express their views, are unjust.

Among other things, then, a conception of justice tells us what legal rights we would have in an ideal society: what *procedural* rights we would have regarding our participation in legal and political institutions—rights with respect to voting, holding political or legal office, to legal representation, and so on; and what *substantive* rights we would enjoy with respect to various non-political activities, such as pursuing our goals, expressing our views, associating with others, engaging in economic transactions, protecting our health, advancing the interests of others, and so on. In democratic societies, a conception of justice also operates as a guide for citizens. For example, when we vote in referendums or for political representatives, we have a duty to advance the cause of justice. Sometimes that will mean voting for legal changes so that the law recognizes the rights we would have in an ideal society. But that is not

---

[1] For a selection of alternative conceptions of legitimacy and its grounds, see Dworkin, *Justice for Hedgehogs*, 317–324; Fabienne Peter, *The Grounds of Political Legitimacy* (Oxford: Oxford University Press, 2023); Quong, *Liberalism without Perfection*, Ch. 4; A. John Simmons, 'Justification and Legitimacy', *Ethics* 109 (1999): 739–771; Zofia Stemplowska and Adam Swift, 'Dethroning Democratic Legitimacy', *Oxford Studies in Political Philosophy* 4 (2018): 3–26.

always the case. Sometimes it will involve voting for legal changes that are less than ideal, but which are the best response to the non-ideal circumstances in which we live. In either case, an account of justice understood as what legal rights and duties would exist in an ideal society is a useful guide to how we ought to vote.[2]

Justice and legitimacy can diverge. There are countless cases in which it is morally wrong for citizens to campaign or vote for a particular policy yet nevertheless morally permissible for the government to enact the same policy if it is the decision of a fair political process. In these cases, the government acts legitimately even if the laws it enacts fail to protect the rights people would enjoy in an ideal society. For example, it is reasonably clear that the arrangements for the distribution of wealth and income in most societies are unjust, but it does not follow that they are illegitimate. Indeed, some believe that if general elections are sufficiently free and fair, and certain other arrangements are in place, then elected governments are morally required to enact and enforce the laws they promised in their election manifestos.

I'll not investigate the conditions that are necessary or sufficient for political legitimacy. If you like, you can assume that a free and fair democratic process gives the elected government a justified right to rule—to enact and enforce the policies it chooses or the policies in its manifesto—at least when its policies are not too unjust.[3] Nevertheless, there are further questions concerning the justice of its activities and the laws we have. We want to know whether the laws the legislature enacts and the government enforces accord with the rights and duties we would have in an ideal society, and whether they accord with the rights and duties we ought to have given the non-ideal circumstances in which we live. It is these questions of justice that will occupy me in this chapter. First, I explore whether an ideal society would protect for parents the legal right to comprehensively enrol their child and the right to a school that helps parents to enrol their child by educating her in the traditions of a particular faith, for example. Second, I address whether parents ought to enjoy such legal rights given the non-ideal, somewhat unjust, circumstances in which we live.

---

[2] For an itemization of the various ways in which a theory of justice might guide us, see Zofia Stemplowska, 'Feasibility: Individual and Collective', *Social Philosophy & Policy* 33 (2016): 273–291.

[3] See, for example, Rawls, whose account of political legitimacy is a procedural one subject to certain substantive constraints given by a theory of justice: see Rawls, *Political Liberalism*, 136–138, 427–428. For perhaps the best available account of legitimate schooling as I understand it here, see Gutmann, *Democratic Education*.

7.1 A Parental Right to Enrol?

Our first question is whether an ideal society would legally permit parents to enrol their children into a controversial conception of the good, such as a set of religious practices. Recall that the enrolment of children consists in making them act in ways demanded by the conception, such as making them worship, for example, and encouraging them to develop beliefs and desires that align with the conception. To keep matters simple, I'll discuss religious enrolment, but we should keep in mind that this is only one kind of comprehensive enrolment: even if religious enrolment is the most visible and historically the form that has generated most debate, parents and others seek to enrol their children into many other conceptions of the good, some of which I'll discuss in the concluding chapter.

I have argued that religious enrolment wrongs children, but that conclusion does not yet encompass the claim that the political community is morally permitted to forbid it or, indeed, to interfere in any way with parents' enrolling activities. We need to explore further the different functions of law and the ideal of self-rule before we have a clear idea of whether the community may prohibit it or interfere with parents' enrolling activities.

Let me first pick out certain state powers that seem relevant to the issue at hand.[4] In Chapter 1, I drew a distinction between the *commands* of the state and its *use of force, coercion, and manipulation*. With respect to the former, the state has the power to demand certain conduct of its citizens. For example, it may prohibit certain activities and, if there is a standing obligation to obey the state's commands, its prohibition of an activity correlates with citizens' having a moral obligation not to engage in it. With respect to the latter, the state has the ability to enforce its commands. In some cases, the police or other agents of the state can prevent prohibited acts from being performed, and they can threaten punishments of various kinds to try to discourage the performance of such acts. In addition to these powers, the state has mechanisms for holding people to account and for issuing public blame: a justice system that seeks to establish whether particular individuals have acted wrongly and, if so, whether they can be held responsible for that wrongdoing. Such arrangements help victims to recognize their status as equally valued citizens and everyone to understand what kinds of behaviour are acceptable and unacceptable; the unpleasantness

---

[4] I am indebted to Victor Tadros's discussion in *Wrongs and Crimes* (Oxford: Oxford University Press, 2016), Ch. 9.

of being publicly blamed and punished also serves to deter people from acting wrongly.

In addition to legal instruments, the state has soft powers at its disposal: powers over educational institutions and various media, which it can use to give guidance, promote good public causes, and discourage wrongful conduct. For example, over the past fifty years or so, governments have used print and broadcast media to encourage citizens to avoid drinking and driving, to wear seatbelts, to give blood, and, more recently, not to smoke near children. And the state can give financial help in the form of direct grants or tax relief to non-governmental organizations that pursue publicly valuable goals. These initiatives sometimes reinforce the communicative and preventive features of the law, but sometimes they seek to shape our conduct in the absence of legal regulation.

Issues concerning the political community's position with respect to religious enrolment are further complicated by the fact that in matters concerning the treatment of children it is inevitable that the state will protect *special* legal rights for certain parties. In many parts of the law, the state polices the boundaries between different individuals by recognizing and enforcing rights enjoyed by everyone—laws prohibiting murder, assault, theft, and so on. By contrast, in childrearing and educational matters states must confer rights on particular people—parents or teachers—which protect their control over specific aspects of particular children's lives against interference by others. For example, in most jurisdictions they give legal custodians the right to decide where a particular child lives, what she eats, how she spends her time, and so on. The state protects these decisions from interference by others who might want to control the child's life.

In §6.1 I argued that some parental control rights over children are justifiable because the institution of the family, which is constituted by parents having some such rights, is justifiable. But it remains to be seen how extensive are the control rights enjoyed by parents. The state might or might not give parents the legal right to choose the kind of schooling their child receives. If it does that, the right in question might merely involve the political community's preventing others from interfering with their choices. Or the parental right might place more demands on the community: in some societies, for instance, citizens are legally required to pay taxes that fund the maintenance of the religious schools parents want for their children. Or, alternatively, parents' legal rights might be rather limited. Parents might, for example, enjoy very few or no legal options with respect to the education their child receives. The state is involved however it decides. As James Dwyer observes, 'any struggle over the content of laws relating to children's education, medical care, or other aspects of child rearing is not between more and less intervention, but rather over the form that state intervention will take—that is, whether the state will confer more or less power on the persons whom it has made legal parents, and conversely how much power the state will repose in its own employees (for example, education agency officials, courts).'[5] Because young children cannot make appropriate decisions regarding how they are raised, such decisions must be made by others, but we need to determine whether it is legally recognized guardians or others who should make them.

Later, I'll examine whether certain instances of religious enrolment should be illegal—enrolment within the home, within religious associations, and within public and private schools. Before doing so, I set out a general argument for independence for children as a *legal requirement*. By this I mean two things. First, a just political community would publicly express that child enrolment is wrong and command parents not to enrol their children into comprehensive doctrines. Second, the state's commands are enforceable in this sense: *parents have no valid complaint against the use of force to prevent them from engaging in religious enrolment*. This conception of enforceability does not imply that the state is always morally permitted to prevent religious enrolment *all things considered*.[6] There might be reasons for the state not to prevent parents from enrolling their children that appeal to children's interests, some of which will be discussed. Nevertheless, even if there is no all-things-considered case for the moral permission to prevent them from enrolling their children, it would be significant if parents lacked a valid complaint against being prevented from so doing. Parent-centred objections to the enforcement of requirements regarding upbringing and education have historically been a fetter on government policy. It is important to establish that, notwithstanding their longstanding influence over policy and the law, parents' claims lack justification.

My argument that independence for children should be a legal requirement so understood is reasonably straightforward. First, consider the expressive and command functions of law. Political liberals like Rawls claim that a just society is one regulated by fair cooperation between citizens who acknowledge each other as free and equal. Everyone has interests in developing and deploying a sense of justice and the capacity independently to form and pursue a particular

---

[5] James G. Dwyer, 'Regulating Child Rearing in a Culturally Diverse Society', in *Philosophical Foundations of Children's and Family Law*, edited by Brake and Ferguson, 277.

[6] For discussion of this distinction in the context of debates about criminalization, see Tadros, *Wrongs and Crimes*, 160.

conception of the good. Those interests justify a claim to a fair share of various resources such as rights, liberties, and socioeconomic opportunities. A just society is one regulated by laws that sustain that kind of social cooperation. Furthermore, for reasons of individual political self-rule, it is appropriate for these arrangements to be pursued *publicly*: a just society is one in which the laws are capable of being seen to be implemented and are ones that do not rest on controversial comprehensive doctrines but rather appeal to the ideal of fair cooperation between free and equal citizens and the public reasons aligned with that conception. In other words, a feature of a just society is that legal and political institutions publicly recognize, and command citizens to respect, the moral claims of free and equal individuals.

I have claimed that the ideal of individual self-rule extends to issues concerning parenting and the raising of children. If I am right about that, then just political institutions would publicly express that position by prohibiting religious enrolment. Given their standing duty to comply with just laws, citizens would, therefore, be under a political obligation not to enrol their children. Deferring the issue of enforcement for now, the state might also deploy its soft powers to encourage conformity with the law. It might, for example, use its control over educational institutions and various media to seek to develop an *independence-respecting ethos* among the adult population. As suggested in previous chapters, independence for children is a conception of upbringing that is partly constituted by the provision of various developmental goods to children to ensure that they acquire the wherewithal to lead just and independent lives. But it also requires parents and other adults to have a particular attitude towards children. It claims that adults should not incorporate children into their ethical or religious plans; rather, when exercising their control over children they should be motivated to act from the public reasons relevant to upbringing. The right attitude, then, involves excluding from consideration the religious ideals that may guide adults in their non-parental lives. The state has a role to play in explaining such an ethos to adults and encouraging them to live by it. For example, it may promote that ethos during ante-natal classes it provides for prospective parents and in other public education campaigns. It may also foster an independence-respect ethos through educational institutions. Teachers are vital agents for the promotion of such an ethos, it seems, because they work with both parents and their children. Part of their role is to guide parents in how they raise their children; part of it is to encourage children to understand their moral status and rights as children and to encourage them to respect the independence of others in their capacities as citizens and possible future parents.

Perhaps some might worry that an ethos of this kind should not be promoted by political institutions, because just institutions must satisfy the requirement that the principles that govern citizens must be capable of being satisfied in a publicly verifiable way. The worry is that it is too hard to be sure that everyone is fulfilling the duties demanded of the independence-respecting ethos. Given the importance of individuals' ruling themselves, which is constituted in part by citizens' being in a position to determine whether their society lives up to its principles of justice, there seems to be an objection to promoting an ethos compliance with which is hard to gauge.[7]

Worries about the public verifiability of an independence-respecting ethos are misplaced, because it is not hard to tell whether individuals are complying with its demands. As suggested, the ethos requires certain conduct of parents and other adults. We can check that the required actions are performed. In particular, the attitudinal requirement of the ethos—that parents should exclude religious reasons from consideration when making decisions for their child—can be verified by parents' disclosing whether they are indeed excluding those reasons.[8] No doubt, issues concerning the public verifiability of principles of justice arise in other domains, such as in cases where the burdens we are duty-bound to bear depend on the burdens borne by others.[9] However, the independence-respecting ethos does not include duties that require us to have comparative information of that kind. Parents and other adults owe it to children to live by the ethos, and their duty to exclude religious reasons is not sensitive to how others act, at least in an ideal world.

Let us turn now to the issue of enforcement. Again, it is reasonably straightforward to establish that the political community is sometimes justified in

---

[7] This possible objection seeks to extend Andrew Williams's Rawlsian publicity objection to the *egalitarian ethos* defended by G. A. Cohen. Williams argues that public verifiability—the idea that for a principle to be a principle of justice it should be specified in such a way that citizens can establish that social and political arrangements satisfy its requirements—is a weighty desideratum of principles of justice. Cohen's egalitarian ethos is incapable of satisfying the desideratum, he argues, because its verification requires individuals to have information about other citizens' occupational choices that is too difficult or costly to gather. Given the Rawlsian foundations of independence for children, I am sympathetic to Williams's appeal to publicity. Nevertheless, for the reasons I go on to set out, I do not believe that a publicity problem arises for the independence-respecting ethos I propose. The debate about the egalitarian ethos and publicity is conducted in the following pieces: Cohen, *If You're an Egalitarian How Come You're So Rich?* (Cambridge, MA: Harvard University Press, 2000); Williams, 'Incentives, Inequality, and Publicity', *Philosophy and Public Affairs* 27 (1998): 225–247; G. A. Cohen, *Rescuing Justice and Equality* (Cambridge, MA: Harvard University Press, 2008), Ch. 8; Andrew Williams, 'Justice, Incentives and Constructivism', *Ratio* (2008): 276–293.

[8] No doubt some will be unable to fully understand the motivations that guide them. But that is the same for any attitudinal moral requirement. In these cases, self-reflection and deliberation with others are bound to improve our self-awareness, as is the case with our understanding of our own implicit biases.

[9] Williams's objection to Cohen's egalitarian ethos focuses on this feature of distributive justice.

preventing parents from enrolling their child into particular comprehensive doctrines. Children are free and equal persons with weighty interests and moral claims related to independence. It is the state's role to protect every citizen's weighty interests and claims. Of course, there are cases in which the state should not prevent religious enrolment, which I discuss below. These are cases where prevention would be futile or set back the realization of weightier demands of justice. Nevertheless, independence for children is enforceable, at least in the sense that parents have no reasonable objection to being prevented from enrolling their children.

It is widely believed that parents have a right to enrol their children into a religion. Following Kagan, in Chapter 6 I drew a distinction between two ways of understanding that view. We can ask whether parents enjoy the *moral option* to enrol their child, which I understand as the combination of a moral permission to enrol and the absence of a moral requirement to enrol; parents enjoy the moral option if they are morally permitted to enrol or not to enrol as they choose. But we might understand the right to enrol as a *moral injunction*.[10] A moral injunction might take the form of forbidding others, including state officials, from preventing, or interfering in other ways with, parents' enrolling activities—this is a negative injunction. Or it might take the form of requiring others to facilitate those activities by, for example, paying for religious schools that help parents to enrol their child or subsidizing religious organizations to reduce the costs of parents' religious enrolment—a positive injunction. Earlier (§6.2), I argued that parents have no right to enrol where that is understood as their enjoying a moral option to enrol or not as they choose. Our present question is whether, notwithstanding the moral wrongness of religious enrolment, parents have interests or claims that justify a right to enrol understood as a moral injunction: do they have interests that are sufficiently weighty to justify a duty on others not to interfere with, or to facilitate, their enrolling conduct? I contend that parents do not have such a right—a right to wrong their children; the political community does not wrong parents by interfering with their enrolling activities.

I'll offer further defence of the enforceability of independence for children by rebutting some arguments for a parental right to wrong their children. At the outset, however, it is worth noting that political liberals accept that citizens sometimes have a right to do moral wrong—a valid claim to a moral injunction

---

[10] For those who like to use Hohfeld's taxonomy of different rights, the moral option to enrol is a Hohfeldian privilege (or liberty right) to enrol and a privilege not to enrol. Moral injunctions with respect to enrolment are Hoheldian claim-rights, at least where we understand those as remaining noncommittal on the issue of whether the holders of claim-rights also enjoy moral options.

that justifies a legal permission to commit certain moral wrongs.[11] For example, consider this case:

> *Evil Paul.* Suppose that Catholicism is the one true faith acceptance of which is transcendently good for people. Paul knows this but tries to persuade other adults to become atheists.

It is clear that, taking the facts about Catholicism and his knowledge of them as given, Paul wrongs others because he knowingly harms them considerably. He acts morally impermissibly because he is required to act with concern for others, at least where that is not costly to him. Still, political liberals would recognize Paul's claim not to be prevented by others, including the state, from engaging in such wrongful conduct. For political liberals draw a distinction between comprehensive and public reasons. Paul's conduct is morally forbidden from a *comprehensive* point of view, but that perspective is excluded from consideration when we are identifying principles to guide the political community. Political liberals appeal to a subset of moral reasons, those related to the idea of fair cooperation between citizens who recognize each other as free and equal. If someone were to ask for legal protection from evil Paul's behaviour, a political liberal community would refuse to give it: to provide such protection would involve its adopting a controversial position on religious matters or what counts as mischief, which it is committed not to do for reasons of maintaining citizens' political autonomy. There is, therefore, a political liberal case for a right to do a (comprehensive) moral wrong.

Still, as suggested above, political liberals would not extend the right to do wrong to those who seek to deny others' claims to independence, which is what I have argued parents do when they enrol their children. Notice that Evil Paul does not violate other *adults'* independence, because we suppose that adults have developed the wherewithal to think for themselves about comprehensive matters, which offers them protection against being manipulated or forced into following a particular conception of the good. (If Paul were to pursue his ambition by hypnotizing them that would be a different matter.) However,

---

[11] There has been a lively debate about whether a right to do wrong is conceptually coherent and, if so, whether there are sound normative arguments for such a right in some cases. See Waldron, 'A Right to Do Wrong'; William Galston, 'On the Alleged Right to Do Wrong: A Response to Waldron', *Ethics* 93 (1983): 320–324; Jeremy Waldron, 'Galston on Rights', *Ethics* 93 (1983): 325–327; David Enoch, 'A Right to Violate One's Duty', *Law and Philosophy* 21 (2002): 355–384; Ori J. Herstein, 'Defending the Right to Do Wrong', *Law and Philosophy* 31 (2012): 343–365; and Renee Bolinger, 'Revisiting the Right to Do Wrong', *Australasian Journal of Philosophy* 95 (2017): 43–57. One unfortunate feature of the debate is that the participants appear not to address the political liberal case for such a right.

if he tried to shape a child's comprehensive life by encouraging her to adopt atheism, there would be a reason for public concern. He would be taking advantage of her lack of the cognitive and psychological capacities necessary to live independently; he would be imposing on her a comprehensive conception she might reasonably reject (and may well reject in adulthood). In short, Paul has no right—no valid claim to a moral injunction—that protects his extending the scope of his goal to encompass children. That is not because his ambitions are mischievous from a comprehensive point of view. He has a right to pursue the comprehensive activities of his choice, but only if that is consistent with respect for others' independence.

How, then, do advocates of parents' rights to engage in religious or ethical enrolment defend their view? Their main argument is that parents have an interest in parenting *authentically* or *with integrity*, which requires them to have discretion over how they raise their child. Altman runs an argument of this kind. He contends that parents have an interest in 'nurturing, educating and counselling' their child, which is independent of the child's interest in being nurtured. For parents to 'participate meaningfully' in these important tasks they must 'offer something of [themselves], not just to be a vehicle through which others act'. The lessons and advice they provide their child must be ones they endorse as valuable: 'The point of shaping another person (to the extent this is possible) is lost if we are compelled to shape that person toward a view of goodness or happiness that we ourselves reject.'[12] According to this view, perhaps parents have an authenticity-based right that correlates with others' at least not preventing them from their raising their child in ways that fail to respect their child's independence.

A similar argument is developed by Moschella who defends parental rights, such as the right of parents to withdraw their child from sex education classes in state-funded schools, as conscience rights. She presents an argument in which parents and states have separate spheres of authority. First, parents have wide-ranging rights that protect their decisions regarding how they raise their child. Second, she argues that the authority of the political community is narrower than many liberals believe it to be. The two parts of her argument combine to defend a division of moral labour between parents and the state. Parents enjoy moral injunctions that protect from interference by others their freedom to make decisions regarding their child's upbringing. The state may

---

[12] Altman, 'Parental Control Rights', 221. Altman notes the similarities between his argument and Galston's in *Liberal Pluralism* (101–102), though he believes that parents have a right to appeal to their ethical views quite generally, whereas Galston appeals to their interest in acting in accordance with their 'deepest commitments'. See Altman, 'Parental Control Rights', 222–223.

intervene only if parents' conduct is abusive, negligent, or is inconsistent with maintaining public order. For Moschella, then, at least as I understand her view, even if we grant that my conception of independence for children is the morally right way for parents to exercise their authority over their child, they have the right to depart from this, just as they have a right to make mistakes about what is conducive to their own well-being.[13]

I take the core of Moschella's argument to be as follows.[14] Parents have primary, pre-political, obligations to 'foster the overall wellbeing of their children'.[15] Such obligations are non-transferable: parents are obligated to provide appropriate care and nurture themselves rather than delegate this work to others. Parental rights against interference allow parents to fulfil their obligations to their children. These rights should be understood as 'conscience rights', which protect parents' rights to raise their child in a way that preserves their integrity, that is, to parent in accordance with their own beliefs about what kind of upbringing they are morally obligated to give her. Moschella accepts that conscience rights are defeated by 'the fundamental rights of others and the prerequisites of public order'.[16] However, she argues at length for a conception of children's rights and a 'civic minimum' that are considerably less demanding than those defended by both the liberal consensus and independence for children. With respect to children's interests, for example, she claims that they have a fundamental right to an upbringing that enables them to live with integrity, which is considerably less demanding than a right to independence.[17]

I'll not repeat the arguments I have given for treating children's claim to independence as a weighty moral consideration, which parents have a duty to respect. The present issue is whether and under what conditions third parties owe it to parents not to prevent them from violating their duties of independence to their children. The issue is, in fact, more general than this. Regardless of whether we take an independence-respecting or a different view of upbringing, suppose that we can identify an upbringing to which children have a weighty and normally decisive moral claim—call this *the morally required*

---

[13] Moschella, *To Whom Do Children Belong?*, 119–121. It is clear that Moschella does not share my view of how parents should exercise the legal options they enjoy. However, her book concerns parents' moral rights understood as moral injunctions rather than the moral requirements and permissions that determine how they ought to exercise their rights.

[14] Her argument is presented over the course of five chapters, and I lack the space to provide a full summary of its various features. For example, some of her arguments for parental rights appeal to the child's interests, others to parents' interests. Here, I focus only on the latter. My aim is to present its main features so that I can mount a challenge to it.

[15] Moschella, *To Whom Do Children Belong?*, 20.

[16] Moschella, *To Whom Do Children Belong?*, 56.

[17] Moschella, *To Whom Do Children Belong?*, Chs. 3 and 4.

upbringing—and several ways of raising children that fall short of this; they are decent ways of parenting, suppose, but fail to satisfy certain moral claims children have that are satisfied by the morally required upbringing. Appeals to authenticity or integrity need to explain why a third party may not prevent parents from failing to provide the morally required upbringing, and why she is morally permitted to intervene only if parents fail to provide a decent upbringing. The explanation appears to be that the third party has a pro tanto reason not to prevent them, because prevention would be bad for parents—it would make them act in a way that lacks authenticity or integrity. True, the third party also has pro tanto reasons to attend to the interests and claims of children. Nevertheless, because she is morally required to respond to both parents and children's interests, the fact that parents have a duty to provide the morally required upbringing does not imply that the third party may always prevent them from departing from that upbringing if they are mistaken about their moral obligations.

The integrity argument for allowing parents to violate their duties to their children fails because it requires parents and third parties alike to take an inappropriate attitude to wrongdoing. Granted, respect for people's independence means allowing individuals to form and act on their own judgement about what is ethically or religiously valuable. Similarly, several ethical conceptions treat acting on one's own judgement and expressing one's agency as an important ingredient of living well: a life well lived is one in which I steer my own course through life even if that path is not as rewarding in other respects as alternative lifestyles third parties could manipulate me to pursue. However, our reasons to care about expressing our judgement and agency are conditional. One elaboration of this thought is provided by Tadros, who writes: 'Certain actions are not valuable as free expressions of agency because of the significance of the reasons against acting in that way. Respect for these values makes valuing one's free performance of such actions inappropriate. This explains the idea that these values constrain. And this explains wrongness.'[18] To identify some action as morally wrong just is to identify free performance of it as inappropriate. In our case, it is inappropriate to value acting on one's beliefs when the beliefs or actions in question violate the independence of others. In this way, our reasons to act with integrity are conditional upon our acting morally permissibly.[19]

---

[18] Tadros, *Wrongs and Crimes*, 41.
[19] There is a rare class of cases where others are not permitted to interfere to prevent moral wrongdoing. These are cases in which conducting ourselves in the right way involves our having to avoid the temptation to act wrongly.

The upshot of treating integrity as conditionally valuable in the way described is that parents have no integrity-based interest in having opportunities to depart from the morally required upbringing, however that is described. And, consequently, a third party has no integrity-based parental interest to weigh in the balance when assessing whether she is permitted to prevent parents from violating their child's independence. To be clear, the rejection of such an interest in integrity in this case does not imply that parents should not be given some discretion. For example, children's interests might be served by parents' having a range of childrearing choices with respect to which they are not monitored by the state. Still, even if there are good reasons for the state not to enforce anti-perfectionist parenting, it remains the case that parents have no authenticity- or integrity-based interest in not being prevented from enrolling their children. Independence for children is enforceable in at least that sense.

If parents have no interest that grounds a right to enrol, then are there other reasons that tell against the state's enforcing anti-perfectionist parenting? Later, I consider whether states should allow parents to choose the religious character of the school their child attends—I argue that religious schools should be phased out; I also consider whether private associations, such as religious organizations, may help parents to enrol their children. But we first need to consider enrolment that is conducted in the home: should the state intervene to stop these instances of religious enrolment, if not for the sake of parents then for other reasons?

A just political community would declare that parents should not make their children practise religious rites within the home or direct them to endorse a particular comprehensive doctrine. That declaration might take the form of a legal instruction. The state might also encourage parents and others to develop an independence-respecting ethos of the kind I have outlined. But there are weighty reasons for the state to refrain from coercively preventing parents from engaging in religious enrolment within the home. This is for two main reasons. First, the use of coercion is a clumsy tool that should be deployed sparingly and carefully, especially given the value of familial intimacy reviewed earlier.[20] And, second, even if the state could prevent religious enrolment by coercive prevention, such a policy would be too costly for the political community to pursue: it would jeopardize the pursuit of weightier demands of justice.[21]

---

[20] Clumsy tool arguments against coercive interference are characteristic of the political moralities elaborated by J. S. Mill and Joseph Raz, among others.

[21] For these and other shrewd notes of caution about the use of coercion to regulate families, see Archard, *The Family*, 71–75.

Let us consider some 'clumsy tool' reasons against state officials' preventing religious enrolment within the home. We need to know how prevention might be effected. In the first place, it would require surveillance. At one extreme, the government could place cameras in people's homes to monitor parents' activities. But that would destroy the parent-child intimacy that children need to develop. As surveyed in §6.1, a child's interests are served by being in families in which parents display ongoing sensitivity to the child's needs so that she becomes a just and independent adult; in particular, she benefits from living with authority figures who take decisions in her interests. That does not imply that parents have an interest in having the opportunity to violate their child's independence, but it does mean that the child has an interest in having parents who are not continually worried about others' holding them to account for their decisions or preventing them from exercising their judgement.

To illustrate, suppose there were a safe and effective chemical we could put in the water that would somehow stop parents from acting in ways that wrong their child by violating her independence. Suppose, in particular, that the chemical does not prevent parents from forming and acting on morally permissible ways of raising their child; it merely blocks them from acting wrongfully should they make moral mistakes or develop wrongful motivations. A state's use of a smart technology of that kind would be morally permissible, I believe, at least in principle.[22] In particular, it would not jeopardize valuable familial intimacy. Parents would still perform the role of being attentive authority figures to their child, and they would not have to worry about being held to account or being prevented from exercising their permissible judgement.

Obviously, such a technology does not exist. In its absence, preventing parents from enrolling their child would have to be done by officials monitoring their activities to identify whether enrolment is happening, and preventing or threatening sanctions when it is. There are decisive objections to such an enforcement regime: it might be hard to prevent state officials from abusing the powers given to them; children might suffer by having parents who become self-conscious about their parenting—even those who have no intention of enrolling their children might be frightened to be themselves, inhibited in revealing what they value out of fear of prosecution, and wary about being

---

[22] The 'at least in principle' qualification is important, because there are countless cases of practices involving the use of technical fixes that are corrupted or which have bad side effects. For a nice discussion, see Emily McTernan, 'Those Who Forget the Past: An Ethical Challenge from the History of Treating Deviance', in *Treatment for Crime: Philosophical Essays on Neurointerventions in Criminal Justice*, edited by David Birks and Thomas Douglas (Oxford: Oxford University Press, 2018).

spontaneous;[23] and sanctions in the form of fines or losing custody may well have negative consequences for their children.

Even putting these concerns to one side, a policing regime to prevent parents from enrolling their child in the home environment would be unjustifiably costly just in virtue of the human resources that would be needed to monitor and enforce anti-perfectionist parenting. Independence for children is a multifaceted ideal in which parental anti-perfectionism is one, but only one, moral requirement. Like the liberal consensus, it favours an education system staffed by highly qualified teachers who have the skills to develop children's knowledge, understanding, and aptitude so that they can fashion their own comprehensive conception. In a world of scarce resources, funding an education system to develop those traits in children takes priority over preventing parents from enrolling their children into a religion. For many different reasons, then, the state should not generally be in the business of enforcing anti-perfectionist parenting within the home.

7.2 Against Religious Schools

Enrolment by schools is a different matter. In this section I argue that in an ideal society, one free of other relevant injustices, the political community is morally permitted to abolish religious schools: it is permitted to coercively enforce a prohibition on directive religious teaching in both state-regulated and private schools.[24] In the next section (§7.3), I give some reasons why, in our unjust world, religious schools might be tolerated, perhaps even encouraged. In other words, although religious schools are objectionable from the perspective of independence for children, society ought not to abolish them here and now, but rather phase them out in conjunction with the introduction of arrangements that replicate the beneficial features of religious schools in our unjust world.

Our question is whether schools that help parents to enrol their children into a religion should be allowed to exist. We can imagine many different educational arrangements that grant more or fewer legal rights regarding education

---

[23] Suppose that a surveillance regime would prevent enrolment and would not, all things considered, be bad for the child from the point of view of independence, but it would make the experience of parenting worse for parents, because they would worry about being held to account. On the view I have defended, such a surveillance regime would be justified.

[24] As should be clear from previous chapters, I focus on religious schools because they are prominent enrolling educational institutions in many societies. If my conception of independence for children is sound, then my argument is that schools that promote and practise atheist beliefs and rites should also be prohibited.

to parents and correspondingly fewer or more rights over schooling to others such as teachers or citizens. At one extreme—we can call this *the model of anti-perfectionist liberal schooling*—the government enforces a prohibition of any kind of comprehensive enrolment within schools; and the prohibition holds regardless of whether the school is publicly or privately funded. In this model, schools offer a curriculum that is directive with respect to moral and political matters, but non-directive with respect to matters concerning religion and ethics. That does not mean that they refuse to engage with comprehensive questions; they regard themselves as required to engage with them, to impart to children the skills and understanding to develop their own independent views as they mature. Nevertheless, anti-perfectionist liberal schools do not aim to promote any particular religious view or to get or invite its students to practise one.

At the other extreme there is *the model of parental choice*, which holds that parents ought to have the legal right to decide what kind of religious education their child receives and, in particular, the right to choose schools that promote particular religious beliefs or observe specific religious rituals. The parental choice model might be elaborated in several ways. First, the right might support the legal option to spend their own income on paying for their child to attend a religious school; or it might involve religious schooling that is publicly funded. Second, there are different possible arrangements regarding the standards that schools chosen by parents are legally required to meet. Some advocates of the liberal consensus, for example, argue for a model of parental choice that protects the child's interest in leading a just and authentic life; others argue for arrangements that allow parents to select schools that control their child's exposure to alternative world views.

The previous section established that an upbringing in line with independence for children is enforceable in the sense that parents have no reasonable objection to being prevented from religiously enrolling their child. However, we also noted reasons why parents should not be prevented by state officials from enrolling their child within the home environment. Here, in a similar fashion, we are asking whether parents may engage others who work in schools to help them to enrol their child: if parents lack an interest that justifies the right to enrol, should the political community nevertheless prefer the model of parental choice for other reasons, such as the maintenance of familial intimacy, the interests of children, or the interests of the wider community? Specifically, are their reasons acceptable to citizens who regard themselves as free and equal that favour the parental choice model over anti-perfectionist liberal schooling?

Some of the reasons for caution with respect to enforcing independence for children within the home do not extend to the school environment. There are good reasons for the political community to put in place a monitoring and inspection regime that provides quality assurance with respect to the education that is offered by different schools. Of course, policymakers need to think carefully about how the inspection regime is configured to ensure that it does not produce perverse incentives or have other negative consequences. For example, evaluating schools by assessing student attainment at different points in children's school career can be a self-defeating way of ensuring that standards are met. This method of assessing schools can lead to schools' refusing to admit students who are likely to perform poorly in the relevant assessments. Because of that possibility, we cannot treat student success in tests as a reliable indicator of quality of teaching in the school, because the results might be explained by its ability to select students who will perform well. Similarly, in certain contexts, highly judgemental inspection regimes can have the effect that, because of the reduced autonomy and job satisfaction they engender, highly capable and committed teachers leave the profession to the detriment of the quality of education students receive. So, any school inspection regime must be carefully calibrated to ensure that it is optimal for promoting the right kind of education. Still, an appropriately designed inspection and enforcement regime is justifiable for various reasons—in the case of the private school market, should one exist, parents benefit from having clear and accurate information about the costs and benefits of different schools; in the state-funded sector, improving educational provision and value for public money depend on identifying more and less successful schools. In both the public and private sectors, the weightiest reason to monitor what schools do is to ensure that children's educational interests are satisfied.

If a system of school monitoring and inspection is required for these and other reasons, inspectors' enforcement of the political community's prohibition on religious enrolment would not have the negative consequences that enforcement within the home would have. That is partly because teachers play a different role in children's lives compared to parents. First, children and teachers do not need to get to know each other intimately and, therefore, children do not need teachers to have the same freedom as parents to be themselves or to act spontaneously. Second, the financial cost of enforcing anti-perfectionism in schools would be negligible. It would represent merely a minor addition to the inspection and enforcement regime that checks whether child safeguarding and other educational standards are satisfied.[25]

---

[25] For similar observations, see Daniel Weinstock, 'For a Political Philosophy of Parent-Child Relationships', *Critical Review of International Social and Political Philosophy* 21 (2018): 351–365, at 363.

If the reasons that tell in favour of our reluctance to enforce anti-perfectionist parenting in the home do not extend to support the model of parental choice, are there other reasons that favour that result? I consider two arguments of that kind: first, an appeal to children's interest in what, following MacMullen, I'll call 'comprehensive consonance'; second, an appeal to the overall benefits to society of having a diversity of schools.[26]

First, the appeal to 'comprehensive consonance'. It might be argued that children's interests are best satisfied if the comprehensive values of the child's parents also animate the school—its composition, ethos, and curriculum, for example.[27] This might be the case for several different reasons, but typically advocates of this argument appeal to a bundle of considerations: the thought that the child needs to be given some kind of provisional identity on the basis of which she can deliberate and learn what it is to have and pursue a conception of the good and that identity-formation should be part of the school's remit; or that, to avoid disorientation, it is better if the school's identity-formation of the child does not compete with the formation that is offered within the family.

According to this argument, then, the educational interests of children within religious families are damaged if they have a school experience that fails to match the religious upbringing they receive within the home. Before assessing this defence of religious schools, let me make two comments about it. First, notice that although these arguments are typically used to defend parental *choice*, it is not clear that they succeed in that respect. If it is genuinely important for a child's development that the messages she receives in school about religion be the same as those within the home, then this is a reason to deny religious parents the option of sending their child to a school that is religiously neutral, or which promotes a religious or comprehensive conception different to the one they endorse. Second, an evaluation of this argument needs to rest on an investigation of the empirical claim that comprehensive consonance between school and home is indeed necessary or helpful for children's development into independent agents. In that investigation, it is important to eliminate noise generated by variables that would be absent in an ideal society. For example, some have argued that religious consonance between school and

---

[26] I draw on my longer discussion in 'Against Religious Schools' in Matthew Clayton, Andrew Mason, and Adam Swift, with Ruth Wareham, *How to Think About Religious Schools: Principles and Policies* (Oxford: Oxford University Press, 2024).

[27] MacMullen, *Faith in Schools?*, 186 and Ch. 8. MacMullen claims that the good of comprehensive consonance might be true for certain schools even if not all schools. For example, he argues that there should be religious or ethical 'consonance between school and home' in primary schools (the first five or six years of school) but not beyond that.

home protects or fosters a sense of self-respect in children who live in a society that generally discriminates against those who practise the particular religion in question.[28] At best, such arguments support the retention of religious schools in non-ideal circumstances, but they are insufficient to justify the existence of religious schools in an ideal society free from discrimination.

I do not know of any noise-free study of the consonance hypothesis, so cannot give a knock-down case against it. Still, it is worth clarifying the argument and recording my belief that it is mistaken. First, we need to clarify the meaning of 'identity-formation'. For the defence of directive religious schooling to work, it needs to be established that to develop the capacity to reflect on, revise, and pursue a particular conception of the good, the child needs to be initiated into a particular comprehensive doctrine. Note, in addition, that the society anti-perfectionist liberals advocate is not hostile to every kind of identity formation. Indeed, they want children to become deeply committed to specific norms of justice—to comply with and support a raft of civil, political, and socioeconomic rights. As suggested earlier (§5.1), to the extent that the argument from consonance relies on the thought that children must know what it is like to be committed to a set of values and norms on the basis of which they can learn to evaluate others they encounter, it is unclear why initiation into liberal values is not enough.

Second, there are stronger and weaker versions of the appeal to comprehensive consonance. A strong version holds that the child's development suffers if her school fails to direct her towards her parents' religious values. Weak comprehensive consonance holds that the school must not *gainsay* her parents' religious convictions. Now, the weak version is of no help to the advocate of directive religious schools, because the 'no gainsaying' requirement is fulfilled by having an anti-perfectionist liberal school that teaches about different religious views and directs children towards various political virtues, but refuses to direct its pupils towards any particular religion or conception of the good. If consonance is compatible with non-direction, then this argument for religious schools fails because anti-perfectionist schools are not in tension with it.

But the strong version seems mistaken. There are countless parents who go out of their way to choose schools that expose their child from a very young age to religious and ethical viewpoints that are different to those they affirm. That might be because they want to ensure that she learns to respect individuals who live differently; or it might be that they want their child to

---

[28] I briefly discuss Michael Merry's argument for this view below.

develop an awareness that their (the parents') conception is one she should learn to evaluate and accept or reject on the basis of an informed evaluation. The consonance argument for religious schools needs to claim that children who go through that kind of anti-perfectionist schooling are less well served than those who attend schools that reinforce the directive religious teaching they receive in the home. When a noise-free study of the comprehensive consonance hypothesis is done, I do not believe it will sustain such a strong claim.

Let us turn to the appeal to diversity in schooling as an argument for the parental choice model. Children are entitled to certain educational outcomes, which, with no attempt to provide an exhaustive list, include the capacity to sustain themselves economically, various moral and political virtues, and the capacity to engage in independent reflection and pursuit of a conception of the good. The diversity argument for religious schools is that an educational regime that includes multiple independent providers pursuing different experiments in schooling, alongside parental choice between the various schools, will tend to promote these educational outcomes better than a regime in which every school is anti-perfectionist in character. As Mill suggests, experiments in living and choice between them is our best bet for exchanging 'error for truth'.[29] Similarly, we might learn from our own and others' educational successes or mistakes: a society that lets a hundred schools blossom will deliver what we want from education better than a schooling regime without publicly funded faith schools. Thus, advocates of religious schools might appeal to the good consequences that follow from there being diverse providers of education with parents choosing between them.

The central reply to the diversity argument is that it would be wrong to straightforwardly adopt an education policy in virtue of the benefits of experimentation for overall societal progress. Mill's appeal to a marketplace of ideas is nested within a utilitarian moral theory that liberal anti-perfectionists reject because it fails to protect the interests and claims of individual persons.[30] In the case of schooling, the worry is that if an educational experiment embodied in a particular school fails, particular individuals are harmed or wronged, perhaps seriously, by being denied an appropriate education. Anti-perfectionist ideals draw a limit regarding the extent of permissible diversity with respect to schools.

---

[29] Mill, *On Liberty*, especially Ch. 2.
[30] That utilitarianism fails to respect what he calls 'the separateness of persons' is in many ways the central thought of Rawls's *A Theory of Justice*.

To be sure, diversity in schooling has its place and, no doubt, there are good arguments against uniform, data-driven approaches to education that have been favoured in education over the past few decades.[31] Some who make the argument from diversity point to the bland uniformity of non-religious schools that exist here and now and their inattention to spiritual, moral, and ethical questions. They point out that religious schools offer something genuinely distinctive. In reply, an anti-perfectionist might observe that in an ideal education system spiritual, ethical, and moral questions would be addressed more systematically than they are under current arrangements and, while directive religious education would not be part of that provision, there would be plenty of opportunity for schools to specialize in different kinds of education and offer tailored educational experiences to different children. The argument for religious schools is most plausible when those schools are compared to anti-perfectionist schools as they operate here and now, but not when compared to such schools as they might be. For now, it is enough to ask why the right kind of diversity in schooling is not possible within a school system that does not include directive religious education.

7.3 The Phased Abolition of Religious Schools

For the reasons given above, I believe an ideal political community would abolish directive religious schools and follow the model of anti-perfectionist liberal schooling. But it does not follow that societies should prohibit religious schools here and now. Even if the religious enrolment of children is morally wrong, we can imagine certain non-ideal conditions in which third parties ought to tolerate, perhaps even facilitate, wrongdoing. To illustrate the general thought, consider the particularly gory hypothetical case described by Tadros:

> *Claw hammer.* I am standing on the shore unable to save a child who is drowning. Only you can save him, by wading in, but you are unwilling to do so, because going into the water would ruin your suit. You point out that if I pass you the claw hammer I have in my possession you will be able to save the child without damaging your suit, by jamming the claw into his eye socket to pull him out.[32]

---

[31] See Matthew Clayton and Daniel Halliday, 'Big Data and the Liberal Conception of Education', *Theory and Research in Education* 15 (2018): 290–305.
[32] Tadros, *The Ends of Harm*, 161f.

Obviously, it would be wrong for you to save the child with the claw hammer, because you are morally required to save him by wading in at the cost of ruining your suit. Still, the fact is that you are unwilling to do your moral duty. Because that is the case, I can either facilitate wrongdoing by giving you the claw hammer or let the child drown. I should give you the claw hammer. Similarly, when we consider school policy for the non-ideal real world in which we live, we must consider certain injustices, including the unjust conduct of parents and others, that would not exist in an ideal world. The presence of those injustices gives us reasons to be cautious about prohibiting religious schools and parental choice more generally. Consequently, although religious schools should eventually be abolished, their elimination should coincide with other developments in education, politics, and society that ensure that the positive features that religious schools bring to current societies are not lost. Here, I identify three features of many contemporary societies that illustrate how the case for abolishing religious schools is more complicated than might be thought.

First, at the most mundane level, religious schools that currently exist contribute resources to the education system of a society. Other things equal, their abolition would diminish, perhaps considerably, the level of funding devoted to the education of children. Many religious schools are privately funded. Other religious schools pay some, but not all, of the costs of their pupils' education. Either way, it is likely that, without putting in place compensatory measures, the prohibition of religious schools would involve fewer resources being devoted to children's schooling. The loss of resources is explained by the fact that parents and religious institutions are prepared to invest more in schools that promote their religious viewpoint compared to those that do not. It is likely that many religious organizations would withdraw from the education sector if they were not legally permitted to run schools that enrol pupils into their particular traditions, rites, and beliefs.

The loss of educational funding that we can expect from prohibiting religious schools is not a serious objection to the argument for abolishing faith schools. Compare the campaign against exploitation in the workplace. Advocates of a minimum wage, for example, face the possibility that if employers are required to pay a decent wage to their workers, they will employ fewer workers. One response to that possibility is for the larger community to ensure that no one has less than an adequate share of resources, whether they are in work or not. Similarly, in our case, the right response to religious organizations or parents who threaten to withdraw money from the education sector if they cannot use it to promote their particular religious view is for the political community to fund an appropriately funded anti-perfectionist liberal education for every child.

The resource issue, then, can easily be resolved in theory. However, it is worth noting that in certain environments—I have in mind societies that maintain low levels of public spending across the board—citizens are unwilling to fund education to the degree required by justice. One can imagine cases in which the level of funding provided by religious organizations is so high, and the appetite of citizens to fill the funding gap that would be left by these organizations' withdrawal from the sector so low, that the satisfaction of independence for children and children's other educational entitlements would be best served by working to regulate religious schools rather than by abolishing them.[33] That would be acquiescence in the face of injustice, but acquiescence is sometimes rational.

Second, some argue that religious schools can be a safe haven for children who suffer religious or racial discrimination. For example, Michael Merry argues that, notwithstanding the risk of religious indoctrination they present, separate Muslim schools are justifiable to combat the harm of stigmatization that Muslim pupils would suffer if they were educated in religiously neutral common schools within existing societies in which discrimination against Muslim minorities is widespread.[34] Muslim schools are safe havens, he claims, for several reasons: they provide environments that are free of discrimination, which, among other things, prevents Muslim pupils from internalizing the stigmatizing dominant culture; they are staffed by teachers who have 'cultural competence' and, therefore, have a better understanding of the challenges faced by Muslim pupils; and they provide environments in which pupils can reflect with others who face similar injustices and consider how to resist discrimination.[35]

Merry's argument should be taken seriously, because, as Rawls suggests, self-respect is perhaps the most important good a society should protect.[36] It is of the utmost value that individuals view themselves as having equal moral importance to others, that they have confidence in their ability to adopt and pursue a reasonable life-plan regardless of its content, and that they do not experience shame for having a particular ethnic heritage or characteristics. If the maintenance of neutral common schools for the sake of individuals' political

---

[33] Some of these issues are explored in the final part of *How to Think About Religious Schools*.
[34] Michael Merry, 'Indoctrination, Islamic Schools, and the Broader Scope of Harm', *Theory and Research in Education* 16 (2018): 162–178.
[35] Merry, 'Indoctrination, Islamic Schools, and the Broader Scope of Harm', 169–170.
[36] Rawls, *A Theory of Justice*, Sec. 67.

autonomy threatened the self-respect of stigmatized groups in societies, then that would be a serious objection to them. The abolition of religious schools should, therefore, be conditional upon arrangements being in place that sustain the self-respect of groups that suffer discrimination in the wider society.

How serious a constraint on the campaign against religious schools is the duty to promote and maintain the self-respect of all pupils? It might be that the duty to promote self-respect speaks in favour of separate schooling for certain groups in certain unjust societies, but not for others in other non-ideal societies. It has been shown, for example, that the educational integration of pupils with different ethnic heritages can be helpful for encouraging trust and respect for others.[37] To the extent that the self-respect of minority groups is threatened by discrimination by the majority in society, which is, in turn, explained by fear, distrust, and misunderstanding, the existence of separate, segregated schools appears to be counterproductive, at least in certain environments. If so, then self-respect for all might be promoted, rather than impeded, by the abolition of religious schools. Still, critics of enrolling religious schools must be mindful of the important consideration of self-respect.

Finally, a common argument for religious schools is that they provide better education in morality compared to non-religious schools, at least those in many educational regimes here and now. A central feature of many religions is that they provide opportunities to reflect on, and codes that inform, how one ought to treat others. For example, many religions recommend or require that individuals be charitable and display concern and respect for others. This represents a directive education in which pupils are encouraged to embrace moral values that ask them to rein in the pursuit of their self-interest for the sake of others.

It is vital for the promotion and maintenance of a just society that schools provide directive moral education that is centred on the recognition that individuals have claims to freedom and equality. Citizens ought to vote for, and in other ways promote, arrangements in which everyone enjoys a fair share of resources as well as rights to participate as equals in politics and civic freedoms to reflect on and pursue their own distinctive conception of the good.

As I have argued, directive religious schools are problematic because they deny individuals political autonomy. Indeed, although it is important for pupils to acquire a sense of morality and justice—a sense of their obligations and duties to others as well as of the rights they enjoy—this sense can be imparted

---

[37] Miles Hewstone, Ananthi Al Ramiah, Katherina Schmid, Christina Floe, Maarten van Zalk, Ralf Wölfer, and Rachel New, 'Influence of Segregation versus Mixing: Intergroup Contact and Attitudes among White-British and Asian-British Students in High Schools in Oldham, England', *Theory and Research in Education* 16 (2018): 179–203.

without the controversial inflection that religions give morality. We do not have to believe in a god to be brought to the view that we ought to distribute resources fairly or to respect other people's choices in life. Rather, the anti-perfectionist liberal model holds that pupils can be taught to adopt the right moral norms without schools' taking a stand on further disputes concerning the existence of gods or their relevance for our moral duties.

Ideally, then, individuals should be taught to embrace liberal values in a religiously neutral way, in a way that does not tie those values to particular religious or ethical doctrines. But how should we proceed if the anti-perfectionist schools we have here and now are poor at encouraging pupils to develop concern and respect for others? In that scenario, we would face a hard choice between, on the one hand, maintaining religious schools that violate the prohibition on enrolment but do a good job of encouraging a sense of justice, and anti-perfectionist schools that are less good at developing their students' moral capacities.

The hard choice is not merely hypothetical. There is sometimes a reluctance on the part of many secular schools in various countries to engage in directive moral education. Many teachers in non-religious schools that exist here and now worry about the fact that there is widespread disagreement about political morality and treat that fact as a reason not to engage in directive teaching in this domain. They say that there is a disagreement about whether everyone should have access to housing, health care, education, and so on, and that fact is a reason for them not to direct their pupils towards a particular view of justice. That is a deeply unfortunate situation, because living together in a just society depends on individuals' coming to embrace the moral norm that universal access to these and other goods is an enforceable entitlement, and directive moral education is essential for that outcome to reliably be achieved.

If we face a hard choice between eliminating religious enrolment in schools and promoting directive moral education that promotes or sustains a just society, we ought to choose the latter. To be clear, the hard choice we face is avoidable and, indeed, many religiously neutral schools no doubt do a good job with respect to liberal moral education. However, where religious schools do better with respect to creating a liberal citizenry compared to anti-perfectionist schools, we need to think twice before prohibiting them. This is another illustration of how the abolition of faith schools needs to proceed in tandem with enhancements to the moral education offered by schools so that the liberal project is not jeopardized.[38]

---

[38] For a nice discussion of these issues in the context of education in Canada, see Andrée-Anne Cormier, 'Must Schools Teach Religions Neutrally? The Loyola Case and the Challenges of Liberal

My remarks on educational resources, anti-discrimination, and moral and political education suggest that the abolition of religious schools here and now may not be appropriate. Nevertheless, even if we should be reluctant to prohibit religious schools under present unjust circumstances, we should work to establish the conditions under which they can be abolished. After all, in a just society all schools would be anti-perfectionist in character and not form part of the institutional framework for the comprehensive enrolment of children.

7.4 Religious Associations

Finally, let us briefly consider the place of religious associations and other organizations, which often practise the comprehensive enrolment of children. Parents do not act in an ethical vacuum. Many direct their child towards particular religious beliefs and practices because they are members of a religious community, and the direction of their children is often informed or guided by the expectations of the organizations that govern those communities. As we know them, religious institutions enrol children by welcoming them as members of the community, by communicating expectations that they (the children) will live by the tenets of the religion, and by encouraging them to accept the teachings of the religion, which sometimes includes formal or informal instruction. Should the state prevent religious associations from engaging in those kinds of activity?

Of course, religious associations are a stable and permissible feature of a just society, one that protects people's freedom to pursue their own religious views in conjunction with others. But I have also argued that the enrolment of children within a religion is morally wrong. If my argument is sound, an ideal state would command religious institutions not to engage in comprehensive enrolment and would take steps to encourage different religions to develop an ethos of non-enrolment of children. But would the state use further powers to discourage such associations from enrolling children into their respective religions?

Religious associations might be thought as lying somewhere between the family and schools with respect to their features. First, they sometimes exhibit

Neutrality in Education', *Religion & Education* 45 (2018): 308–330. The relationship between religious instruction and the development of an individual's sense of justice has been a key debate in the history of US education. For a nuanced discussion of that history, see Benjamin Justice and Colin Macleod, *Have a Little Faith: Religion, Democracy, and the American Public School* (Chicago: Chicago University Press, 2016).

a certain kind of intimacy between members of their community, though it is doubtful that children benefit from the community leaders' having the same kind of opportunity to exercise discretion and spontaneity as their parents. Second, in comparison with schools, while religious associations are subject to legal regulation, they are typically not under the gaze of well-resourced bodies charged with ensuring that they satisfy the legal requirements that apply to them. In addition to these features, associations afford adults the opportunity to pursue their distinctive comprehensive beliefs with other adults. Even if parents have no interest in having the opportunity to make use of their religious community to enrol their children, they do have interests in privacy with respect to their affairs with other adults.

As well as these ideal-world considerations, the reasons that speak in favour of retaining religious schools in certain unjust environments might extend to religious associations. Depending on the environment, considerations of self-respect, combatting discrimination, and providing moral education might be reasons not to interfere in the activities of religious communities, even those that practise the enrolment of children.

Given the plethora of reasons in play, any final determination of what powers the state should deploy to discourage religious associations from comprehensively enrolling children will involve fine, context-sensitive, balancing judgements. I do not have a clear sense of how to do that. But we might note certain powers that the state could use to promote independence for children within religious associations. First, in many jurisdictions, religious associations benefit from their status as charities that enjoy exemptions from certain kinds of taxation in virtue of their public value. To qualify, the state in question asks charities to show how their activities constitute a public benefit. No doubt there are various criteria we might use to identify what counts as a public benefit. The anti-perfectionist liberal view I have outlined gives a distinctive account: we might augment our interpretation of 'public benefit' by adding independence for children to the mix. Second, states sometimes give religious associations certain legal powers. For example, in many societies the law allows people to have a legally recognized marriage conducted according to the rites of their religion. It might be that the power of the state to delegate legal functions of that kind should be dependent on the institution's agreeing to respect the independence of children. Finally, religious institutions are typically employers. They offer contracts to priests, rabbis, imams, pujaris, granthis, and so on, to lead their communities. It might be that respect for children's independence should be incorporated into the laws regulating the duties of office holders alongside laws that safeguard children's other interests.

Thus, incorporating a concern to protect children from comprehensive enrolment through the selective use of subsidies, recognition, and employment law might be attractive. Although I cannot defend concrete proposals for the regulation of religious institutions, it seems clear that the observations about enforcement with respect to parents and schools will be useful guides for thinking about the activities of religious institutions. In an independence-respecting society, the self-understanding of such institutions with respect to their role in the upbringing of children would be very different to that which they exhibit here and now. Instead of seeing their role in terms of helping parents to induct their children into their community and encouraging children to adhere to the tenets of the religion, religious associations should see themselves as part of the background culture in which, alongside groups representing other non-religious doctrines, they non-directively educate the young about the content of different comprehensive practices and beliefs so that children can, in due course, make well-informed choices with respect to the various doctrines that are available. Various legal instruments might be used to advance that vision of society.

8
Conclusion

Anti-Perfectionist Parenting beyond Religion

Anti-perfectionist liberalism extends to parenting. Reasons given by comprehensive doctrines should be excluded from consideration when we are identifying what parents are morally permitted or required to do to or for their child. In addition, parents ought not to enrol their child into a particular conception of the good even when their doing so is compatible with her having an open future. These two ideas distinguish what I call 'independence for children' from the liberal consensus as well as more permissive parentalist views with respect to children's upbringing. The core idea of independence for children, that everyone is entitled to rule herself, is a conception of upbringing that involves paternalism without perfectionism. The ideals that inform how children are raised must be ones that are capable of retrospective endorsement by free and equal citizens, which in turn supports parental anti-perfectionism. Such a view is morally compelling, I argue, but it also constitutes a powerful alternative conception of parenting to those that have dominated our thinking about children and the family to date. Family life should take the form of parents' non-directively exploring the world of religious and ethical value with their child, rather than making her practise comprehensive activities or trying to steer her to endorse particular conceptions of the good. In virtue of its safeguarding responsibilities with respect to their lives, the state also has a role to play in protecting children's independence, I argue. Nevertheless, the view I have elaborated applies to parents directly. Parents are often duty-bound to respect their child's independence even in societies that do not legally prohibit or prevent comprehensive enrolment.

For the most part, when elaborating my argument for parental anti-perfectionism I focus on questions about theology and religion to illustrate the implications of independence for children. But there are many other conceptions of the good such as those concerning gender, work, consumption, and appearance. How should anti-perfectionist parents engage with these conceptions? How does independence for children extend beyond the case of religion?

As discussed in previous chapters, anti-perfectionist liberals distinguish between public and comprehensive reasons. As I understand them, public reasons are those reasons given by our status as 'free and equal' individuals and, particularly, our interest in setting and pursuing our own comprehensive ends and developing and deploying a sense of justice, which includes respect for others' end-setting and political autonomy. As I have argued, these are the reasons that count when elaborating a conception of parenting and political morality more generally.

Comprehensive reasons include religious and ethical reasons for belief or action that relate, among other things, to how we ought to live our lives and what counts as a good life when questions about what we owe to each other are bracketed. Independence for children contends that these reasons must be excluded from consideration in an account of upbringing, and parents qua parents must take an anti-perfectionist attitude towards them.

When it comes to a particular issue, then, we need to figure out what are the public and comprehensive reasons in play. I finish my elaboration of independence for children with some brief tentative remarks about various matters about which parents need to engage with their children.

8.1 Consumption and Materialism

It is undeniable that there are influential non-religious comprehensive social norms regarding how we live our lives, which are promoted by parents and other institutions and sustained by the expectations of large numbers in society. Materialism is a powerful ethical norm in many contemporary societies, which shapes people's ambitions with respect to work and consumption. Parents and schools often encourage children to work hard and to form ambitions to pursue well-paid, status-conferring careers. Although slogans such as 'Be the Best You Can Be', 'Everyone is an Achiever' and 'Quest for Excellence', which are sometimes used as school mottos, could strictly speaking be neutral between different conceptions of the good, the way they are commonly deployed delivers the message that a good life is one in which individuals maximize their chances of securing a university education and well-paid occupations that sustain high levels of material consumption. Schools and parents who support them thereby issue more or less explicit guidance as to what a successful life involves. (As theorists of 'the hidden curriculum' have long emphasized, many schools also promote the capitalist work ethic of hard work and deference to employers through their emphasis on hierarchy, dress codes, discipline, and a curriculum that offers little scope for student choice.[1] I discuss work ethics below.)

Social norms surrounding material consumption are also intentionally cultivated by businesses and corporations through advertising and are reinforced by the explicit expectations or implicit biases of parents, peers, and adults. From Wollstonecraft to the recent burgeoning literature on appearance norms and discrimination, we know that there exist powerful norms surrounding the clothes people wear and how they appear, for example.[2] Conduct that goes against these powerful norms is often discouraged, frowned upon, treated as an affront to the wider social group, and at the extreme treated as a reason to exclude a person from the group in question. Many of these reactions can be viewed as attempts to enrol individuals into particular conceptions of the good, either for the benefit of the individuals themselves or for the sake of those who do the enrolling.

What is to be done about comprehensive norms concerning consumption? First, we should note that certain public reasons are in play. Many norms that express, aim, or tend to promote injustices ought to be challenged. For example, conceptions that encourage material consumption that is incompatible with our duty to live sustainably or to be appropriately responsive to the moral claims of future generations should be challenged. Children have an interest in being raised in a way that enables them to accept and conform with their duties to others. For that reason, their upbringing should encourage them to consider the impact of their choices on the lives of future individuals and to embrace lifestyles that involve having fewer children than many do, eating a largely plant-based diet, and emitting low levels of greenhouse gases.[3]

There are countless other injustices that are explicitly or implicitly encouraged by materialist social norms. Citizens have duties of justice to vote for and comply with tax and spending policies that ensure a fair distribution of resources within society and between different societies. Although independence for children does not take a stand on the merits of materialism *within*

---

[1] See, for example, Samuel Bowles and Herbert Gintis, *Schooling in Capitalist America: Educational Reform and the Contradictions of Economic Life* (London: Routledge and Keegan Paul, 1976).

[2] Mary Wollstonecraft, 'A Vindication of the Rights of Woman', in *A Vindication of the Rights of Men; A Vindication of the Rights of Woman; An Historical and Moral View of the French Revolution*, edited by Janet Todd (Oxford: Oxford University Press, 1993); Clare Chambers, *Sex, Culture, and Justice: The Limits of Choice* (University Park, PA: Penn State University Press, 2008); Heather Widdows, *Perfect Me: Beauty as an Ethical Ideal* (Princeton, NJ: Princeton University Press, 2018); Andrew Mason, *What's Wrong with Lookism? Personal Appearance, Discrimination, and Disadvantage* (Oxford: Oxford University Press, 2023).

[3] For policy-relevant discussion, see Seth Wynes and Kimberly A. Nicholas, 'The Climate Mitigation Gap: Education and Government Recommendations Miss the Most Effective Individual Actions', *Environmental Research Letters* 12 (2017), 074024.

the limits of justice, it takes a firm stand against raising children in ways that allow them to believe that the poverty and inequalities that prevail in most societies are not serious injustices. Even if a liberal society would not criticize a person who develops ambitions to wear fine clothes, drive a plush car, and so on, parents and others are duty-bound to educate their children to understand that the pursuit of any comprehensive ambition is morally constrained by what we owe to others.

With respect to permissible materialist conceptions of the good, the ideal of independence for children has at least two concerns. First, it claims that the comprehensive enrolment of children wrongs them. Second, it objects to the closing of their minds. It is worth pausing to remind ourselves of the difference between these two ways of violating children's independence. Comprehensive enrolment wrongs children because it involves the use of power or authority to induce children to pursue ends that can reasonably be rejected and may well be rejected by them when they become adults. But children's independence is also threatened when the options they face are unduly limited by the intentional or unintentional activities of others. For example, a school curriculum closes children's minds when it fails to introduce them to alternative markers of success compared to a life of material consumption.

Many prominent critics of materialist conceptions of the good present an apparently more straightforward argument against their being promoted by parents or schools.[4] They argue that materialist lifestyles are bad for those who follow them. Some psychologists and economists of happiness, for example, show how people's welfare, understood in terms of self-reported subjective satisfaction scores, is diminished by having materialist ambitions. Note, however, that the ideal of independence operates without a comprehensive conception of harm and, therefore, avoids such arguments. We are morally permitted to live less good lives than we might. What matters is that our lives are our own, that they reflect our own independent choices and judgements, provided they are consistent with fulfilling our duties to others. The worry about dominant materialist norms is not that they reduce individuals' well-being, but that they constitute wrongful comprehensive enrolment or prevent meaningful reflection on alternative possible lifestyles.[5]

---

[4] Tim Kasser, 'Materialistic Values and Well-Being: Problems and Policy', in *Policies for Happiness*, edited by Stefano Bartolini, Ennio Bilancini, Luigino Bruni, and Pier Luigi Porta (Oxford: Oxford University Press, 2016); Richard Layard and Judy Dunn, *A Good Childhood: Searching for Values in a Competitive Age* (London: Penguin Books, 2009).

[5] For a similar view, though not as it pertains to parenting, see Tom Parr, 'Work Hours, Free Time, and Economic Output', *The Philosophical Quarterly* 74 (2024): 900–919.

8.2 Work Ethics

The central question: is it just for parents to encourage their child to adopt a particular work ethic; if so, what kind of ethic regarding her occupational ambitions and how hard she should work (at school, say)? At one extreme, we have the Protestant work ethic, which Max Weber famously suggested has an affinity with 'the spirit of capitalism'—hard work in the market to accumulate wealth to give oneself assurance of one's own salvation.[6] The other extreme is the Homeric work ethic—I refer to the denizen of the fictional American town of Springfield, rather than the great Greek poet: 'Lisa, if you don't like your job you don't strike. You just go in every day and do it really half-assed. That's the American way';[7] and, 'If something's hard to do, then it's not worth doing'.[8]

When considering work ethics we have certain public reasons to guide us. Our interests in developing a sense of justice and in political autonomy justify imparting to children a motivation to work hard at acquiring the relevant understanding of this sphere of morality and the motivation to live by it. In virtue of that interest, children should be steered away from the Homeric ethic at least when it is presented as a general conception of how one should orientate oneself to the world. Nevertheless, when limited to advice about one's career, there might be an argument to treat the Homeric view as a permissible conception on which parents should not take a stand. That would be the case if the life of a slacker is not incompatible with developing the motivation to fulfil one's duties of justice to others.

An alternative view is that anti-perfectionist liberalism supports the cultivation of a work ethic of *public service*, a motivation to work hard for everyone's benefit. Suppose we have identified the goods owed to free and equal citizens, including education, health case, security from violence and other hazards. Does it not follow that parents and teachers ought to shape the work preferences of the young so that they grow up to make work choices that enable the political community to supply these goods reasonably cheaply? In such a society, because of their work preferences, few financial incentives would be required to induce people to take on these roles. Parents might, for example, encourage the young to develop and exercise their powers in a socially

---

[6] Max Weber, *The Protestant Ethic and the Spirit of Capitalism* (London: Routledge, 1987).
[7] Swinton O. Scott III (director) and Jennifer Crittenden (writer), *The Simpsons*, Season 6, Episode 21.
[8] Wes Archer (director) and Jeff Martin (writer), *The Simpsons*, Season 3, Episode 22.

productive way: steer them to form ambitions to be teachers, doctors, nurses, police officers, or wealth producers.[9]

Such a view is, I believe, mistaken because the cultivation of a public service work ethic in the young can be reasonably rejected. The emphasis on the value of producing goods or reducing the costs to others of the supply of public and socioeconomic benefits makes individuals serve a social good they have no public duty to serve. No doubt, individuals have a duty to bear a fair share of the costs to realize and sustain just institutions, and part of that duty is to campaign and vote for institutions that ensure that the effects of good and bad luck regarding marketable skill are fairly shared between citizens. But, beyond that, individuals are not under a duty to embrace occupational ambitions that advance the material or health-related interests of others.[10]

In sum, children's upbringings should include direction towards a certain attitude towards work, but there might be considerable room for parents not to take a stand on various different conceptions of work, leisure, and their importance in life. Such a stance would mean that children might be more likely to adopt and pursue working lives that fail to benefit themselves or fail to maximize socioeconomic benefits to others, but these outcomes are the inevitable effect of respecting individuals' independence.

8.3 Gender

Following the same reasoning, we can distinguish between conceptions of gender that fall foul of public reason, which children should be steered away from by parents and teachers, and those that are compatible with public reason with respect to which parents should be non-directive when raising their children.

How should we identify conceptions of gender that are impermissible at the bar of public reason? There are some clear cases. Certain conceptions of gender have as their primary aim the cultivation and maintenance of inegalitarian public relations and the social norms that sustain them. Certain comprehensive doctrines, including certain religions, that advocate that women

---

[9] The argument that an ethic of public service should be promoted in children chimes with G. A. Cohen's claim that justice supports the adoption of an 'egalitarian ethos'. See his *If You're an Egalitarian, How Come You're So Rich?*; *Rescuing Justice and Equality*; and *Why Not Socialism?* (Princeton, NJ: Princeton University Press, 2009). For further discussion, see Joshua Cohen, 'Taking People as They Are', *Philosophy and Public Affairs* 30 (2001): 363–386.

[10] For reasons advanced earlier (§7.1), there would also be publicity-related concerns about cultivating an ethos of public service.

should not pursue public roles—as representative politicians, judges, or police officers, for example—are constitutively impermissible. Encouraging children to endorse such doctrines wrongs them, not least because they assert that girls and women lack a claim to develop and exercise a sense of justice.[11]

What about the gendered division of labour with respect to caregiving and waged work? Many have noted that women are disadvantaged by the gendered division of labour that is characteristic of many families. In her influential account, Susan Moller Okin argues for a society in which parents exhibit an equal division of caregiving and waged work. Nevertheless, she recognizes that the political community ought to allow adults to pursue their particular reasonable conceptions of the good, which may include a gendered view of labour between partners, at least to some degree. In the latter context, she argues for various legal arrangements—reforms to childcare rules, how schools operate, how earnings from waged employments are paid to adult partners, and reforms to divorce laws, among others—to mitigate women's vulnerability caused by a gendered division of labour.[12]

Rawls has a similar view. Thinking through his own conception of justice, 'justice as fairness', he distinguishes between voluntary and involuntary inequality regarding the division of labour within families, and he argues that political liberalism does not prohibit voluntary inequality provided 'it does not result from or lead to injustice' specified in terms of his principles of justice.[13] Although he does not specify the details of what he has in mind, at least some voluntary inequality is permitted, he claims, because it is 'connected with basic liberties, including the freedom of religion'.[14]

As observed in Chapter 3, Rawls does not argue for *parental* anti-perfectionism. Still, his remarks about how to conceive the distinction between public and comprehensive reasons in the context of the gendered division of labour are instructive for the ideal of independence for children. At least within some boundaries, those who embrace comprehensive views that prescribe different roles for men and women within the family are permitted to pursue their goals in their own lives, at least when their doing so is consistent with the maintenance of a just society.

---

[11] Wollstonecraft, *A Vindication of the Rights of Woman*. Wollstonecraft's feminist critique focuses on how constructed gender norms prevent women from fulfilling their public duties to others in society, including children. Unsurprisingly, there are various features of Wollstonecraft's view in *Vindication* that are perfectionist in character. An interesting question is whether, duly revised, the central features of her view—an account of virtue as duty-fulfilment and the development and deployment of one's reason as a constitutive of virtue—can be reformulated as anti-perfectionist ideals.
[12] Susan Moller Okin, *Justice, Gender, and the Family* (New York: Basic Books, 1989), Ch. 8.
[13] Rawls, 'The Idea of Public Reason Revisited', 599.
[14] Rawls, 'The Idea of Public Reason Revisited', 600.

No doubt there are many further questions to address, not least how to draw the boundary between permissible and impermissible inequality between parents, and what kinds of political intervention are justified to achieve equal citizenship for men and women.[15] One prominent question is whether children who grow up in gendered households, even those with parents who exhibit an anti-perfectionist attitude to parenting, find it unreasonably difficult or costly to form, reflect on, and pursue their own authentic conception of the importance or unimportance of gender in their own lives. If it were unreasonably hard for them to do so, then this would be a public reason supporting a more equal division of labour between parents.

Here, I do not attempt to engage with that question or other issues related to how our family and paid work lives must be structured to satisfy children's claims to a just and voluntary future. The central claim I want to make is that, even if certain gendered views of the division of labour within the family are compatible with public reason, parents should take an anti-perfectionist stance towards them when raising their children. If a particular set of parents believe that men and women should specialize in the labour they undertake, with men having responsibility for waged work and women responsibility for caregiving, that view is excluded as a reason within political morality and, I argue, parental morality. This position holds even if we suppose that their comprehensive view is sound. Parents should not be enrolling their children into gendered labour practices within the family. They should not be expecting or asking their children to follow the gendered division of labour they themselves practise within their relationship as partners.[16]

Does this mean that the presumption is that the household work that children can reasonably be expected to do should be shared equally between children regardless of gender? I believe such a rule of thumb is sound. My view asserts that it is important for all children to become acquainted with the various permissible conceptions of gender within society. Certain conceptions advocate a gender-based specialization of labour within the household. Others, like Okin's, demand an equal split of all forms of labour between partners. In an age-appropriate way, all children should be introduced to and scrutinize the different conceptions of the relationship between gender and labour. But prior to making their own decisions about these matters, there are good

---

[15] See Watson and Hartley, *Equal Citizenship and Public Reason*, especially Part 2; Gina Schouten, *Liberalism, Neutrality, and the Gendered Division of Labor* (Oxford: Oxford University Press, 2019); Anca Gheaus, 'Political Liberalism and the Dismantling of the Gendered Division of Labour', *Oxford Studies in Political Philosophy* 9 (2023): 153–182.

[16] For a fuller elaboration of this argument, notwithstanding her doubts about my view, see Gheaus, 'Political Liberalism and the Dismantling of the Gendered Division of Labour', Sec. 6.7.

public reasons for family life to be governed by a principle of equality that asserts that girls and boys have equal standing, equal rights, and equal duties.

Like religious views, conceptions of gender can be viewed as comprehensive doctrines. Parents should be steering children away from those conceptions that fall foul of the demands of public reason rooted in our interests as free and equal persons. With respect to conceptions that are consistent with public reason, in an ideal world parents would take an anti-perfectionist stance and not gender their children. In such a world, parents would be entitled to identify themselves as they believe appropriate—to identify as a man, woman, gender fluid, non-binary, or genderless, for example. But that entitlement does not extend to their having the right to choose to raise their children to conform to, or to believe they have, a particular gender identity or, indeed, to endorse a particular conception of what gender consists in.

What principles, then, should govern an anti-perfectionist upbringing regarding gender? A considerable amount turns on whether we live in a society that is free of discrimination and other kinds of injustice. In an ideal society, the three principles I outlined as constitutive of independence for children would operate. First, children would be given the wherewithal and exposed in an age-appropriate way to the variety of conceptions of gender. Second, parents would take an anti-perfectionist stance towards gender. And, third, parents and others would be increasingly respectful of the decisions of children as they develop the capacity to make reflective and informed decisions about their own lives. No doubt, the practical and policy-related implications of these principles need working out in much more detail. But the nature of the arrangements supported by independence for children should be reasonably clear.

In a non-ideal world like ours, which exhibits considerable gender-based violence, discrimination, and injustice, it is harder to identify the principles and policy implications of independence for children. That is partly because, like the liberal consensus and many perfectionist views, the ideal is multifaceted and, when elaborating it, certain basic principles are taken as read, such as the social conditions of self-respect, the protection of basic liberties, and a fair distribution of socioeconomic goods. Those protections cannot be assumed in contemporary societies, and we know there are contexts in which disastrous or seriously disadvantageous consequences for children or parents would follow if parents did not get their children to follow particular gender norms, or they increasingly allowed them to follow their own emerging views about gender, or they sought to ensure that they are exposed to alternative conceptions of gender. Notwithstanding the fact that some societies have made considerable progress in recent decades with respect to gender matters, there are countless lamentable features of many contemporary societies that make it hard to figure out how to make progress with the project of promoting and respecting independence for children. So, although I treat the principles of independence for children as applicable to parenting regardless of the political culture of different societies, the distinctive social and political character of a particular society surely makes a difference to how they are to be implemented in practice.

8.4 Diet

What does an anti-perfectionist diet for children look like? May parents feed their child meat and dairy products? May or must they give their child an exclusively vegetarian or vegan diet? May they exclude particular items from their child's diet for religious reasons, such as food that is not kosher or halal?

The contours of independence for children are now familiar. There are several public reasons to guide us: children need a balanced diet that protects their health as children and enables them to grow mentally and physically. That public reason is indeterminate with respect to diet: it can be satisfied by an omnivorous diet that does not exclude particular kinds of meat or seafood; a purely vegetarian, vegan, or kosher diet can be equally as good. Another dietary public reason stems from our duties to others. We have already noted climate-based reasons that favour a largely plant-based diet, perhaps one that also has wild venison on the menu;[17] and no doubt there are public reasons that derive from our duty to share food with others across the world. There are also reasons of independence—both the ethical and moral aspects of independence—to learn about the gastronomic features of different societies and comprehensive doctrines: to try foods that have cultural or religious significance for people.

A simple independence-respecting view is that parents should offer their child a diet that is balanced and compatible with honouring our duties to others who live in the present and future. Beyond that, it asserts that parents' comprehensive convictions regarding food should be set aside, and they should introduce their child, or allow her to be introduced, to the variety of dietary conceptions in society and worldwide. The simple independence view

---

[17] George Monbiot, 'I Shot a Deer—And I Still Think It Was the Ethical Thing to Do', *The Guardian*, 19 February 2020.

claims that parents who restrict their child's diet to foods that are vegan, vegetarian, kosher, or halal, for example, wrong their child, because they impose on her particular comprehensive views about what they ought to eat.[18]

The simple view is partly, but not entirely, right. Religious, aesthetic, and gastronomic reasons to control the food one's child eats should be set aside by parents. Nevertheless, the view is too simple, because it overlooks the fact that some non-human animals have moral claims to various kinds of treatment, indeed claims that have similar moral stringency to the independence-based claims of citizens and children. If that is the case, then veganism, vegetarianism, or some such diet might be morally required of all humans. Let me explain.

Many argue that some non-human animals have a normally decisive moral right to life, a right that places humans under a duty not to kill them, at least for food. In the way they understand it, that argument is a moral conception, a conception of what we owe to each other when the class of individuals in focus extends beyond humans. Other moral conceptions of our treatment of non-human animals have been proposed, such as the view that farming practices as we know them are morally wrong because they do not adequately attend to the interests of animals, or the view that animals must be slaughtered humanely, or the claim that it is morally wrong for humans to create non-human animals for food because of the pain and suffering they are bound to experience.[19]

I'll not offer a view of morality as it pertains to our treatment of animals. I merely note that certain conceptions of animals' claims argue that our killing them—in some conceptions, our creating them for food—is seriously morally wrong. If those conceptions are sound, it is hard to believe that our claim to independence—to decide our own diets on the basis of experiencing different kinds of food, and not to be governed by others' views about what we should eat—defeats our duty to avoid serious moral wrongdoing.

Issues concerning our treatment of non-human animals are like those that arise when parents propose to baptize their children (see §5.5), because they

---

[18] In his interesting article, Daniel Butt offers an argument for parents' giving their child a vegetarian diet, an argument that appeals to a version of the moral relevance of retrospective rejection. His thought is that if an adult comes to believe that eating meat is morally wrong, her being fed meat as a child would compromise her moral integrity in a way that being fed a vegetarian diet would not. See Butt, 'Corrupting the Youth: Should Parents Feed their Children Meat', *Ethical Theory and Moral Practice* 24 (2021): 981–997. If, for now, we put aside the moral claims of animals I go on to discuss, I take a different view, because appeals to integrity rest on a particular comprehensive conception of harm, and comprehensive views are excluded within my independence-respecting view: see my 'Is Ethical Independence Enough?'.

[19] The literature on moral questions concerning non-human animals is vast, and I'll not attempt to discuss it. One particularly insightful contribution is Jeff McMahan's 'Eating Animals the Nice Way', *Daedalus* 137 (2008): 66–76.

point to possible limits of the ideal of independence. In the case of baptism, the argument of many who are devout is that failure to baptize a child risks her eternal damnation. If they are right, then the ideal of independence for children is defeated by the child's interest in avoiding that disastrous outcome. Similarly, if advocates of animal rights are correct in thinking that we seriously wrong an animal by rearing and killing it for food, then it is hard to believe that the child's claim to independence defeats our duty to avoid wronging animals.

In the case of baptism, my reply was that independence does not risk disastrous outcomes for the child because the theological arguments that make that a prospect are implausible. Independence for children is attractive in the case of religion because we do not live in a world in which living independently involves such high-stakes gambles with respect to our eternal salvation. In the case of our treatment of non-human animals, however, I take a different view because arguments for our having stringent duties to end many practices of farming animals for food are convincing. For that reason, I believe parents are morally required to provide their children with a diet that is compatible with the stringent moral duties we have to non-human animals.

I have merely sketched some brief thoughts about how the ideal of independence for children informs everyday parenting decisions in a few selected cases that go beyond religion. There are many further questions about consumption, work, gender, and diet that need addressing, as well as other issues to consider, including sexuality, body image, and cultural and leisure pursuits. And, as noted, the important distinction between ideal and non-ideal contexts considerably complicates the task of identifying the implications of independence for everyday parenting. I hope those attracted to the ideal of independence for children will investigate these important questions.

Bibliography

Altman, Scott. 'Parental Control Rights'. In *Philosophical Foundations of Children's and Family Law*, edited by Elizabeth Brake and Lucinda Ferguson (Oxford: Oxford University Press, 2018).
Archer, Wes (director), and Jeff Martin (writer). *The Simpsons*, Season 3, Episode 22, 'The Otto Show' (20th Century Fox, 1992).
Arneson, Richard. 'Liberalism, Distributive Subjectivism, and Equal Opportunity for Welfare'. *Philosophy and Public Affairs* 19 (1990): 158–194.
Arneson, Richard, and Ian Shapiro. 'Democratic Autonomy and Religious Liberty: A Critique of Wisconsin v. Yoder'. In *NOMOS XXXVIII: Political Order*, edited by Russell Hardin and Ian Shapiro (New York: New York University Press, 1996).
Archard, David. 'Children, Multiculturalism, and Education'. In *The Moral and Political Status of Children*, edited by David Archard and Colin Macleod (Oxford: Oxford University Press, 2002).
Archard, David. *Children: Rights and Childhood*, 2nd edn. (London: Routledge, 2004).
Archard, David. *The Family: A Liberal Defence* (Basingstoke: Palgrave Macmillan, 2010).
Archard, David. 'Children, Adults, Autonomy and Well-Being'. In *The Nature of Children's Well-Being*, edited by Alexander Bagattini and Colin Macleod (Dordrecht: Springer, 2015).
Arjo, Dennis. 'Public Reason and Childrearing: What's a Liberal Parent to Do?', *Journal of Philosophy of Education* 48 (2014): 370–384.
Badman, Graham. *Report to the Secretary of State on the Review of Elective Home Education in England* (London: The Stationary Office, 2009).
Banaji, Mazarin, and Anthony Greenwald. *Blindspot: Hidden Biases of Good People* (New York: Bantam Books, 2016).
Bargh, John, and Tanya Chartrand. 'The Unbearable Automaticity of Being'. *American Psychologist* 54 (1999): 462–479.
Bargh, John, Mark Chen, and Laura Burrows. 'Automaticity of Social Behaviour: Direct Effects of Trait Construct and Stereotype Activation on Action'. *Journal of Personality and Social Psychology* 71 (1996): 230–244.
Barraza, Jorge A., and Paul J. Zak. 'Empathy toward Strangers Triggers Oxytocin Release and Subsequent Generosity'. *Annals of the New York Academy of Sciences* 1167 (2009): 182–189.
Barry, Brian. *Culture and Equality* (Cambridge: Polity, 2001).
Benatar, David. *Better Never to Have Been: The Harm of Coming into Existence* (Oxford: Oxford University Press, 2006).
Benatar, David. 'The Misanthropic Argument for Anti-Natalism'. In *Permissible Progeny: The Morality of Procreation and Parenting*, edited by Sarah Hannan et al. (Oxford: Oxford University Press, 2015).
Betzler, Monika. 'Enhancing the Capacity for Autonomy: What Parents Owe Their Children to Make Their Lives Go Well'. In *The Nature of Children's Well-Being*, edited by Alexander Bagattini and Colin Macleod (Dordrecht: Springer, 2015).

Billingham, Paul. 'Convergence Justifications Within Political Liberalism: A Defence'. *Res Publica* 22 (2016): 135–153.
Bolinger, Renee. 'Revisiting the Right to Do Wrong'. *Australasian Journal of Philosophy* 95 (2017): 43–57.
Bou-Habib, Paul. 'A Theory of Religious Accommodation'. *Journal of Applied Philosophy* 23 (2006): 109–126.
Bou-Habib, Paul. 'The Moralised View of Parental Partiality'. *Journal of Political Philosophy* 22 (2014): 66–83.
Bou-Habib, Paul. 'The Integrity of Religious Believers'. *Critical Review of International Social and Political Philosophy* 22 (2020): 81–93.
Bou-Habib, Paul, and Serena Olsaretti. 'Autonomy and Children's Well-Being'. In *The Nature of Children's Well-Being: Theory and Practice*, edited by Alexander Bagattini and Colin Macleod (Dordrecht: Springer, 2015).
Bowles, Samuel, and Herbert Gintis. *Schooling in Capitalist America: Educational Reform and the Contradictions of Economic Life* (London: Routledge and Keegan Paul, 1976).
Bradstock, Andrew. *Radical Religion in Cromwell's England: A Concise History from the English Civil War to the End of the Commonwealth* (London: I. B. Tauris, 2011).
Brennan, Samantha. 'Children's Choices or Children's Interests: Which Do Their Rights Protect?' In *The Moral and Political Status of Children*, edited by David Archard and Colin Macleod (Oxford: Oxford University Press, 2002).
Brennan, Samantha. 'The Goods of Childhood and Children's Rights'. In *Family-Making: Contemporary Ethical Challenges*, edited by Françoise Baylis and Carolyn Mcleod (Oxford: Oxford University Press, 2014).
Brennan, Samantha, and Colin Macleod. 'Fundamentally Incompetent: Homophobia, Religion, and the Right to Parent'. In *Procreation, Parenthood, and Educational Rights: Ethical and Philosophical Issues*, edited by Jaime Ahlberg and Michael Cholbi (New York: Routledge, 2017).
Brennan, Samantha, and Robert Noggle. 'The Moral Status of Children: Children's Rights, Parents' Rights, and Family Justice'. *Social Theory and Practice* 23 (1997): 1–26.
Bridges, David. 'Non-paternalistic Arguments in Support of Parents' Rights'. *Journal of Philosophy of Education* 18 (1984): 55–61.
Brighouse, Harry. *School Choice and Social Justice* (Oxford: Oxford University Press, 2000).
Brighouse, Harry, and Adam Swift. *Family Values: The Ethics of Parent-Child Relationships* (Princeton, NJ: Princeton University Press, 2014).
Brighouse, Harry, and Adam Swift. 'Family Values Reconsidered: A Response'. *Critical Review of International Social and Political Philosophy* 21 (2018): 385–405.
Buchanan, Allen. 'Cognitive Enhancement and Education'. *Theory and Research in Education* 9 (2011): 145–162.
Buchanan, Allen, Dan W. Brock, Norman Daniels, and Daniel Wikler. *From Chance to Choice: Genetics and Justice* (Cambridge: Cambridge University Press, 2000).
Butt, Daniel. 'Corrupting the Youth: Should Parents Feed their Children Meat?' *Ethical Theory and Moral Practice* 24 (2021): 981–997.
Callan, Eamonn. 'McLaughlin on Parental Rights'. *Journal of Philosophy of Education* 19 (1985): 111–118.
Callan, Eamonn. *Creating Citizens: Political Education and Liberal Democracy* (Oxford: Clarendon Press, 1997).
Callan, Eamonn. 'Autonomy, Child-Reading and Good Lives'. In *The Moral and Political Status of Children*, edited by David Archard and Colin Macleod (Oxford: Oxford University Press, 2002).

Cameron, Christina. 'Clayton on Comprehensive Enrolment'. *Journal of Political Philosophy* 20 (2012): 341–352.
Casal, Paula. 'Love Not War: On the Chemistry of Good and Evil'. In *Arguing about Justice: Essays for Philippe Van Parijs*, edited by Axel Gosseries and Philippe Vanderborght (Louvain-la-Neuve: Presses Universitaires de Louvain, 2013).
Catholic Church. *Catechism of the Catholic Church*. Available at https://www.vatican.va/archive/ccc_css/archive/catechism/p2s2c1a1.htm.
Chambers, Clare. *Sex, Culture, and Justice: The Limits of Choice* (University Park, PA: Pennsylvania State University Press, 2008).
Chan, Tak Wing, and Matthew Clayton, 'Should the Voting Age be Lowered to Sixteen? Normative and Empirical Considerations'. *Political Studies* 54 (2006): 533–558.
Clayton, Matthew. 'Individual Autonomy and Genetic Choice'. In *A Companion to Genethics*, edited by Justine Burley and John Harris (Oxford: Blackwell, 2002).
Clayton, Matthew. *Justice and Legitimacy in Upbringing* (Oxford: Oxford University Press, 2006).
Clayton, Matthew. 'How Much Do We Owe to Children?' In *Permissible Progeny? The Morality of Procreation and Parenting*, edited by Sarah Hannan, Samantha Brennan, and Richard Vernon (New York: Oxford University Press, 2015).
Clayton, Matthew. 'Liberal Equality: Political not Erinaceous'. *Critical Review of International Social and Political Philosophy* 19 (2016): 416–433.
Clayton, Matthew. 'Is Ethical Independence Enough?' In *Religion in Liberal Political Philosophy*, edited by Cecile Laborde and Aurelia Bardon (Oxford: Oxford University Press, 2017).
Clayton, Matthew, and Daniel Halliday. 'Big Data and the Liberal Conception of Education'. *Theory and Research in Education* 15 (2018): 290–305.
Clayton, Matthew, Andrew Mason, and Adam Swift, with Ruth Wareham. *How to Think About Religious Schools: Principles and Policies* (Oxford: Oxford University Press, 2024).
Clayton, Matthew, and David Stevens. 'When God Commands Disobedience: Political Liberalism and Unreasonable Religions'. *Res Publica* 20 (2014): 65–84.
Clayton, Matthew, and Andrew Williams, 'Distributive Justice and Subjective Health Assessment'. In *Measuring Health and Medical Outcomes*, edited by Crispin Jenkinson (London: UCL Press, 1994).
Cohen, G. A. 'On the Currency of Egalitarian Justice'. *Ethics* 99 (1989): 906–944.
Cohen, G. A. *If You're an Egalitarian, How Come You're So Rich?* (Cambridge, MA: Harvard University Press, 2000).
Cohen, G. A. *Rescuing Justice and Equality* (Cambridge, MA: Harvard University Press, 2008).
Cohen, G. A. *Why Not Socialism?* (Princeton, NJ: Princeton University Press, 2009).
Cohen, Howard. *Equal Rights for Children* (Totowa, NJ: Rowman & Littlefield, 1980).
Cohen, Joshua. 'Taking People as They Are'. *Philosophy and Public Affairs* 30 (2001): 363–386.
Cohen, Joshua. 'Establishment, Exclusion, and Democracy's Public Reason'. In *Reasons and Recognition: Essays on the Philosophy of T. M. Scanlon*, edited by Jay Wallace, Rahul Kumar, and Samuel Freeman (New York: Oxford University Press, 2011).
Colburn, Ben. *Autonomy and Liberalism* (London: Routledge, 2010).
Cormier, Andrée-Anne. 'On the Permissibility of Shaping Children's Values'. *Critical Review of International Social and Political Philosophy* 21 (2018): 333–350.
Cormier, Andrée-Anne. 'Must Schools Teach Religions Neutrally? The Loyola Case and the Challenges of Liberal Neutrality in Education'. *Religion & Education* 45 (2018): 308–330.

Cormier, Andrée-Anne, and Mauro Rossi, 'Is Children's Wellbeing Different from Adults' Wellbeing?'. *Canadian Journal of Philosophy* 49 (2019): 1146–1168.
Crockett, Molly J. 'The Neurochemistry of Fairness'. *Annals of the New York Academy of Sciences* 1167 (2009): 76–86.
Daniels, Norman. *Just Health Care* (Cambridge: Cambridge University Press, 1985).
De Dreu, Carsten K. W., Lindred L. Greer, Gerben A. Van Kleef, Shaul Shalvi, and Michel J. J. Handgraaf. 'Oxytocin Promotes Human Ethnocentrism'. *Proceedings of the National Academy of Sciences* 108 (2011): 1262–1266.
De Wispelaere, Jurgen, and Daniel Weinstock. 'The Grounds and Limits of Parents' Cultural Prerogatives: The Case of Circumcision'. In *The Nature of Children's Well-Being*, edited by Alexander Bagattini and Colin Macleod (Dordrecht: Springer, 2015).
Dreben, Burton. 'On Rawls and Political Liberalism'. In *The Cambridge Companion to Rawls*, edited by Samuel Freeman (Cambridge: Cambridge University Press, 2003).
Dworkin, Ronald. *Sovereign Virtue: The Theory and Practice of Equality* (Cambridge, MA: Harvard University Press, 2000).
Dworkin, Ronald. *Justice for Hedgehogs* (Cambridge, MA: Harvard University Press, 2011).
Dworkin, Ronald. *Religion without God* (Cambridge, MA: Harvard University Press, 2013).
Dwyer, James G. 'Regulating Child Rearing in a Culturally Diverse Society'. In *Philosophical Foundations of Children's and Family Law*, edited by Elizabeth Brake and Lucinda Ferguson (Oxford: Oxford University Press, 2018).
Dwyer, James G., and Shawn F. Peters. *Homeschooling: The History and Philosophy of a Controversial Practice* (Chicago: University of Chicago Press, 2019).
Eideslon, Benjamin. *Discrimination and Disrespect* (Oxford: Oxford University Press, 2015).
Elster, Jon. *Sour Grapes: Studies in the Subversion of Rationality* (Cambridge: Cambridge University Press, 1983).
Enoch, David. 'A Right to Violate One's Duty'. *Law and Philosophy* 21 (2002): 355–384.
Ernest-Jones, Max, Daniel Nettle, and Melissa Bateson. 'Effects of Eye Images on Everyday Cooperative Behavior: A Field Experiment'. *Evolution and Human Behavior* 32 (2011): 172–178.
Farson, Richard. *Birthrights* (London: Collier Macmillan, 1974).
Feinberg, Joel. 'The Child's Right to an Open Future'. In *Freedom and Fulfilment: Philosophical Essays* (Princeton, NJ: Princeton University Press, 1992).
Foot, Philippa. 'The Problem of Abortion and the Doctrine of the Double Effect'. *Oxford Review* 5 (1967): 5–15.
Franklin-Hall, Andrew. 'On Becoming an Adult: Autonomy and the Moral Relevance of Life's Stages'. *The Philosophical Quarterly* 63 (2013): 223–247.
Franklin-Hall, Andrew. 'What Parents May Teach Their Children: A Defense of Perfectionism in Childrearing'. *Social Theory and Practice* 45 (2019): 371–396.
Fowler, Tim. *Liberalism, Childhood and Justice* (Bristol: Bristol University Press, 2020).
Galston, William. 'On the Alleged Right to Do Wrong: A Response to Waldron'. *Ethics* 93 (1983): 320–324.
Galston, William. *Liberal Pluralism: The Implications of Value Pluralism for Political Theory and Practice* (Cambridge: Cambridge University Press, 2002).
Gaus, Gerald. *The Order of Public Reason* (Cambridge: Cambridge University Press, 2011).
Gerhardt, Sue. *Why Love Matters: How Affection Shapes a Baby's Brain*, 2nd edn. (London: Routledge, 2015).
Gheaus, Anca. 'The "Intrinsic Goods of Childhood" and the Just Society'. In *The Nature of Children's Well-Being: Theory and Practice*, edited by Alexander Bagattini and Colin Macleod (Dordrecht: Springer, 2015).

Gheaus, Anca. 'Parental Genetic Shaping and Parental Environmental Shaping'. *The Philosophical Quarterly* 67 (2017): 263–281.
Gheaus, Anca. 'Biological Parenthood: Gestational, Not Genetic'. *Australasian Journal of Philosophy* 96 (2018): 225–240.
Gheaus, Anca. 'Children's Vulnerability and Legitimate Authority Over Children'. *Journal of Applied Philosophy* 35 (2018): 60–75.
Gheaus, Anca. 'The Best Available Parent'. *Ethics* 131 (2021): 431–459.
Gheaus, Anca. 'Political Liberalism and the Dismantling of the Gendered Division of Labour'. *Oxford Studies in Political Philosophy* 9 (2023): 153–182.
Gheaus, Anca. 'Enabling Children to Learn from Religions Whilst Respecting Their Rights: Against Monopolies of Influence'. *Journal of Philosophy of Education* 58 (2024): 120–127.
Giesinger, Johannes. 'Parental Education and Public Reason: Why Comprehensive Enrolment is Justified'. *Theory and Research in Education* 11 (2013): 269–279.
Glover, Jonathan. *What Sort of People Should There Be?* (Harmondsworth: Penguin, 1984).
Gutmann, Amy. *Democratic Education* (Princeton, NJ: Princeton University Press, 1987).
Hand, Michael. *A Theory of Moral Education* (London: Routledge, 2017).
Hannan, Sarah. 'Why Childhood is Bad for Children'. *Journal of Applied Philosophy* 35 (2018): 11–28.
Hannan, Sarah, and Richard Vernon. 'Parental Rights: A Role-Based Approach'. *Theory and Research in Education* 6 (2008): 173–189.
Hansen, Thomas. 'Parenthood and Happiness: A Review of Folk Theories Versus Empirical Evidence'. *Social Indicators Research* 108 (2012): 29–64.
Harris, John. 'The Political Status of Children'. In *Contemporary Political Philosophy: Radical Studies*, edited by Keith Graham (Cambridge: Cambridge University Press, 1982).
Harris, John. 'Liberating Children'. In *The Liberation Debate: Rights at Issue*, edited by Dan Cohn-Sherbok and Michael Leahy (London: Routledge, 1996).
Harris, John. 'Reply to Purdy'. In *The Liberation Debate: Rights at Issue*, edited by Dan Cohn-Sherbok and Michael Leahy (London: Routledge, 1996).
Harris, John. *Enhancing Evolution: The Ethical Case for Making Better People* (Princeton, NJ: Princeton University Press, 2010).
Hellman, Deborah. *When is Discrimination Wrong?* (Cambridge, MA: Harvard University Press, 2013).
Herstein, Ori J. 'Defending the Right to Do Wrong'. *Law and Philosophy* 31 (2012): 343–365.
Hewstone, Miles, Ananthi Al Ramiah, Katherina Schmid, Christina Floe, Maarten van Zalk, Ralf Wölfer, and Rachel New. 'Influence of Segregation versus Mixing: Intergroup Contact and Attitudes among White-British and Asian-British Students in High Schools in Oldham, England'. *Theory and Research in Education* 16 (2018): 179–203.
Heyd, David. *Genethics: Moral Issues in the Creation of People* (Berkeley, CA: University of California Press, 1994).
Hirst, Paul H. (2010) 'From Revelation and Faith to Reason and Agnosticism'. In *Religious Upbringing and the Costs of Freedom,* edited by Peter Caws and Stefani Jones (University Park, PA: Pennsylvania State University Press, 2010).
Hobbes, Thomas. *Leviathan*, ed. Richard Tuck (Cambridge: Cambridge University Press, 1991).
Holt, John. *Escape from Childhood: The Needs and Rights of Children* (New York: Ballantine Books, 1975).
Hurka, Thomas. *Perfectionism* (Oxford: Oxford University Press, 1996).
Justice, Benjamin, and Colin Macleod. *Have a Little Faith: Religion, Democracy, and the American Public School* (Chicago: Chicago University Press, 2016).
Kagan, Shelly. *The Limits of Morality* (Oxford: Oxford University Press, 1989).

Kamm, F. M. *The Trolley Problem Mysteries*, ed. Eric Rakowski (New York: Oxford University Press, 2016).
Kasser, Tim. 'Materialistic Values and Well-Being: Problems and Policy'. In *Policies for Happiness*, edited by Stefano Bartolini, Ennio Bilancini, Luigino Bruni, and Pier Luigi Porta (Oxford: Oxford University Press, 2016).
Kitzmiller v. Dover Area School District, 400 F. Supp. 2d 707 (M.D. Pa. 2005).
Kymlicka, Will. *Liberalism, Community and Culture* (Oxford: Oxford University Press, 1989).
Laborde, Cécile. *Liberalism's Religion* (Cambridge, MA: Harvard University Press, 2017).
Lamont, William. 'The Muggletonians 1652–1979: A "Vertical" Approach'. *Past & Present* 99 (1983): 22–40.
Layard, Richard, and Judy Dunn, *A Good Childhood: Searching for Values in a Competitive Age* (London: Penguin Books, 2009).
Lecce, Steven. 'How Political is the Personal? Justice in Upbringing'. *Theory and Research in Education* 6 (2008): 21–45.
Leland, R. J. 'Civic Friendship, Public Reason'. *Philosophy and Public Affairs* 47 (2019): 72–103
Levinson, Meira. *The Demands of Liberal Education* (Oxford: Oxford University Press, 1999).
Lister, Andrew. *Public Reason and Political Community* (London: Bloomsbury, 2013).
Locke, John. *Two Treatises of Government*, student edn., ed. Peter Laslett (Cambridge: Cambridge University Press, 1988).
Lott, Tommy L. 'Patriarchy and Slavery in Hobbes's Political Philosophy'. In *Philosophers on Race: Critical Essays*, edited by Julie K. Ward and Tommy L. Lott (Malden, MA: Blackwell, 2002).
Luke. *Gospel According to Luke*. In *The Bible*, New revised standard version (Oxford: Oxford University Press, 1989).
Macedo, Stephen. *Diversity and Distrust: Civic Education in a Multicultural Democracy* (Cambridge, MA: Harvard University Press, 2000).
Mackie, J. L. *Ethics: Inventing Right and Wrong* (Harmondsworth: Penguin, 1977).
Macleod, Colin. 'Conceptions of Parental Autonomy'. *Politics & Society* 25 (1997): 117–140.
Macleod, Colin. 'Liberal Equality and the Affective Family'. In *The Moral and Political Status of Children*, edited by David Archard and Colin Macleod (Oxford: Oxford University Press, 2002).
Macleod, Colin. 'Parental Responsibilities in an Unjust World'. In *Procreation and Parenthood*, edited by David Archard and David Benatar (Oxford: Oxford University Press, 2010).
Macleod, Colin. 'Primary Goods, Capabilities and Children'. In *Measuring Justice: Primary Goods and Capabilities*, edited by Harry Brighouse and Ingrid Robeyns (Cambridge: Cambridge University Press, 2010).
Macleod, Colin. 'Agency, Authority and the Vulnerability of Children'. In *The Nature of Children's Well-Being: Theory and Practice*, edited by Alexander Bagattini and Colin Macleod (Dordrecht: Springer, 2015).
McMahan, Jeff. 'Eating Animals the Nice Way'. *Daedalus* 137 (2008): 66–76.
MacMullen, Ian. *Faith in Schools? Autonomy Citizenship, and Religious Education in the Liberal State* (Princeton, NJ: Princeton University Press, 2007).
Mason, Andrew. *Levelling the Playing Field: The Idea of Equal Opportunity and its Place in Egalitarian Thought* (Oxford: Oxford University Press, 2006).

Mason, Andrew. *Living Together as Equals: The Demands of Citizenship* (Oxford: Oxford University Press, 2012).
Mason, Andrew. *What's Wrong with Lookism? Personal Appearance, Discrimination, and Disadvantage* (Oxford: Oxford University Press, 2023).
McLaughlin, T. H. 'Parental Rights and the Religious Upbringing of Children'. *Journal of Philosophy of Education* 18 (1984): 75–83.
McTernan, Emily. 'Those Who Forget the Past: An Ethical Challenge from the History of Treating Deviance'. In *Treatment for Crime: Philosophical Essays on Neurointerventions in Criminal Justice*, edited by David Birks and Thomas Douglas (Oxford: Oxford University Press, 2018).
Merry, Michael. 'Indoctrination, Islamic Schools, and the Broader Scope of Harm'. *Theory and Research in Education* 16 (2018): 162–178.
Mill, J. S. *On Liberty, Utilitarianism and Other Essays*, 2nd edn., ed. Mark Philp (Oxford: Oxford University Press, 2015).
Mills, Christopher. 'The Case for Restricted Perfectionism in Upbringing'. *Social Theory and Practice* 49 (2023): 709–738.
Monbiot, George. 'I Shot a Deer—And I Still Think It Was the Ethical Thing to Do'. *The Guardian*, 19 February 2020.
Moreau, Sophia. *Faces of Inequality: A Theory of Wrongful Discrimination* (New York: Oxford University Press, 2020).
Moschella, Melissa. *To Whom Do Children Belong? Parental Rights, Civic Education and Children's Autonomy* (Cambridge: Cambridge University Press, 2016).
Mozert v. Hawkins, 827 F.2d 1058 (6th Cir. 1987).
Mullin, Amy. 'Children, Paternalism and the Development of Autonomy'. *Ethical Theory and Moral Practice* 17 (2014): 413–426.
Munoz-Dardé, Véronique. 'Is the Family to be Abolished Then?' *Proceedings of the Aristotelian Society* 99 (1999): 37–56.
Nagel, Thomas. *The View from Nowhere* (New York: Oxford University Press, 1986).
Nettle, Daniel, Kenneth Nott, and Melissa Bateson, "'Cycle Thieves, We Are Watching You': Impact of a Simple Signage Intervention against Bicycle Theft". *PLoS ONE* 7 (2012): e51738.
Neufeld, Blain, and Gordon Davis. 'Civic Respect, Civic Education, and the Family'. *Educational Philosophy and Theory* 42 (2010): 94–111.
Niker, Fay. *Living Well by Design: An Account of Permissible Public Nudging* (University of Warwick, 2017).
Nozick, Robert. *Anarchy, State and Utopia* (Oxford: Blackwell, 1974).
Nussbaum, Martha. *Liberty of Conscience: In Defense of America's Tradition of Religious Equality* (New York: Basic Books, 2008).
Okin, Susan Moller. *Justice, Gender, and the Family* (New York: Basic Books, 1989).
Parfit, Derek. *Reasons and Persons* (Oxford: Oxford University Press, 1984).
Parfit, Derek. 'Equality or Priority?' In *The Ideal of Equality*, edited by Matthew Clayton and Andrew Williams (Basingstoke: Macmillan, 2000).
Parfit, Derek. *On What Matters*, Volumes One and Two (Oxford: Oxford University Press, 2011).
Parr, Tom. 'Work Hours, Free Time, and Economic Output'. *The Philosophical Quarterly* 74 (2024): 900–919.
Peter, Fabienne. *The Grounds of Political Legitimacy* (Oxford: Oxford University Press, 2023).
Peto, Thomas. *Children's Rights: A Liberal Framework* (Oxford University, 2018).

Project Implicit. Available at https://implicit.harvard.edu/implicit/takeatest.html.
Purdy, Laura. *In Their Best Interests? The Case Against Equal Rights for Children* (Ithaca, NY: Cornell University Press, 1992).
Quinn, Warren. *Morality and Action* (Cambridge: Cambridge University Press, 1993).
Quong, Jonathan. 'The Scope of Public Reason'. *Political Studies* 52 (2004): 233–250.
Quong, Jonathan. *Liberalism without Perfection* (Oxford: Oxford University Press, 2011).
Quong, Jonathan. 'What is the Point of Public Reason?' *Philosophical Studies* 170 (2014): 545–553.
Ramaekers, Stefan, and Judith Suissa. *The Claims of Parenting: Reasons, Responsibility, and Society* (Dordrecht: Springer, 2012).
Rawls, John. *Political Liberalism*, paperback edn. (New York: Columbia University Press, 1996).
Rawls, John. 'The Idea of Public Reason Revisited'. In *Collected Papers* (Cambridge, MA: Harvard University Press, 1999).
Rawls, John. *A Theory of Justice*, rev. edn. (Cambridge, MA: Harvard University Press, 1999).
Rawls, John. *Justice as Fairness: A Restatement* (Cambridge, MA: Harvard University Press, 2001).
Raz, Joseph. *The Morality of Freedom* (Oxford: Oxford University Press, 1986).
Raz, Joseph. *Ethics in the Public Domain* (Oxford: Oxford University Press, 1995).
Raz, Joseph. *Practical Reason and Norms*, with a new postscript (Princeton, NJ: Princeton University Press, 1990).
Reich, Rob. *Bridging Multiculturalism and Liberalism in American Education* (Chicago: University of Chicago Press, 2002).
Richards, Norvin. 'Raising a Child with Respect'. *Journal of Applied Philosophy* 35 (2018): 90–104.
Ripstein, Arthur. 'Beyond the Harm Principle'. *Philosophy and Public Affairs* 34 (2006): 215–245.
Ripstein, Arthur. *Force and Freedom: Kant's Legal and Political Philosophy* (Cambridge, MA: Harvard University Press, 2009).
Rousseau, Jean-Jacques. *On the Social Contract*, ed. Roger Masters, trans. Judith Masters (New York: St Martin's Press, 1978).
Sandel, Michael. *Liberalism and the Limits of Justice* (Cambridge: Cambridge University Press, 1982).
Savulescu, Julian, and Nick Bostrom (eds.), *Human Enhancement* (Oxford: Oxford University Press, 2009).
Scanlon, T. M. *What We Owe to Each Other* (Cambridge, MA: Harvard University Press, 1998).
Scanlon, T. M. *Moral Dimensions: Permissibility, Meaning, Blame* (Cambridge, MA: Harvard University Press, 2008).
Scanlon, T. M. *Being Realistic About Reasons* (Oxford: Oxford University Press, 2014).
Schapiro, Tamar. 'What Is a Child?' *Ethics* 109 (1999): 715–738.
Schouten, Gina. *Liberalism, Neutrality, and the Gendered Division of Labor* (Oxford: Oxford University Press, 2019).
Schrag, Francis. 'Justice and the Family'. *Inquiry* 19 (1976): 193–208.
Schrag, Francis. 'Diversity, Schooling, and the Liberal State'. *Studies in Philosophy and Education* 17 (1998): 29–46.
Scott III, Swinton O. (director), and Jennifer Crittenden (writer). *The Simpsons*, Season 6, Episode 21, 'The PTA Disbands' (20th Century Fox, 1992).

Shiffrin, Seana. 'Moral Autonomy and Agent-Centred Options'. *Analysis* 51 (1991): 244–254.
Shoeman, Ferdinand. 'Rights of Children, Rights of Parents, and the Moral Basis of the Family'. *Ethics* 91 (1980): 6–19.
Simmons, A. John. 'Justification and Legitimacy'. *Ethics* 109 (1999): 739–771.
Skelton, Anthony. 'Children and Well-Being'. In *The Routledge Handbook of the Philosophy of Childhood and Children*, edited by Anca Gheaus, Gideon Calder, and Jurgen Wispelaere (London: Routledge, 2019).
Stemplowska, Zofia. 'Feasibility: Individual and Collective'. *Social Philosophy & Policy* 33 (2016): 273–291.
Stemplowska, Zofia and Adam Swift. 'Dethroning Democratic Legitimacy'. *Oxford Studies in Political Philosophy* 4 (2018): 3–26.
Swift, Adam. *How Not to be a Hypocrite: School Choice for the Morally Perplexed Parent* (London: Routledge, 2003).
Swift, Adam. 'Parents' Rights, Children's Religion: A Familial Relationship Goods Approach'. *Journal of Practical Ethics* 8 (2020): 30–65.
Tadros, Victor. *The Ends of Harm: The Moral Foundations of Criminal Law* (Oxford: Oxford University Press, 2011).
Tadros, Victor. 'Orwell's Battle with Brittain: Vicarious Liability for Unjust Aggression'. *Philosophy and Public Affairs* 42 (2014): 42–77.
Tadros, Victor. 'Wrongful Intentions without Closeness'. *Philosophy and Public Affairs* 43 (2015): 52–74.
Tadros, Victor. *Wrongs and Crimes* (Oxford: Oxford University Press, 2016).
Terbeck, Sylvia, Guy Kahane, Sarah McTavish, Julian Salvulescu, Philip J. Cowen, and Miles Hewstone. 'Propranolol Reduces Implicit Negative Racial Bias'. *Psychopharmacology* 222 (2012): 419–424.
Thaler, Richard, and Cass Sunstein. *Nudge: Improving Decisions about Health, Wealth and Happiness* (New York: Penguin, 2009).
Thomson, Judith Jarvis. 'Physician-Assisted Suicide: Two Moral Arguments'. *Ethics* 109 (1999): 497–518.
Thomson, Judith Jarvis. 'Turning the Trolley', *Philosophy and Public Affairs* 36 (2008): 359–374.
Tillson, John. *Children, Religion and the Ethics of Influence* (London: Bloomsbury, 2019).
Tomlin, Patrick. 'Saplings or Caterpillars: Trying to Understand Children's Well-Being'. *Journal of Applied Philosophy* 35 (2018): 29–46.
Tomlin, Patrick. 'The Value of Childhood'. In *The Routledge Handbook of the Philosophy of Childhood and Children*, edited by Anca Gheaus, Gideon Calder, and Jurgen Wispelaere (London: Routledge, 2019).
Tooley, Michael. 'Abortion and Infanticide'. *Philosophy and Public Affairs* 2 (1972): 37–65.
Vallentyne, Peter. 'The Rights and Duties of Childrearing'. *William and Mary Bill of Rights Journal* 11 (2003): 991–1010.
Vallier, Kevin. *Liberal Politics and Public Faith: Beyond Separation* (London: Routledge, 2014).
Waldron, Jeremy. 'A Right to Do Wrong'. *Ethics* 92 (1981): 21–39.
Waldron, Jeremy. 'Galston on Rights'. *Ethics* 93 (1983): 325–327.
Wall, Steven. *Liberalism, Perfectionism and Restraint* (Cambridge: Cambridge University Press, 1998).
Wall, Steven. 'Is Public Justification Self-Defeating'. *American Philosophical Quarterly* 39 (2002): 385–394.

Wannarka, Rachel, and Kathy Ruhl. 'Seating Arrangements Promote Positive Academic and Behavioural Outcomes: A Review of Empirical Research'. *Support for Learning* 23 (2008): 89–93.

Watson, Lori, and Christie Hartley, *Equal Citizenship and Public Reason: A Feminist Political Liberalism* (New York: Oxford University Press, 2018).

Weber, Max. *The Protestant Ethic and the Spirit of Capitalism* (London: Routledge, 1987).

Weinstock, Daniel. 'A Freedom of Religion-Based Argument against Religious Schools'. In *Religion and the Exercise of Public Authority*, edited by B. Berger and R. Moon (Oxford: Hart, 2016).

Weinstock, Daniel. 'How the Interests of Children Limit the Religious Freedom of Parents'. In *Religion in Liberal Political Philosophy*, edited by Cécile Laborde and Aurélia Bardon (Oxford: Oxford University Press, 2017).

Weinstock, Daniel. 'On the Complementarity of the Ages of Life'. *Journal of Applied Philosophy* 35 (2018): 47–59.

Weinstock, Daniel. 'For a Political Philosophy of Parent-Child Relationships'. *Critical Review of International Social and Political Philosophy* 21 (2018): 351–365.

Weithman, Paul. 'Convergence and Political Autonomy'. *Public Affairs Quarterly* 25 (2011): 327–348.

White, John. *Education and the Good Life: Beyond the National Curriculum* (London: Kogan Page, 1990).

Widdows, Heather. *Perfect Me: Beauty as an Ethical Ideal* (Princeton, NJ: Princeton University Press, 2018).

Williams, Andrew. 'Incentives, Inequality, and Publicity'. *Philosophy and Public Affairs* 27 (1998): 225–247.

Williams, Andrew. 'Justice, Incentives and Constructivism'. *Ratio* 21 (2008): 476–493.

Williams, Andrew. 'Constructivism in Political Philosophy'. In *The Stanford Encyclopedia of Philosophy* (Spring 2024 Edition), edited by Edward N. Zalta and Uri Nodelman, URL= <https://plato.stanford.edu/archives/spr2024/entries/constructivism-political/>.

Williams, Bernard. 'A Critique of Utilitarianism'. In Bernard Williams and J. J. C. Smart, *Utilitarianism: For and Against* (Cambridge: Cambridge University Press, 1973).

Wisconsin v. Yoder, 406 US 205 (1972).

Wollstonecraft, Mary. *A Vindication of the Rights of Woman*. In *A Vindication of the Rights of Men; A Vindication of the Rights of Woman; An Historical and Moral View of the French Revolution*, edited by Janet Todd (Oxford: Oxford University Press, 1993).

Wynes, Seth, and Kimberly A. Nicholas. 'The Climate Mitigation Gap: Education and Government Recommendations Miss the Most Effective Individual Actions'. *Environmental Research Letters* 12 (2017), 074024.

Index

For the benefit of digital users, indexed terms that span two pages (e.g., 52–53) may, on occasion, appear on only one of those pages.

acceptability requirement 19
Achilles and Hector 70–71
affection 76–78 *see also* familial intimacy
age-based discrimination 49–50
alienation 69–70, 75–76, 159–61
Altman, Scott 177
altruism 77–78
anti-perfectionist liberalism 19, 22–24, 55–68, 196
Antigone 136
appeal to cost to parents 13, 157–61
Archard, David 13n.19, 51–52
Arjo, Dennis 83–84
attitudes 44–46, 52–53, 85–88, 96–102, 173–75
authenticity 118–19, 120, 177
automaticity 34–35
autonomy
    personal 32, 38–39, 40–41, 42–43, 58, 123–24
    political *see* political autonomy

baptism of children 6, 135, 137–38, 161–62, 206–7
best interests of the child 15–17
Bridges, David 13n.18
Brighouse, Harry and Adam Swift 141–44, 147, 148, 152–53, 157–58
burdens of judgement 59, 67

cannabis 3–4
capacity for a conception of the good 42–44
Catholic Church 135, 137–38
charitable status 194
child liberation 46–53
childhood goods 16–17, 127–28, 130–32

children's development 43, 50–53, 75–76, 106–7, 127, 132, 143, 145–47
children's moral claims 5–10, 25, 121–23, 174
    balancing with parents' claims 157–61, 177–80
    to family life 63–64, 141–43
    respect for views 50–52
church/state separation 27–28
citizenship 74–76
Claw Hammer 188–89
coercion 3–4, 6–7, 63–64, 171, 180
Cohen, Joshua 74, 123
communitarianism 77
compelled service 89–96
comprehensive doctrines 8–10, 59, 83–84
    and public reason 56–57, 197
consent 12
Cormier, Andrée-Anne 140, 153
Crusoe, Robinson 8

democracy 55–56, 57
    and political legitimacy 169
    and public reason 55–56
diet 205–7
dignity 16, 118, 120–21
    compared to self-rule argument 123–25
    and parental anti-perfectionism 121–23
    and political anti-perfectionism 120
directive parenting/teaching 6–10, 33–34
    contrasted with non-directive 6
    and enrolment 6, 85–88, 170–82
    and independence for children 27, 40–46, 63–68, 85–88, 91–96, 125–38, 170–82
    kinds of 6–7

*I thank Katherine Watson for preparing the index.

discrimination
  age-based 49–50
  schools as protection from 190–91
  see also racist selector
distributive justice 26, 59–60, 174
drowning child in a pond 36–37, 38–39
drug laws 3–4
Dworkin, Ronald 117–23
Dwyer, James 171–72

education
  ethical 86–88, 105–6, 127–34
  science 132–34
  see also moral education; religious schools
endorsement, ethical 28–29
enforcement
  of independence for children 174–76
  of morality 3–4, 18–19, 29–30, 33, 36–38, 93n.8, 93–94, 170–71
  reasons against 181–82
enrolment
  and additive account of independence 31–32
  and anti-perfectionism 23–24, 128–29
  comprehensive 7, 91–96, 112–13
  defined 6
  ethical and religious 6, 7, 9–10, 24–26, 85–88, 128, 170, 175
  and intention 6, 85–88, 103–4
  and moral development 129–30
  moral and political 7
  and parentalism 10–12
equality
  and democratic citizenship 74–76
  and moral status 12–13
  and public reason 75–76
ethical scepticism 110, 112–14
ethical subjectivism 114–16
ethics,
  and morality 7–8, 109, 110–16
  and religion 8–10
ethos, independence-respecting 173–74
Evil Paul 176–77
evolution 132–34

familial intimacy 20, 77–78, 139–54, 157, 158–59
  and enrolment 144–47
  and parental spontaneity 152–53
  and parents' revelation of conception of the good 148–52
family,
  and anti-perfectionism 142–44
  as a coercive institution 63–64
  value of 139, 141–42
Feinberg, Joel 1–2n.1
flourishing 14–17, 125–34
  and dignity 123–25
  subjectivist accounts 114–16
food *see* diet
Fowler, Tim 14–15
Franklin-Hall, Andrew 129–30
freedom
  of association 55–56, 57–58
  of children 46–53
  of expression 55–56, 57–58
  of parents 155–56
  of religion 13, 19, 55–56, 57–58
funding of schools 21, 189–90

Galston, William 32n.6
gender 9–10, 201–5
genetic selection 166
Gheaus, Anca 141
Glancing Blow 92
global normative scepticism 112, 113–14
good life 8, 28, 43–44, 117–18, 142–43

Hand, Michael 6n.6
harm
  to children 83–84, 125–34, 135, 137–38
  to parents 13, 16, 143–44, 147, 152–53, 156–57
  to third parties 15–16
high stakes, problem of 134–38, 161–62
Hobbes, Thomas 4n.3, 12, 136
Holt, John 47–48, 52
home-school consonance 185–87
homeschooling 3
human flourishing *see* flourishing

intentions 85–88, 96–102
  and liability 96–97, 100–1
  and moral permissibility 96–102
  and public reason 85–86
  and third-party intervention 96–98
intimacy *see* familial intimacy

justice
    distributive 17–18, 26, 33
    and legitimacy 167–69

Kagan, Shelly 155, 175
Kitzmiller v Dover Area School District (2005) 5n.4

law 3–5, 46–48, 60–61, 170–71
legal rights,
    and moral rights 10–11, 21–26, 155–56
    and the treatment of children 171–73, 176–77
legitimacy 167–69
liberal consensus 1–2, 21–26
    and independence for children 27
    'open future' 1, 21, 23
    and perfectionism 22
liberalism 55–56
    anti-perfectionist *see* anti-perfectionist liberalism
    convergence and consensus conceptions 60–63
    limits of independence 134–38, 161–62
living well 8, 22, 28, 43–44, 117–23
Local Schooling case 45, 88, 91–92, 96–97, 99, 101–2
Locke, John 13n.19

Macleod, Colin 127–28, 141, 165–66
MacMullen, Ian 21
manipulation 3, 6–7, 29–30, 38–39, 122–23
materialism 9–10, 197–99
means principle 163
Merry, Michael 190–91
Mill, John Stuart 187
moral capacities 29, 33, 37, 42–44, 48, 50, 52–53, 69–70, 72–73, 92n.6
moral duties 90–91, 93–95
moral education 27, 37–38, 52–53, 58, 78–80, 104–7, 129, 192
    and accomplishment 38–39
    and alternatives 33–36
    coerced-party interests 37–38
    and political autonomy 38
    third-party interests 36–37
moral options
    compared to moral injunctions 175

    and parentalism 10–12
    and parents 4–5, 27–28, 154–63
    see also legal rights
moral right to control one's learning 47–48
moral status 12–13, 156
morality and ethics 7–8
Moschella, Melissa 11, 177–78
motives 44–46, 85
Mozert v Hawkins (1987) 5n.4
Muggletonians 45–46, 109–10, 148, 149, 150–51
musicianship 128–29

Neufeld, Brian and Gordon Davis 64n.17
neurointerventions 35–36, 38–39
non-directive parenting 6, 9
non-parental influences on children 102–7, 197–98
    no attempt v. plural attempt regime 105–6
    compared to non-social influences 106–7
Nose Job 71–73
nudging 6–7, 29–30, 35, 39, 48

Okin, Susan Moller 202, 203–4
open future 1, 10, 21–23
    rejected by parentalism 11

parental anti-perfectionism 40–46, 63–68, 77, 78–84, 125–34, 139–40, 196
parental authority 171–72
parental choice
    as a legal right 170–82
    as a moral right 156–63, 165–66
    and schools 183–87
parental integrity 159–61, 177, 179–80
parental morality 3–10, 155
    conceptions of 10
    and the law 3–5, 155–56
    principles applying directly to parents 4–5, 96–102, 124, 149–54
    proprietarian conception 13, 156
parental perfectionism 14–17, 20, 95–96, 111
parental rights
    appeal to welfare cost 157–59
    appeal to integrity/conscience 159–61
    and duties 161

parental rights (cont.)
  fiduciary moral rights 156–61
  legal right to enrol 170–82
  non-fiduciary moral rights 156–57, 162–63
parental wrongdoing 24–26, 45, 68–69, 85–86, 96–102
parentalism 10–14
  and the appeal to cost 13
  and independence for children 14
  and moral status 12–13
  and perfectionism 17, 20
parents' interests 16, 154–63
Parfit, Derek 17n.28, 18n.30
paternalism 37
perfectionism 13, 14–20
  rejection of 19
phased abolition of religious schools 188–93
political anti-perfectionism 40–41, 56–57, 120
political authority 3–5, 170–71
  and moral education 38
  and political autonomy 58–60
  and problem of high stakes 136–38
political morality 3–5, 17–19, 40–41
political obligation 3–4
political perfectionism see perfectionism
posthumous mistreatment 70–71, 72–73
present capacity view 72–73
present rejection view 70–72
procreation 164–66
public reason(s) 56–57, 66, 85–88
  and affection 76–78
  and democracy 74–76

Quinn, Warren 89

racist selector 36–37, 99, 100–1
Rawls, John 54
  burdens of judgement 59, 65
  capacity for conception of the good 42, 58
  comprehensive doctrines 8–9, 59, 84, 129–30
  distributive justice 59, 172–73
  gender 202
  just society 172–73
  political autonomy 38, 54–55, 57–58
  public reason 56–57, 61–63, 65, 77n.30, 135–36
religion,
  comprehensive doctrine 8–10, 56–57, 58, 162–63
  open future 1–2, 43–44
  parenting 14–15, 17, 25–26, 27–28, 41, 43–44, 66–67, 95–96, 140, 143–44, 148, 162–63
  personal autonomy 58
  political autonomy 59–61, 77–78, 82
  public reason 40–41, 56–57, 84
religious associations/institutions 27–28, 193–95
religious rights see freedom of religion
religious schools 21, 97–98, 182–93
  abolition 25–26, 182–88
  and discrimination 190–91
  funding of 21, 25–26, 189–90
  phased abolition 188–93
retrospective rejection 64–83, 91–92, 130–32
Richards, Norvin 102–3
right to do wrong 175–80
right to make ethical mistakes 13
Rousseau, Jean-Jaques 38, 54, 58–59

Sandel, Michael 77
Scanlon, T. M., 98–99
school
  curriculum 132–34, 199
  ethos 197–98, 200–1
  uniform 51–52
schools 82–83, 182–88
  and consonance with home 185–87
  two models 182–83
  see also funding of schools; religious schools
science 132–34
self-justifying paternalism 66–67
self-regarding duties 16
self-respect 118
sense of justice 37
state surveillance 25–26, 180–82

Sunday Schooling 86–88
Swift, Adam 16n.25

Tadros, Victor 89–91, 94–95, 96, 179, 188–89
Thomson, Judith Jarvis 98–99
Tooley, Michael 13n.16
Trolley Problem 88–96, 99, 101

usurpation 29–31, 103–4, 119, 122–23

Wall, Steven 80–81
Weinstock, Daniel 21n.34, 145–46, 148
well-being 16–17
   adults 142, 143–44
   children 126–27, 128, 132–35, 137–38, 178, 199
Wisconsin v Yoder (1972) 5n.4
withdrawal from lessons 3
work 200–1, 202, 203–4